MW00991105

EMORY UNIVERSITY STUDIES IN LAW AND RELIGION

John Witte Jr., General Editor

BOOKS IN THE SERIES

Faith and Order: The Reconciliation of Law and Religion
Harold J. Berman

Rediscovering the Natural Law in Reformed Theological Ethics
Stephen J. Grabill

*The Ten Commandments in History:
Mosaic Paradigms for a Well-Ordered Society*
Paul Grimley Kuntz

Theology of Law and Authority in the English Reformation
Joan Lockwood O'Donovan

*Suing for America's Soul: John Whitehead, The Rutherford Institute,
and Conservative Christians in the Courts*
R. Jonathan Moore

Political Order and the Plural Structure of Society
James W. Skillen and Rockne M. McCarthy

*The Idea of Natural Rights:
Studies on Natural Rights, Natural Law, and Church Law, 1150-1625*
Brian Tierney

The Fabric of Hope: An Essay
Glenn Tinder

SUING FOR AMERICA'S SOUL

*John Whitehead, The Rutherford Institute, and
Conservative Christians in the Courts*

R. Jonathan Moore

William B. Eerdmans Publishing Company
Grand Rapids, Michigan / Cambridge, U.K.

Published 2007 by
Wm. B. Eerdmans Publishing Co.
2140 Oak Industrial Drive N.E., Grand Rapids, Michigan 49505 /
P.O. Box 163, Cambridge CB3 9PU U.K.

Printed in the United States of America

12 11 10 09 08 07   7 6 5 4 3 2 1

Library of Congress Cataloging-in-Publication Data

Moore, R. Jonathan.
Suing for America's soul: John Whitehead, the Rutherford Institute,
and conservative Christians in the courts / R. Jonathan Moore.
p.   cm. — (Emory University studies in law and religion)
Includes bibliographical references.
ISBN: 978-0-8028-4044-8 (pbk.: alk. paper)
1. Christianity and law. 2. Law (Theology). 3. Practice of law —
United States. 4. Christian conservatism — United States.
5. Whitehead, John W., 1946- 6. Rutherford Institute.   I. Title.

BR115.L28M67   2007
261.70973 — dc22

2006039042

www.eerdmans.com

Contents

Foreword

In the Art Institute of Chicago there is a large gallery devoted to the Thorne Miniature Rooms. Meticulously detailed, crafted on a scale of one inch to one foot, rooms from castles, historic homes, chapels, and places of business have been re-created. These models, situated in small boxes, are so subtly lit in various shades of afternoon sun streaming through windows or candles on tables that the viewer senses what it would have been like to inhabit the full-scale room. Indeed, many visitors report that the Thorne replicas allowed them to access elements of the space that they had not noticed upon visiting the original full-scale rooms. By concentrating on the miniaturized versions, viewers could see important characteristics that might have otherwise been overlooked.

Similarly, recall the way art history books often reproduce a large and "busy" scene — picture Brueghel's portrayal of a village feast — in its entirety. Then, on the next page, the book takes one feature, such as a single wheelbarrow or a figure's nose, and labels it "Village Scene: Detail." In the same vein, a favorite *New Yorker* cartoon depicts an everyday scene featuring an ordinary man on his porch as he leaves for work, with the caption "The Milky Way: Detail." Reducing to manageable size a complex reality allows us to grasp critical details and better understand a broader context.

In this book, Jonathan Moore has provided us with a comparable close-up that reveals a much wider world. Newspaper and journal articles abound that deal with grand-scale phenomena such as the United States Supreme Court, the Christian Right, evangelical legal societies, and more. Readers who try to stay on top of all this soon find their eyes glazing over, the mind wandering, the spirit growing tired. But by taking The Rutherford Institute as his subject, Moore reduces things to manageable size while still illuminating the grand scene. By narrowing our focus to John Whitehead and his legal advocacy endeavors, he helps readers comprehend much more of what is happening in this increasingly busy corner of the church-state arena.

One final reference to scale and distance comes from Stephen Toulmin's *Cosmopolis: The Hidden Agenda of Modernity* (Free Press, 1990). Toulmin notes that in our connected, webbed, global world scene, we have seen an apparently paradoxical attentiveness shown to the immediate, the local, the cut-to-size, the graspable. Mass media and directories point to phenomena that have to be called cosmic, or at least global, and, from there on down, national. On those scales we speak of global searches for justice, efforts to represent the undernoticed, the interests of interest groups that through mass media and the Internet bid for attention by pointing to almost incomprehensibly large bureaucracies, congresses, and forces.

Along comes Moore with an accent on The Rutherford Institute, an agency that came to its prime by stirring the interest in the local and stirring up the locals. Often in its legal and representational endeavors, it chose causes that some dismissed as trivial and very limited, at the expense of "page 1" and "prime-time" interests. John Whitehead and Company in their most effective times worked with local instances and drew attention, thus effecting some national change.

To illustrate a political dimension of such localism, this comes to mind: in 1994, during an off-year election that seemed to portend little national consequence, the Republicans swept into offices from county road commissioner to governor. The still fairly new president, Bill Clinton, immediately took pains to say that nothing national was at stake and that the election returns should not be seen as a referendum on his stewardship of the presidential office. Then he quoted Congressman "Tip" O'Neill's maxim: "All politics is local." The next day unfriendly columnist Bill Safire said that, while never before had he agreed with Clinton and O'Neill, he did this time. "Yes, all politics is local," Safire wrote. "What you two have not noticed is that today the local IS the national." Issues of bedroom and clinic and town hall get projected upon a very large screen where far-distant people look and find themselves and their interests portrayed.

The adducing of these metaphors, analogies, or examples before we get to the substance of Moore's book should not make readers worry that they won't catch on to the connections between local and national, between particular and general, embedded within this analysis. These comparisons are motivated only by my desire to urge readers to exercise their

imaginations from page 1 on, because they will soon grasp that national issues are at the center of the plot.

Never heard of The Rutherford Institute? The Moral Majority, the
Christian Coalition, the American Civil Liberties Union, People for the
American Way — agencies on both or all sides of contemporary political issues are familiar. But Rutherford? As Moore develops his story, based on extensive and intensive research, it sometimes appears that John Whitehead
engaged in a kind of stealth campaign. While he was *very* ambitious, agi-
tated, and sure of himself, he was effective in part because he flew under
the radar, as it were, until he got in range of courts where he could achieve
some victories or make his point amid setbacks.

Never heard of John Whitehead? Jerry Falwell, Pat Robertson, and
any number of secular legal figures such as Alan Dershowitz or Lawrence
Tribe come to mind as frontline figures in the third of a century just past.
But John Whitehead? Many will not have heard of him, because he belongs
to a subculture whose complexity the outsider cannot always comprehend.
That subculture is the complex of Christian and "Judeo-Christian" law
schools, legal aid societies, filers of amicus curiae briefs. Within it are people who deal with legal issues that affect the whole culture, but the consequences of their activities are often not felt until they have made their
point, or even won their point.

Never heard of Christian Reconstructionism? Other worldviews and
programs are more familiar. Zionism, environmentalism, and more recently, thanks to the multimillion-selling *Left Behind* series, millennialism
have entered the public consciousness. But Reconstructionism? That
sounds like something to do with the building trades. Yet Moore shows
how at some stages Whitehead and The Rutherford Institute have been informed by and identified with this theological perspective — a worldview
that, if more widely known, would be genuinely disturbing to much of the
larger public. Watch for it as Moore describes it.

Here, as at many other points in this introduction, I find myself step-
ping back from the brink, able to resist the strong temptation to tell
Moore's story. It's as if I am thinking, "I can't wait until he tells about Reconstruction, which you will find illuminating or threatening or bizarre,
unless you are committed to its camp, so let me tell it now." No, the story is
his. I am backstage, figuratively ready to pull at the ropes as he moves his
props onstage and begins narrating.

It won't spoil the author's creative analysis, however, if I do some of
my own backgrounding. Here is why I see this "miniature," "close-up,"

"detail," or "case study" to be important, and some understanding of it to be urgent. It happens that some decades ago, perhaps best dated from the early 1960s, great numbers of Americans began to react to a pattern of actions of the United States Supreme Court. In *Engel v. Vitale* (1962) and *Abington School District v. Schempp* (1963), the Court ruled unconstitutional the officially led devotional practices of Bible reading and prayer in public schools. Ever since, opinion polls find 70 to 80 percent of the people critical of such decisions — signs, in their mind, of judicial activism that robs them of cherished practices. The invention of the term "secular humanism" and its entry into discourse about the Supreme Court and about "elites" served to fire them in their discontent and nurture their readiness to do something about the situation.

One could reach back even further to the 1940s, when with the warrant of "incorporation" the Supreme Court sought to assure that states comply with federal judiciary decisions. This approach led many to fear the encroachment of federal governmental powers on local scenes, and, again, publics in a reactive mood were ripe for plucking by counteractive interest groups. Still, it took those cases from the early 1960s to galvanize the opposition. And when *Roe v. Wade*, the abortion decision of 1973, carried the Supreme Court action further into realms perceived as moral, more and more people believed that "secular humanism" was winning out over God and the godly and needed to be resisted.

It was against that background that a number of Christian legal organizations began to form. Some of them, we will find out, served first as inspiration for and then as competitors to John Whitehead and his colleagues at The Rutherford Institute. At first these organizations were regarded as marginal, almost eccentric agitations in the eyes of those accustomed to the workings of an often unchallenged liberal society. Then the agitators began to win some of their cases, to the point that those who favored the liberal way had to worry about the diminution of rights and the rise of theocratic movements (which is what Reconstructionism is). Among the more gifted discerners of the signs of these times was John Whitehead.

Here, as elsewhere, I am strongly tempted to begin to tell the story of exactly what Whitehead saw and why he organized. Questions come to mind: How could he achieve so much without being more visible, more at the center of debates on talk shows and television panels? Why did he so often go his own way, when coalitions and alliances might have advanced his power and position? Moore's last chapter spins out the tale and suggests answers to more questions. Why did Whitehead in more recent years change strategies and sometimes sound enervated, passive, withdrawn, or even revisionist? And finally: Can the story of Whitehead and The Rutherford Institute provide some clues as to how we should regard the prospects of similar movements in a political climate congenial to at least mild "Reconstructionist" and strong "Strict Constructionist" interpretations of American foundings and the legal system? The answer is: yes, it can.

So, read on.

MARTIN E. MARTY
Fairfax M. Cone
Distinguished Service Professor Emeritus
The University of Chicago

∾ 1 ∽

Contexts

Nothing is more certain in modern society than the principle that there are no absolutes.

Chief Justice Fred Vinson, 1951[1]

If the Judeo-Christian principles that served as the source of all law governing this republic are not recovered in the near future, the conflict that will naturally emerge over the changes sweeping across the cultural landscape like a fire storm will destroy the structure of our country and its institutions.

John W. Whitehead, 1994[2]

In September 1994 Paula Jones alleged in a lawsuit that President Bill Clinton, while governor of Arkansas, had sexually harassed her. In 1997, three years into the case, after much public scrutiny and private legal wrangling, Clinton offered to settle with Jones for $700,000. The plaintiff's lawyers, Joseph Cammarata and Gilbert K. Davis, strongly urged her to accept the settlement, but Jones resisted because Clinton refused to include a full apology. Frustrated by her unwillingness to accept their advice, Jones's attorneys — who had advocated her cause from Little Rock, Arkansas, all the way to the United States Supreme Court — formally withdrew from the

1. Chief Justice Fred Vinson, quoted in *Barron's*, 18 June 1951, 60.
2. John W. Whitehead, *Religious Apartheid: The Separation of Religion from American Public Life* (Chicago: Moody Press, 1994), 12.

case. Abandoned by her original counsel, Paula Jones again found herself seeking legal representation.[3]

In his office not far from Washington, D.C., in Charlottesville, Virginia, lawyer John W. Whitehead observed these developments with interest. Fifteen years before, he had founded The Rutherford Institute (TRI), a nonprofit legal organization, to support people who felt their religious liberties threatened. In the years since, TRI's advocates had assisted scores of clients — usually, but not always, fellow Christians — with an impressive range of concerns. Public school students who wanted to read the Bible or pray together, employees who had been admonished for wearing Christian symbols as jewelry, adherents of creation science who insisted that evolution cede its curricular monopoly, abortion clinic picketers — all had found an eager and capable ally in The Rutherford Institute.

Despite this variety, however, in the organization's early years Whitehead and his associates rarely strayed from the boundaries of the First Amendment's religion clauses when deciding which cases to pursue. TRI initially operated not as a legal Wal-Mart with something for everyone, but instead as an advocacy boutique, servicing customers embroiled in situations where religious freedom seemed at stake. So in 1997, even someone borrowing John Whitehead's evangelical Christian spectacles could have been forgiven for not seeing how Paula Jones and her case fit within The Rutherford Institute's previously defined mission.

However, in the first fifteen years Whitehead had steadily adjusted his organization's ocular prescription, slowly expanding his vision of the causes TRI should support. By the mid-1990s he had come to view religious rights as merely one subset of a whole host of freedoms currently threatened by an invasive, omnipresent, and secularist federal government. As Whitehead looked at Jones's predicament, he saw not merely a "he said, she said" argument about sexual harassment; in fact, *Jones v. Clinton* revealed to him yet again the American federal government's interest in suppressing individual liberties. Despite all appearances to the contrary, TRI's founder did in fact perceive a religious dimension to this dispute. Reflecting upon his decision to assist Jones, Whitehead described his rationale: "The Paula Jones story seemed like a clear assault on Christ's view of how men and women should relate to each other in the workplace. I thought it would be a great opportunity for Christians to say, 'We really

---

3. Peter Baker, "Paula Jones Lawyers Ask to Quit Case: 'Fundamental Differences' Cited after Apparent Collapse of Settlement," *Washington Post,* 9 Sept. 1997, A1.

do care about sexual harassment in the workplace.' In my opinion, we were long overdue for the first foray of Christians into a significant sexual harassment case."[4] Not only had Jones been harassed, but Christ himself had been offended; Christians should therefore stand with her, as witnesses, in defense of Christian values. This case represented one small part in a much broader morality play, one in which Jesus Christ stood firmly in support of individual dignity over against the satanic, sexually voracious power of the state. Having cloaked the two antagonists with cosmic, symbolic significance, Whitehead and TRI offered to represent Jones against the president. And, having toiled in semi-obscurity for fifteen years, Whitehead moved closer to the limelight his critics quickly accused him of coveting.

Before the inevitable and immediate media attention gained by appearing at Paula Jones's side, few people outside of the conservative Christian orbit had heard of John Whitehead or The Rutherford Institute.[5] One longtime observer of the Christian Right noted that until the Jones episode, "To most Americans, Whitehead was a total nonentity."[6] By this time, however, TRI had been in operation for fifteen years and in fact had until recently been the most active among a growing host of similarly minded legal organizations.[7] Several groups with comparable missions and conservative Christian constituencies were on the scene by 1997. The oldest such organization with a nationally noticeable profile, the Christian Law Association, appeared in 1969. The Christian Legal Foundation, founded in 1961, dedicated a distinct institutional arm to religious freedom issues by forming the Center for Law and Religious Freedom in 1976. The Rutherford Institute, created in 1982, soon found itself amid an increasingly crowded field: the National Legal Foundation, formed in 1985; the Liberty Counsel,

4. John W. Whitehead, *Slaying Dragons: The Truth behind the Man Who Defended Paula Jones* (Nashville: Nelson, 1999), 4.

5. The Rutherford Institute first attracted attention from mainstream print media in 1994; see Andrea Gerlin, "With Free Help, the Religious Turn Litigious," *Wall Street Journal*, 17 Feb. 1994, B1. The evangelical magazine *Christianity Today* noted the emergence of TRI and similar organizations a year earlier; see Tim Stafford, "Move Over, ACLU: A Host of New Public-Interest Law Firms Are Helping American Christians Fight for Their Religious Liberties," *Christianity Today*, 25 Oct. 1993.

6. Robert Boston, *Close Encounters with the Religious Right: Journeys into the Twilight Zone of Religion and Politics* (Amherst, N.Y.: Prometheus Books, 2000), 142.

7. Boston, of Americans United, noted that until the American Center for Law and Justice was founded in 1992, "Whitehead ran what was probably the nation's largest and most active Religious Right legal group" (*Close Encounters*, 142).

chartered in 1989;[8] the American Center for Law and Justice, affiliated with religious broadcaster and erstwhile presidential candidate Pat Robertson, incorporated in 1992; and the Becket Fund, founded in 1994. Also in 1994, a collective of over thirty conservative Christian leaders — most already directing their own parachurch organizations — formed the Alliance Defense Fund to coordinate financing and strategy for the kinds of legal activities in which these other organizations were already engaged.[9]

Although conservative Protestants had long devoted time and energy to religious organizations outside the boundaries of denominational institutions, these legal advocacy endeavors constituted a new breed of special-interest groups in American culture. Despite decades upon decades of parachurch activities, only in the last half of the twentieth century did conservative Protestants devote organizations specifically to pursuing constitutional claims.[10] Why did they turn their attention to the American courts? What historical factors influenced the particular timing of this development?

The Rutherford Institute represents a particularly important organiza-

8. Begun as a project within an Orlando law firm, it formally allied with Jerry Falwell Ministries in 2000.

9. Founders included Focus on the Family's James Dobson, D. James Kennedy of Coral Ridge Ministries, the American Family Association's Donald Wildmon, and Bill Bright of Campus Crusade for Christ; TRI declined to join. For more on TRI's relationship with rival institutions, see chapter 3.

10. In American history, Christians had certainly organized around causes with legal dimensions before the 1970s. For example, the Woman's Christian Temperance Union, founded in 1874, was one of many religiously motivated organizations that sought the legal prohibition of alcohol. The American Protective Association, founded in 1887, sought to limit Catholic immigration and citizenship rights. Earlier, other associations sought the abolition of slavery or an amendment to the Constitution acknowledging God's sovereignty over the new republic. However, such groups did not coalesce around a particular interpretation of the First Amendment's religion clauses, nor did they intentionally organize in such a way as to take advantage of specialized legal expertise or to press specifically legal concerns. These earlier activist groups and organizations, like TRI, reacted to a perceived cultural dilemma, but the specifically *legal* nature of TRI's response was driven in large part by the magnified importance of U.S. courts — particularly the Supreme Court — for resolving (or, in some cases, creating) those conflicts. Unlike earlier voluntary associations, Christian legal advocacy organizations saw the misapplication of American law as both the cause of and the potential solution to that dilemma in all its manifestations. Therefore, these late twentieth-century organizations differ from earlier ones both in their raison d'être and in their devotion not to a narrowly defined cause but to a broader philosophical approach to religious freedom and establishment issues. These distinctions are discussed further below.

tion to examine because its younger peers imitated some of its tactics. Indeed, while "other New Christian Right public interest law firms have since adopted a similarly assertive stance," Steven P. Brown has contended, "it was Whitehead who pioneered the religious conservatives' proactive approach to law."[11] A close examination of The Rutherford Institute — its founder, published materials, and court activities — helps to explain the rise of conservative Christian legal advocacy groups in late twentieth-century America. Evangelical Protestants during this era perceived themselves as defenders of the sacred spheres of family, church, and community, spheres increasingly and unjustifiably encroached upon by an out-of-control, hostile-to-religion government. To protect themselves they marched headlong into the nation's legal system, one of the key engines propelling secularism's perceived advance. Conservative Protestants saw legal activism as a critical means to reverse secularism's unwelcome victories and, in so doing, to rehabilitate America's true religious character. To preserve the Christian character of the country in which they once felt at home, evangelicals entered the courts to thwart the antireligious designs of a many-tentacled "octogovernment."[12]

Christian legal activism, as examined through The Rutherford Institute, reveals a great deal about evangelical Protestantism in late twentieth-century America. Increased wealth, education, and confidence allowed conservative Protestants the relative luxury of legal activism. However, like most luxuries, this was indulged only at great cost. The activities of Whitehead and TRI serve as an instructive example of the potential dangers of legal activism. For in pressing cultural issues in the courts, religious conservatives both intellectually compromised treasured beliefs and ultimately fortified the secular order they so wanted to resist.

*   *   *

Three intersecting but distinct stories frame the emergence of The Rutherford Institute. First, TRI and similar organizations must be located within the American tradition of voluntary religious activity to highlight what makes them both familiar and unique. Next, these groups must be

---

11. Steven P. Brown, *Trumping Religion: The New Christian Right, the Free Speech Clause, and the Courts* (Tuscaloosa: University of Alabama Press, 2002), 35.

12. Whitehead believed that the American people "are steadily building 'the octogovernment,'" and "its tentacles reach into every stream of life in seeking to control." See John W. Whitehead, *The Separation Illusion: A Lawyer Examines the First Amendment* (Milford, Mich.: Mott Media, 1977), 147.

grounded in the narrative of fundamentalists and evangelicals in America, for only by understanding the changing nature of conservative Christianity's relationship to the (perceived) American cultural center can the motivations for forming legal advocacy groups be fully grasped. Finally, the history of church-state jurisprudence in the United States helps illuminate just why conservative Christians turned to specifically *legal* activities. These three stories provide the appropriate contexts for exploring the rise of The Rutherford Institute and explaining the consequences of its activities.

1. Something Old, Something New:
Voluntary Organizations in American Religious History

Since America's founding, Protestants have funneled their religious energies into voluntary, extradenominational institutions, making the parachurch[13] organization a historically familiar landmark on the American religious landscape. Drawing upon the religious energies of the Second Great Awakening, evangelicals pioneered dozens of parachurch groups in the antebellum period. First organized at local and state levels, many such organizations had become by the 1820s national in scope. They ranged widely in purpose, dealing with missions, social reform, antislavery advocacy, or charitable causes. Catholic convert Orestes Brownson complained that "matters have come to such a pass that a peaceable man can hardly venture to eat or drink, to go to bed or get up, to correct his children or kiss his wife" without the guidance of some voluntary society.[14] From Sunday school education to foreign missions to Bible distribution, nary a social cause existed without a religious special-interest group devoted to it.[15]

13. Bruce L. Shelley defines "parachurch groups" as "voluntary, not-for-profit associations of Christians working outside denominational control to achieve some specific ministry or social service"; see Daniel G. Reid et al., eds., *The Dictionary of Christianity in America* (Downers Grove, Ill.: InterVarsity, 1990), s v "Parachurch Groups (Voluntary Societies)." Unless otherwise noted, I intend for "parachurch groups," "paradenominational institutions," and "voluntary religious organizations" to all indicate equivalent phenomena.

14. Quoted in Winthrop S. Hudson and John Corrigan, *Religion in America*, 6th ed. (Upper Saddle River, N.J.: Prentice-Hall, 1999), 158.

15. On voluntary organizations in the nineteenth century, see, for example, Mark A. Noll, *A History of Christianity in the United States and Canada* (Grand Rapids: Eerdmans, 1992), 169, 229; Peter W. Williams, *America's Religions: Cultures and Traditions* (Urbana: University of Illinois Press, 1998; reprint, Illini Books), 176-78; and Syd-

No matter how disparate their specific goals, together these voluntary societies constituted a "Benevolent Empire" bent on Christianizing America. In his book *Barbarism the First Danger,* nineteenth-century Congregationalist pastor Horace Bushnell wrote floridly of this goal: "The Wilderness shall bud and blossom as the rose before us; and we will not cease, till a christian nation throws up its temples of worship on every hill and plain; till knowledge, virtue and religion, blending their dignity and their healthful power, have filled our great country with a manly and happy race of people, and the bands of a complete christian commonwealth are seen to span the continent."[16] No matter how they differed doctrinally, few Protestant reformers would have disdained Bushnell's vision. Almost all "believed firmly in the continuation and extension of Christian civilization" throughout America.[17] The voluntary society, for the most part blissfully independent of denominations and their theological particularities, proved to be a uniquely capable vehicle for common moral endeavor.[18] Evangelicals wholeheartedly embraced this mode of operation as part of the Master's master plan. As one scholar has explained, "In the American context, where the separation of church and state required all religious work to be conducted by voluntary means, the voluntary society seemed to be just what God intended."[19]

Even as Christians began to separate more clearly into theological right and left near the end of the nineteenth century, paradenominational institutions continued to stand at the center of conservative Protestantism. Dwight L. Moody (1837-99), his era's most successful evangelist, developed an independent missionary empire, headquartered in Chicago, which included a variety of organizations targeted to specific tasks.[20] William Bell

---

ney E. Ahlstrom, *A Religious History of the American People* (New Haven: Yale University Press, 1972), 422-28.

16. Quoted in Robert T. Handy, *A Christian America: Protestant Hopes and Historical Realities* (New York: Oxford University Press, 1971), 27.

17. Handy, *A Christian America,* 56.

18. Some scholars have questioned the "benevolent" nature of this empire, suggesting that evangelical leaders encouraged voluntary societies less as vehicles for improving America and more as instruments of social control. On this debate see Lois W. Banner, "Religious Benevolence as Social Control: A Critique of an Interpretation," *Journal of American History* 50 (1973): 23-41.

19. Bruce L. Shelley, "Evangelicalism," in *The Dictionary of Christianity in America,* 413-16.

20. On Moody's decision to start the school that became Moody Bible Institute, see James F. Findlay, Jr., *Dwight L. Moody: American Evangelist, 1837-1899* (Chicago: University of Chicago Press, 1969), 310-38. For Moody's centrality to American evangelical-

Riley established a similar spiritual domain in Minneapolis.[21] Bible institutes formed a critical institutional component of these ministries, serving as "denominational surrogates" where education, fellowship, and mission training could take place in a theologically proper environment. Moody Bible Institute constituted the fundamentalist surrogate par excellence, with a sphere of influence unmatched by any other agency during the 1930s and 1940s.[22] Throughout the first half of the twentieth century, evangelicals and fundamentalists continually turned to independent organizations to express religious impulses.

Conservative Protestants redirected their spiritual commitments toward parachurch institutions not only because they felt alienated by the increasingly liberal tenor of denominational endeavors, but also because they could accomplish more goals outside of traditional religious structures. For fundamentalists and evangelicals before midcentury, parachurch institutions served as "channels for dissent and for alternative activities."[23] During this period religious conservatives "created a host of new agencies and retrofitted many older ones to do their work, and their work prospered."[24]

At midcentury parachurch organizations continued to serve as preferred locations for conservative Christian activity.[25] Indeed, after the Second World War religious special-interest groups multiplied with amazing rapidity, in part because this mode of activity also became more popular among Roman Catholics and mainline Protestants.[26] Ever since colonists had settled the New World, denominations had always far outnumbered parachurch organizations; however, by the 1970s the number of parachurch institutions had surpassed the number of denominations for the first time.[27] The numerical gap between the two organizational modes

---

ism, see George M. Marsden, *Fundamentalism and American Culture: The Shaping of Twentieth-Century Evangelicalism, 1870-1925* (Oxford: Oxford University Press, 1980), 32-39.

21. See William Vance Trollinger, Jr., *God's Empire: William Bell Riley and Midwestern Fundamentalism* (Madison: University of Wisconsin Press, 1990).

22. Joel A. Carpenter, *Revive Us Again: The Reawakening of American Fundamentalism* (New York: Oxford University Press, 1997), 17.

23. Shelley, "Evangelicalism."

24. Carpenter, *Revive Us Again*, 31.

25. William Martin, *With God on Our Side: The Rise of the Religious Right in America* (New York: Broadway Books, 1996), 5.

26. Carpenter, *Revive Us Again*, 32.

27. Robert Wuthnow, *The Restructuring of American Religion: Society and Faith Since World War II* (Princeton: Princeton University Press, 1988), 103. By 1988 there

only continued to grow. By the early 1990s there were well over ten thousand parachurch groups in the nation.[28] Not surprisingly, evangelicals and fundamentalists, old pros in this arena, helped to fuel this phenomenon.[29]

Despite the continuing ubiquity and importance of religious special-interest groups, students of American religion, according to Robert Wuthnow, "have generally paid little attention to these kinds of organizations."[30] Still less have scholars spent time examining particular subsets of parachurch institutions to determine the significance of engaging in particular kinds of activities. Since Wuthnow's observation in 1988, only two authors have devoted book-length treatments exclusively to the contemporary parachurch phenomenon — and both books were written by and for evangelicals.[31]

To explain the rise of parachurch institutions devoted to specifically *legal* activities calls for more than understanding the role of voluntary organizations in American religious history; it also requires an appreciation for the changing relationship between conservative Christianity and American public culture. Once the unquestioned stewards of a monolithic public America, conservative Protestants by the mid–twentieth century found themselves — or at least perceived themselves as — displaced from the culture's center. The rise of conservative Christian legal groups occurs against this particular narrative backdrop. The story of Protestantism's "Righteous Empire" and its decline contextualizes late twentieth-century evangelical self-understanding and provides important clues to explaining parachurch proliferation and its subspecies, conservative legal activism.

---

were about eight thousand nationally incorporated nonprofit associations that met the IRS definition of a religious organization but were not churches or denominations themselves. Contrast this with around two hundred denominations (Wuthnow, 108).

28. Shelley, "Evangelicalism."

29. See, for example, J. Alan Youngren, "Parachurch Proliferation: Caught in Traffic," *Christianity Today*, 6 Nov. 1981, who complained of the "unchecked" and "extravagant proliferation" of parachurch groups. There are so many, Youngren wrote, that "Their effect is like that of the algae in the fish pond: when they have multiplied enough, everything around them will be killed off."

30. Wuthnow, *Restructuring*, 101.

31. See Jerry White, *The Church and the Parachurch: An Uneasy Marriage* (Portland, Ore.: Multnomah, 1983), and Wesley K. Willmer and J. David Schmidt, *The Prospering Parachurch: Enlarging the Boundaries of God's Kingdom* (San Francisco: Jossey-Bass, 1998). Noting the evangelical flavor of these works is not meant to diminish their worth — *The Prospering Parachurch* in particular provides an intelligent, comprehensive analysis — but rather to suggest the need for more perspectives on this phenomenon.

2. Conservative Protestants and the American Story

2.1. Pursuing a (Protestant) Christian America

In American history the nineteenth century, both religiously and culturally, belonged to evangelical Protestants. One historian has argued that the period between 1800 and 1865 can be described as "Evangelical America," a time when conservative Christian theology "held sway across almost the entire ecclesiastical landscape." Evangelicalism not only reigned in the churches, it also ruled in the nation, functioning as "America's public theology" during this era. Evangelical convictions fueled political activities, voluntary organizations, and denominational endeavors. In short, the United States "was thoroughly dominated by evangelical Protestants . . . because so much of the visible public activity, so great a proportion of the learned culture, and so many dynamic organizations were products of evangelical conviction."[32] In its first century, America was undoubtedly a Christian, and specifically an evangelical Protestant, country.[33]

But what does "evangelicalism" mean in this context? At the most general level, nineteenth-century evangelicals broadly agreed upon a "commitment to the Bible as its religious authority and on the gospel of Christ's saving work as the church's central message."[34] Beyond this common belief — one that cut across all manner of Christian denominational and associational lines, both liberal and conservative — evangelicals shared several more specific tenets. Most prominently, they emphasized having a personal conversion experience. They also customarily believed in a trinitarian God, in humanity's sinfulness and need for redemption, in Christ's substitutionary atonement for humanity's innate depravity, in regeneration and repentance through the Holy Spirit, in the importance of the moral life, in a coming millennial kingdom, and in a final divine judgment.[35] As well, evangelicals either embraced or grudgingly accepted the

---

32. Noll, *History of Christianity*, 241-43.

33. For a discussion of evangelicalism's overwhelming numerical strength, see Richard Carwardine, *Evangelicals and Politics in Antebellum America* (Knoxville: University of Tennessee Press, 1997), 4-6.

34. Shelley, "Evangelicalism." This is not meant to paper over the very real differences among evangelicals, especially in the postbellum period. Shelley identifies at least seven separate evangelical traditions in American religious history, and depending on who does the slicing and dicing, there certainly could be even more.

35. Carwardine, *Evangelicals and Politics*, 2-3.

principle of religious freedom.[36] This constellation of values, most elements of which evangelicals could trace back to the Protestant Reformation, shone brightest over the public horizon of nineteenth-century America. During this era evangelicalism embodied the religious and cultural mainstream. As William McLoughlin has contended, the story of American evangelicalism during the nineteenth century is in fact the story of America itself.[37]

Scholars have often referred to this situation of Protestant cultural dominance as an "establishment." After the Revolution, one historian has explained, "a *de facto* establishment grew where the old legal one had fallen."[38] In this informal arrangement, "the leading Protestant denominations worked together selectively through various voluntary associations in an effort to bring their nation more fully into accord with their understanding of what a Christian state and society should be."[39] Protestant leaders and government officials commonly cooperated; if these people were not one and the same, they often belonged to the same religious fellowships. Most American elites considered the nation to be rooted "in the premises of Protestant Christianity," and they felt it their duty "to make that civilization more fully Christian."[40] Even those Protestants who heartily applauded the new constitutional order of disestablishment assumed that religion and government would continue to be closely connected. For example, nineteenth-century church historian Philip Schaff consistently sought to maintain a distinction between the civil and religious spheres, but he saw nothing wrong with Sabbath laws, prayer in school, and other similar markers of church-state intimacy.[41] Most Protestants assumed that American public culture would and should reflect their own religious sensibilities.

A series of challenges confronted the evangelical Protestant empire as the nineteenth century progressed. Regional differences emerged, enervating Protestant reform efforts and dampening dreams of a postmillennial kingdom on earth. The Civil War ratified and intensified those disparities.

---

36. Robert T. Handy, *Undermined Establishment: Church-State Relations in America, 1880-1920* (Princeton: Princeton University Press, 1991), 10.

37. William G. McLoughlin, introduction to *The American Evangelicals, 1800-1900: An Anthology*, ed. William G. McLoughlin (New York: Harper and Row, 1968), 1.

38. Martin E. Marty, *Righteous Empire: The Protestant Experience in America*, 1st ed. (New York: Dial Press, 1970), 44.

39. Handy, *Undermined Establishment*, 7.

40. Handy, *Undermined Establishment*, 11.

41. Handy, *Undermined Establishment*, 20.

As the nation split and both sides claimed the same religious texts and symbols, hopes for perpetuating a unified Protestant empire ran headlong into an increasingly bifurcated religious reality.[42]

More permanent and crippling challenges to the nineteenth-century Protestant consensus came in the form of growing religious pluralism. New religious movements diversified the nation, and some began to gain real cultural strength. Founded in 1830 by Joseph Smith, the Church of Jesus Christ of Latter-day Saints — the Mormons — quickly grew in numbers and visibility.[43] Controversy followed them everywhere; in the first two decades the Saints were chased out of New York, Ohio, Missouri, and Illinois. A revelation sanctioning polygamy in 1843 brought the Mormons under increasing government scrutiny, so adherents soon lit out for the Utah Territory, where there was no law against plural marriage. Congress, under rising public pressure, sought to fix that "problem" by passing the Morrill Anti-Bigamy Act in 1862. Government enforcement and harassment steadily increased in an effort to end polygamy. In 1878 a church challenge to the ban on plural marriage made its way to the United States Supreme Court. As they awaited the official decision early the next year, the Mormons, who believed the U.S. Constitution to be divinely inspired, had high hopes that the Court would restore their religious liberty.

But in Reynolds v. United States, all nine justices agreed that Congress had the right to outlaw polygamy as "subversive of good order."[44] That Mormons asserted a religious obligation to practice plural marriage was no excuse. In another case twelve years later, after further battles and litigation, the Court echoed its earlier sentiments: "Bigamy and polygamy are crimes by the laws of all civilized and Christian countries. . . . Few crimes are more pernicious to the best interests of society and receive more general or more deserved punishment. . . . To call their advocacy a tenet of religion is to offend the common sense of mankind."[45] A revelation in 1890, the Woodruff Manifesto, called upon the Latter-day Saints to suspend the practice of plural marriage; this paved the way for Utah to become a state six years later. From outside the church, it looked as though Mormons had

42. Marty, Righteous Empire, 57-66.

43. For the story of Mormons in America, see especially Jan Shipps, Mormonism: The Story of a New Religious Tradition (Urbana: University of Illinois Press, 1985), and Richard N. Ostling and Joan K. Ostling, Mormon America: The Power and the Promise (New York: HarperCollins, 1999).

44. Reynolds v. United States, 98 U.S. 145 (1878).

45. Davis v. Beason, 133 U.S. 333, 342 (1890).

been forced to capitulate to broader Protestant sensibilities. Domesticated under duress, "mainstreamed," the Latter-day Saints were much less frequently viewed as potentially disruptive outsiders.[46] Protestants felt they had met and repelled a significant threat to their barely informal moral consensus. By bringing the Mormons to heel, Protestants believed that "a peril to their dream for a Christian America had been overcome."[47]

Further challenges to Protestantism's "Righteous Empire" awaited, however, most formidably in the growth of Roman Catholicism. Like Mormons, Catholics in the nineteenth century grew much more visible and — to Protestants — culturally threatening. From 1830 to 1860 the number of Catholics in America increased by 900 percent, and by 1860 Roman Catholicism constituted the nation's single largest denomination.[48] By the middle of the nineteenth century, Catholic numbers had jumped enough to frighten America's evangelical Protestants, who "were seriously concerned about a papist takeover" of the country.[49] Suspect due to foreign birth, languages, and customs, Catholic immigrants constantly had their civic credentials questioned by other Americans. Protestants intensely distrusted the "Roman" part of Roman Catholicism, fearing that Catholic loyalties to a "foreign potentate" (as Protestants often referred to the pope) would trump national allegiance. The official church's preference for the established-church model of political organization only heightened Protestant paranoia.

Not surprisingly, bursts of anti-Catholicism served to unite Protestants, at least temporarily, often during or just after periods of intense immigration. In the 1850s the Know-Nothings, an anti-Catholic and antiforeigner political party, gained widespread attention and captured several city and state governments.[50] Again in the late 1880s anti-Catholicism took on institutional form when many Protestants joined or sympathized with the American Protective Association (APA), which pledged to defend "true Americanism" against foreign — meaning Catholic — influences.[51]

46. See R. Laurence Moore, *Religious Outsiders and the Making of Americans* (New York: Oxford University Press, 1986), 25-47.

47. Handy, *Undermined Establishment*, 36.

48. Jay P. Dolan, *The American Catholic Experience: A History from Colonial Times to the Present,* 1992 paperback ed. (Notre Dame, Ind.: University of Notre Dame Press, 1985), 356.

49. Dolan, *The American Catholic Experience,* 295.

50. Dolan, *The American Catholic Experience,* 202.

51. Edwin S. Gaustad, ed., *A Documentary History of Religion in America,* 2nd ed. (Grand Rapids: Eerdmans, 1993), 2:262. The APA may not have been as popular with

Relations between Protestants and Catholics grew especially heated in the arena of education, in large part because nowhere was the informal Protestant establishment more real or more pervasive than in America's public schools. Hardly bastions of religious neutrality, nineteenth-century common schools, deliberately undergirded by evangelical principles, provided the kind of cultural unity that the theologically divided and officially disestablished denominations could not. President Abraham Lincoln had once offered that "The philosophy of the classroom is the philosophy of the government in the next generation." Protestants clearly agreed and suffused public education with their distinctive Christian ethos. With religious devotions, prayers, and textbooks heavily leavened with evangelical values, America's public schools made little secret of what kind of Americans their students were expected to become.[52]

This situation naturally accentuated an already present tendency for Roman Catholics to prefer parochial over public education. Protestant schools adjusted little for their fellow Christians, insisting that Catholics conform to already established educational mores. Unwelcome in public schools except on Protestant terms, Catholics began to seek public funds for their own educational institutions. Protestants naturally doubted that parochial schools would be proper schools of democracy, and resisted. Some cities found common ground when it came to funding both public and parochial schools, but rarely without controversy.[53] Conflicts ensued across the country, from the Atlantic Ocean to the Mississippi River. In the early 1870s a protracted battle broke out between Protestants and Catholics in Cincinnati. By the end of this lengthy civic conflict, soon known as the "Cincinnati Bible War," Protestants had stepped up devotional Bible-reading in the public schools and left parochial schools without any public assistance.[54]

Protestants as most scholars have assumed; see Les Wallace, *The Rhetoric of Anti-Catholicism: The American Protective Association, 1887-1911* (New York: Garland, 1990).

52. James W. Fraser, *Between Church and State: Religion and Public Education in a Multicultural America* (New York: St. Martin's Press, 1999), esp. 9-104.

53. One such compromise, which came to be known as the Poughkeepsie Plan, saw some states subsidize Catholic schools by paying salaries and building costs during the hours of secular instruction. After this period, Catholics and Protestants could turn to religious subjects in the same buildings. Various municipalities, from New York to New Mexico, adopted this educational compromise; see Fraser, *Between Church and State*, 62-65.

54. Handy, *Undermined Establishment*, 40. Protestants and Catholics largely agreed

Roman Catholics had more success in securing government funds for evangelizing Native Americans. More accomplished and generally more interested in Indian missions than Protestants, Catholics had gained control of federal monies for evangelism by the end of the 1880s. Theirs was a short-lived monopoly, however; by 1900 Protestants had successfully pressured Congress to withdraw the program's funding.[55] As in education, Protestants saw Catholics as competitors for cultural hegemony. No matter how lackluster their interest in evangelizing America's native peoples, Protestants had no intention of permitting "papists" to pick up the slack.

In the twentieth century Roman Catholics continued to cascade into American culture, keeping Protestant anxieties over losing cultural dominance never far below the surface. The number of Catholics in America increased from twelve million in 1900 to over nineteen million in 1920, and in response to continuing Catholic growth, nativism flared up with cyclical regularity.[56] In fact, by midcentury anti-Catholicism had become the only attitude that Protestants still seemed to share. Despite increasing fragmentation and division, Protestants cobbled together a more-or-less united front against Democrat Al Smith's presidential candidacy in 1928, the appointment of an American ambassador to the Vatican, and John F. Kennedy's successful presidential run.[57] These episodic Protestant attempts to prevent Catholics from gaining cultural footholds served more to highlight the dissipation of Protestantism's cultural capital than to signal some kind of renaissance. Kennedy's elevation to the presidency in 1960 provided an unequivocal signal to even the most hopeful Protestant chauvinists that their establishment was, undoubtedly, more relic than reality.[58]

---

about the importance of piety in educating children, but they used different versions of the Christian Bible. Using the Protestant Bible exclusively for devotional readings — a common educational practice well into the twentieth century — was a clear way for evangelicals to signal just who was in charge of the local public schools.

In the particular Cincinnati case, moderates existed amid the heated rhetorical skirmishes between Catholics and Protestants. Though its compromise was eventually overturned on appeal, the Cincinnati School Board voted voluntarily to end the practices of Bible reading and singing hymns in the city's public schools; see Fraser, *Between Church and State,* 110-11.

55. Handy, *Undermined Establishment,* 46-47.

56. Handy, *Undermined Establishment,* 150-51.

57. On how anti-Catholicism unified otherwise divided Protestants, see Martin E. Marty, *Modern American Religion,* vol. 3, *Under God, Indivisible, 1941-1960* (Chicago: University of Chicago Press, 1996), 108-12.

58. For Protestant attitudes toward Smith's presidential run, see Martin E. Marty,

Roman Catholicism represented only the most prominent proof of America's increasing religious pluralism. In the late nineteenth century and well into the twentieth, both Judaism and Eastern Orthodoxy also began to emerge publicly. Although hardly a real threat to Protestant numerical strength, other religions in their new visibility reminded Protestants that their moral monopoly was fast disappearing. Looking back on that turn-of-the-century period, historian Robert Handy noted: "Little seen at the time, the informal hegemony that the Protestant movement had long held over American religious and cultural life by its numerical pluralities and the power of its organizational networks was weakened. The voluntary establishment was being undermined."[59]

As the Protestant establishment's edifice began to crumble, pressure came not just from growing religious pluralism. Protestantism also experienced internal tumult, leading to deep divisions that pan-Protestant anti-Catholicism could only sporadically help to veil. From the 1880s through the 1920s, internecine conflicts erupted over Darwin's theory of evolution, higher biblical criticism, and the proper relationship between church and culture. These disagreements soon divided Protestantism further into fast-hardening conservative and liberal camps.

Liberals, termed "modernists" in this era, shared three general characteristics: a self-conscious and deliberate adaptation of religious ideas to modern culture; a belief that God "is immanent in human cultural development and revealed through it"; and the belief "that human society is moving toward realization . . . of the Kingdom of God."[60] According to Shailer Mathews, dean of the University of Chicago Divinity School from 1908 to 1933 and author of *The Faith of Modernism*, at its heart modernism consisted of "the use of the methods of modern science to find, state and use the permanent and central values of inherited orthodoxy in meeting the needs of a modern world."[61] Mathews and his fellow modernists sought to embrace contemporary culture, trying to incorporate the new findings of science and biblical criticism into their religious understanding — and altering the latter when required.

Modern American Religion, vol. 2, *The Noise of Conflict, 1919-1941* (Chicago: University of Chicago Press, 1991), 241-49. On Protestant resistance to sending an ambassador to the Vatican, see Marty, *Under God, Indivisible,* 107-10, 98-210.

59. Handy, *Undermined Establishment,* 189.

60. William R. Hutchison, *The Modernist Impulse in American Protestantism* (Durham, N.C.: Duke University Press, 1992), 2.

61. Quoted in Marty, *The Noise of Conflict,* 204.

By adapting faith to new knowledge and changed circumstances, modernists reshaped or jettisoned many of the tenets held dear by nineteenth-century evangelicals. Conservative Protestants — heirs to that theological legacy — naturally reacted with consternation. Initially conservatives opposed liberals with remarkable vigor and more-than-occasional vitriol, casting the conflict in stark, Manichean terms. Whatever liberalism had become, most conservative Protestants agreed, it certainly was not "true" Christianity.[62] Theologian J. Gresham Machen, writing in 1923, argued that "What the liberal theologian has retained after abandoning to the enemy one Christian doctrine after another is not Christianity at all, but a religion which is so entirely different from Christianity as to belong in a distinct category."[63] The modernist Mathews returned the compliment, dismissing fundamentalists like Machen as his "contemporary ancestors."[64]

This religious competition between liberals and conservatives appeared on many cultural levels and in many forms.[65] At stake, from beginning to end, was nothing less than the power to shape the wider culture.[66] In the early twenties fundamentalists seemed strong, even poised for victory. But by 1926 conservatives, having lost institutional control even where they had been most influential, had clearly been defeated.[67] Some contemporary observers speculated — critics hoped fervently — that Protestant conservatives, denominationally denatured and culturally humiliated, would now fade slowly into oblivion. This seemed all the more likely once conservatives began squabbling among themselves. Through the first quarter of the twentieth century, Protestant evangelicals had generally seemed of one mind, but now it became clear that their common antipathy to ascendant theological liberalism had masked deep, long-standing fissures. With their own religious family riven by conflict, many doubted that Christian conservatives could ever reemerge as a serious public force.

---

62. Hutchison, *Modernist Impulse*, 258.

63. J. Gresham Machen, *Christianity and Liberalism* (New York: Macmillan, 1923), 6-7, quoted in Hutchison, *Modernist Impulse*, 262.

64. Quoted in Sidney E. Mead, *The Lively Experiment: The Shaping of Christianity in America* (New York: Harper and Row, 1963), 186.

65. See Marty, *Under God, Indivisible*, esp. 17-92, 208-36.

66. Marty, *The Noise of Conflict*, 9.

67. Marsden, *Fundamentalism and American Culture*, 184-95, and Bradley J. Longfield, *The Presbyterian Controversy: Fundamentalists, Modernists, and Moderates* (Oxford: Oxford University Press, 1991).

2.2. Regrouping and Reorganizing

In the early nineteenth century most evangelicals had believed that by re-forming society they might help usher in the coming kingdom of God; this naturally invested their voluntary efforts with special importance, even ur-gency. Having inherited this same Calvinist New Light tradition that urged all Christians to transform the culture surrounding them, evangelicals after the Civil War continued to pour their energies into voluntary agencies and social reform. But as the twentieth century neared, incongruous theological streams began to run together in a way that complicated conservative Protestant enthusiasm for engaging American culture. A renewed focus on personal evangelism, combined with the increasing identification of social reform with theological liberalism, caused many conservatives to eschew reform activities. So disinterested in social reform did this group eventually become, and so complete seemed the transformation, that historians would later describe this change as the "Great Reversal."[68]

John Nelson Darby's theological innovation provided the most criti-cal catalyst for the conservatives' inward turn. A Plymouth Brethren leader in England, Darby popularized a new and unique way to understand the plot of millennial history, one that greatly affected evangelical attitudes to-ward the world. According to his scheme — known as premillennial dispensationalism — God had divided history into seven separate seg-ments. The present age represented a relatively brief historical parenthesis between the sixth and final dispensations; in the final epoch Christ would return with his saints to earth to establish his millennial kingdom.[69]

The most crucial consequence of Darby's dispensationalism was that it severed the earlier link between Christian social reform and Christ's mil-lennial reign. Previously, Christians believed they had an important role to play in creating God's kingdom on earth; for Darby, in contrast, God had al-ready established the dispensational historical pattern, and no human ac-tivity could alter that plan. The seventh and final dispensation would begin on God's own terms, in God's own time. While Christians might divine clues from the Bible about how this millennial plot would unfold, they could do nothing to affect it. Christians would better spend their time in-

---

68. On the "Great Reversal" and its close correlation with the rise of social-gospel liberalism, see Marsden, *Fundamentalism and American Culture,* 85-92.

69. Timothy P. Weber, *Living in the Shadow of the Second Coming: American Premillennialism, 1875-1925* (New York: Oxford University Press, 1979).

creasing the population of heaven by evangelizing than trying to remediate contemporary worldly problems. In fact, Darby asserted, God had foreordained the world's inevitable decline as a foreshadowing of Christ's return. This theological perspective gave premillennialists "a real stake in the unraveling of modern life," and they pointed to each new sign of social disorder as proof of their eschatological aptitude.[70] Since dispensationalists "had little or no room for social or political progress" in their theology of the end times, they disengaged from American culture.[71]

Evangelist Dwight L. Moody, a "principal progenitor" of American fundamentalism, vividly illustrated the theological consequences of Darby's dispensationalism. He summarized his Christian message as the "3 Rs: Ruin by Sin, Redemption by Christ, and Regeneration by the Holy Spirit." Emphasis on individual conversion stanched any impulse toward broader social reform.[72] "I look upon this world as a wrecked vessel," Moody said. "God has given me a lifeboat and said to me, 'Moody, save all you can.'" The Chicago-based evangelist perceived the wider culture as wrecked beyond repair, a ship about to go under rather than a vessel to be refitted and restored.

Although dispensational premillennialism probably secured the theological allegiance of only a minority of conservative Protestants, in terms of social behavior the differences between dispensationalists and others could hardly be distinguished. Any conservatives with lingering doubts about the dubiousness of public moral activism quieted themselves as social reform became increasingly identified with theological liberalism. Few conservative Protestants wanted to risk becoming tainted by liberal contact or being mistaken by fellow conservatives as closet liberals, guilty by association.[73]

Though modernism gave conservative Protestants a foil against which to define themselves, a distinct fundamentalist movement did not really emerge until the period between 1917 and 1925. The First World War (1914-18) played a critical role, both enhancing the plausibility of conservative Protestants — the horrific event fit neatly into a dispensational eschatology that foretold, and in a sense looked forward to, the world's decline — and damaging liberal optimism about the inevitability of social progress. This widened the divide between conservative and liberal Protestants, and it

70. Weber, *Living in the Shadow*, 82-87; quotation on 83.
71. Marsden, *Fundamentalism and American Culture*, 66.
72. Marsden, *Fundamentalism and American Culture*, 33-42.
73. Weber, *Living in the Shadow*, 105-10.

emboldened the former to press more energetically for the rightness and desperate necessity of their theological perspective.

Historian George Marsden has defined fundamentalism as "militantly anti-modernist Protestant evangelicalism," and during this postwar period, that militancy emerged in full force. In July of 1920 Curtis Lee Laws, the editor of the Baptist *Watchman-Examiner,* first minted the moniker for this new movement. "We suggest," Laws wrote, "that those who still cling to the great fundamentals and who mean to do battle royal for the fundamentals shall be called 'Fundamentalists.'" The label hearkened back to *The Fundamentals,* a series of essays published between 1910 and 1915.[74] Although a set of rather uncontroversial and predictable statements reflecting traditional Christian theology, this series supplied Protestant separatists with a substantive symbol around which to rally.

The formation of the World's Christian Fundamentals Association in 1919 provided the "spark that helped to generate a nationwide movement."[75] Fundamentalists in America, convinced of the correctness of their cause, focused their energies on driving liberalism out of several denominations and preventing the teaching of evolution in public schools. Conservative success in both tasks appeared possible. Liberal preacher and national celebrity Harry Emerson Fosdick delivered a sermon in 1922 with the title "Shall the Fundamentalists Win?" But despite fundamentalist confidence, the next few years would answer a resounding no to Fosdick's question. Fundamentalists soon lost two key battles for control of denominational machinery in the northern Presbyterian and northern Baptist churches, and the loosely gathered coalition began to disintegrate. The Scopes trial in 1925 — and the public ridicule of fundamentalism it engendered — served to ratify the movement's cultural defeat.[76] Militant,

---

74. George M. Marsden, ed., *The Fundamentals: A Testimony to the Truth,* ed. Joel A. Carpenter, 4 vols., Fundamentalism in American Religion, 1880-1950 (New York: Garland, 1988).

75. Marsden, *Fundamentalism and American Culture,* 158.

76. John T. Scopes, put on trial in Dayton, Tenn., for teaching evolution in violation of state law, was actually convicted of the crime (the case was later overturned on a technicality). The cultural verdict, however, was decidedly the opposite, as famed litigator Clarence Darrow intellectually outdueled the theologically conservative William Jennings Bryan during court testimony. On the Scopes trial and its importance, see Ronald L. Numbers, *The Creationists: The Evolution of Scientific Creationism* (Berkeley: University of California Press, 1992), and Edward J. Larson, *Summer of the Gods: The Scopes Trial and America's Continuing Debate over Science and Religion* (New York: Basic Books, 1997).

separatist, defensive, disillusioned — fundamentalists retreated from publicly pressing their case, and their national influence seemed irreversibly diminished.[77]

Rather than disappearing, however, over the next fifteen years fundamentalists caught their collective breath and reorganized. Alienated from denominations by liberal triumphs, conservative Christians retreated to local congregations and other independent institutions. They developed and strengthened a network of autonomous organizations that effectively functioned as denominational surrogates. In essence, they developed an insular subculture, a religious "shelter belt" protected from the howling secular weather outside. By the 1940s, having regrouped and reenergized, conservative Protestants were poised to publicly reassert themselves.[78]

For a time parachurch organizations provided a kind of neutral ground that all Christian conservatives could share.[79] However, in the 1940s disagreement developed between those who believed good Christians should shun all contact with liberals and those who thought mere contact would not necessarily cause spiritually fatal contamination. Conflict between separatist and nonseparatist conservatives grew more intense, and each side began to develop parallel institutions.[80] Those who maintained, and sometimes intensified, their desire to remain spiritually untainted came to define fundamentalism. The American Council of Christian Churches, founded in 1941 by the vituperative Carl McIntire, became the organizational standard-bearer for religious separatism. The National Association of Evangelicals, founded the next year, symbolically gathered in those conservative Protestants who maintained a more moderate attitude toward participating in endeavors beyond their immediate theological circle. Dubbed "new evangelicals" or "neo-evangelicals," they remained loyal to traditional theological principles — those beliefs and emphases that had united nineteenth-century evangelicals — but they eschewed fundamentalist militancy. Evangelicals a century earlier would have found it absurd to separate themselves from the wider public culture, the new evangelicals asserted — in fact, they *were* public culture. The new evangelicals insisted that they were not really "new" at all; instead, they rejected separatism as a theological "innovation" and reclaimed that older

---

77. Marsden, *Fundamentalism and American Culture*, 141-95.

78. Carpenter, *Revive Us Again*, 206-32.

79. Carpenter, *Revive Us Again*, 54.

80. To justify their stance, separatists relied upon Paul's admonition to the Corinthians: "Come out from among them, and be ye separate" (2 Cor. 6:17 KJV).

evangelical heritage of combining traditional Christian principles with robust civic engagement.[81]

In terms of cultural relevance and prominence, new evangelicals soon left the fundamentalists behind. Fuller Seminary, founded in 1947 in part to combat fundamentalism's intellectual stagnation, institutionally embodied the movement's cooperative spirit.[82] Billy Graham became the personal incarnation and most visible exemplar of the new evangelicalism. As his evangelistic career took flight at midcentury, the charismatic preacher became slowly but surely more promiscuous in cooperating publicly with other Protestants. Graham had decided that his call to spread God's word did not prevent him from interacting with fellow Christians. Separatists like Bob Jones, Sr., and John R. Rice strongly disagreed. As Graham prepared to launch his first revival campaign in New York City in 1957, they complained loudly that his local planning committee included theological liberals. The charge was true, but by this time Graham did not care. "My own position was that we should be willing to work with all who were willing to work with us," he recalled in his autobiography. "Our message was clear, and if someone with a radically different theological view somehow decided to join with us in a Crusade that proclaimed Christ as the way of salvation, he or she was the one who was compromising personal convictions, not we."[83] With the New York City campaign, Graham left his fundamentalist brethren behind for good; given his unrepentant ecumenism, separatists claimed they were happy to see him go. In the end, separatists wanted to separate even from theological kin who associated with nonseparatists. Those who remained constituted a small, if continuously vocal, conservative minority.

Flush with Graham's increasingly visible success — which included his very public cultivation of the nation's political elite — conservative Protestants at midcentury found themselves restored to the center of American life, or if not that, at least to public relevance. Evangelicalism was again mainstream.[84] "Not for more than a century," asserted sociologist

81. Carpenter, *Revive Us Again,* 141-60, and Marty, *Under God, Indivisible,* 435-48.

82. George M. Marsden, *Reforming Fundamentalism: Fuller Seminary and the New Evangelicalism* (Grand Rapids: Eerdmans, 1987).

83. *Just as I Am: The Autobiography of Billy Graham* (San Francisco: HarperSanFrancisco, 1997), 303-4. The two best biographies of Billy Graham are Marshall Frady, *Billy Graham: A Parable of American Righteousness* (Boston: Little, Brown, 1979), and William Martin, *A Prophet with Honor: The Billy Graham Story* (New York: Morrow, 1991).

84. When describing nonfundamentalist conservative Protestants after 1950, I drop the "new" from "new evangelicals" and refer to them as simply "evangelicals."

William Martin, had evangelicals "felt so closely in tune with and wielded as much influence over the national ethos and culture."[85] This helps explain why the fifties so often served as a nostalgic touchstone in late twentieth-century evangelical rhetoric. For conservative Protestants a generation or two later, the traditional, *Father Knows Best* era came to signify the last time they could plausibly claim that America — or at least an important, esteemed part of it — truly belonged to them.

The ideal world of the 1950s, whether real or a convenient fiction, did not last long.[86] By the mid-1970s evangelicals believed that their nation had become a much darker place. They characteristically detailed a litany of intervening political and social upheavals: civil rights, the Vietnam War, student protests, Watergate, the sexual revolution, no-fault divorce, relaxed abortion restrictions, drug experimentation, feminism and the Equal Rights Amendment — the list of culturally destructive horrors often continued indefinitely. Religious conservatives might have become distressed by even one of those cultural events, so for them, not surprisingly, this combination of troubles indicated a society spiraling speedily out of control. As one scholar has observed, the changes that occurred during the notorious sixties seemed to evangelicals "to point toward chaos and destruction of all they cherished." This time retreating and regrouping was not an option; the taste of cultural success still lingered: "They had no intention . . . of giving up without a fight. They preferred an America they had known, and not that long ago. They determined to recover and conserve it, however long that might take."[87]

As part of their attempt to restore America in their image, conservative Christians reasserted themselves in the political arena.[88] Although po-

---

"New" only for a time, they quickly became just "evangelicals" again once their separation from separatists became clear.

85. Martin, *A Prophet with Honor,* 47.

86. On the ideal of the 1950s versus reality, see Stephanie Koontz, *The Way We Never Were: American Families and the Nostalgia Trap* (New York: Basic Books, 1992).

87. Martin, *With God,* 75.

88. The rise of the so-called New Christian Right has been exhaustively documented. The best examinations include Martin, *With God on Our Side* (both the book and the PBS television documentary of the same name); Michael Lienesch, *Redeeming America: Piety and Politics in the New Christian Right* (Chapel Hill: University of North Carolina Press, 1993); Robert Booth Fowler and Allen D. Hertzke, *Religion and Politics in America: Faith, Culture, and Strategic Choices* (Boulder, Colo.: Westview, 1995), esp. 133-51; Sara Diamond, *Spiritual Warfare: The Politics of the Christian Right* (Boston: South End Press, 1989); Sara Diamond, *Not by Politics Alone: The Enduring Influence of the*

litical and social activism drew the most attention, it was during this period that conservatives also began to form legal special-interest groups. By the late 1970s and early 1980s, many evangelicals — and even some very visible, entrepreneurial fundamentalists, who had shed enough of their dispensationalist skin to politically reengage — had become convinced that rescuing American culture demanded legal as well as political activism. Turning to the courts made particularly good sense precisely because judges had delivered some of religious conservatism's most bitter defeats. Seeing church-state developments since midcentury through the eyes of Christian conservatives provides the third and final context for understanding why organized legal advocacy became so important.

3. Godless Courts? Church-State Cases and the "Stealing of America"

According to many evangelicals and fundamentalists, American courts systematically denuded American public life of religious activities and symbols during the last half of the twentieth century. In ejecting religious conservatives from the nation's cultural center, the courts had unjustifiably attacked the very nature of American identity itself. As well, the courts assisted an increasingly secularist federal government in encroaching upon spheres of life once reserved to families and religious communities. While the courts busied themselves with stripping the public terrain of Christian totems, the federal government expanded its power over individual lives in an attempt to secularize all aspects of American life. This constituted a two-front war against religious conservatives, in their estimation, prosecuted by the very institutions that claimed to protect their freedoms.

A full appreciation of these conservative complaints can come only by contextualizing them within the history of church-state relations in America. Indeed, to defend themselves in twentieth-century cultural wars, conservative Christians evoked not just the 1950s but also the 1780s. According to them, history clearly demonstrated that the new nation's founders designed a constitutional framework dependent for legitimacy and success upon religion — specifically Christianity or the "Judeo-Christian

Christian Right (New York: Guilford Press, 1998); and Steve Bruce, The Rise and Fall of the New Christian Right: Conservative Protestant Politics in America, 1978-1988 (New York: Oxford University Press, 1988).

tradition." How accurate this understanding actually is depends on a particular, arguable interpretation of certain historical truths.

Similar to Albert Schweitzer's famous characterization of the search for the historical Jesus, the quest for the "real" understanding of church and state in the founding era yields enough disagreement for conservatives and liberals alike to look deeply into this historical well and discover their own reflections. The original Constitution barely mentioned religion at all, touching upon the subject only in banning religious tests for public office.[89] The First Amendment addressed the matter explicitly, ensuring that the new republic would have no established national church and guaranteeing the free exercise of religion. When the new American states ratified the Bill of Rights in 1791, many retained their colonial religious establishments with little hue or cry. Some scholars have argued that, in religious matters, this was in fact *all* the First Amendment had been designed to do: the new states could still behave as they pleased in church-state arrangements.[90] "So far as the U.S. Constitution was concerned," Leonard Levy has asserted, "the states were free to re-create the Inquisition or to erect and maintain exclusive establishments of religion."[91] Steven Smith has argued similarly that the First Amendment represented a purely jurisdictional statement, one binding only upon the federal government.[92]

Thomas Curry, in an exhaustive examination of church-state arrangements in the American colonies, has concurred with Smith and Levy that the First Amendment is best viewed as a "declaration of no power" for the federal government in religious matters.[93] But in contrast to Levy, who con-

---

89. Article VI reads: "The Senators and Representatives [and others] . . . shall be bound by Oath or Affirmation, to support this Constitution; but no religious Test shall ever be required as a Qualification to any Office or public Trust under the United States." The authors of the Constitution did proclaim the document written "in the Year of Our Lord 1787," but only a handful of religious conservatives have pointed to this as proof of America's Christian foundation.

90. Steven D. Smith, *Foreordained Failure: The Quest for a Constitutional Principle of Religious Freedom* (New York: Oxford University Press, 1995), has offered the most persuasive case that the First Amendment's disestablishment clause was purely a jurisdictional statement that confined the federal government in religious matters. See especially "The Jurisdictional Character of the Religion Clauses," 17-43.

91. Leonard W. Levy, *The Establishment Clause: Religion and the First Amendment*, 2nd rev. ed. (Chapel Hill: University of North Carolina Press, 1994), 147.

92. Smith, *Foreordained Failure.*

93. Thomas J. Curry, *The First Freedoms: Church and State in America to the Passage of the First Amendment* (New York: Oxford University Press, 1986), 208.

tended that the founders opposed both exclusive and nonpreferential establishments of religion, Curry claims the debates surrounding the First Amendment did not concern the meanings of "establishment" or "free exercise." Instead, the founders engaged in "a discussion about how to state the common agreement that the new government had no authority whatsoever in religious matters."[94] Curry insists that the First Amendment simply and directly proclaimed that the secular government could not interfere with the right to the free exercise of religion — a right not defined or conferred by the sovereign, but one that already resided with individuals by virtue of their humanity.[95]

Such seemingly precious historical distinctions came to matter enormously in the twentieth century, as the U.S. Supreme Court decided that the Bill of Rights applied to the states. In doing so, what did disestablishment mean? Levy has argued that "by an establishment of religion the framers meant any government policy that aided religion or its agencies, the religious establishments."[96] Therefore, an originalist understanding of the First Amendment requires the rejection of not just a church-state model wherein the state prefers one religion over others, but also a model wherein the state may offer general assistance to religion in a nonpreferential fashion. Curry, however, argues that this unfairly projects a contemporary understanding of establishment back into the founding period. Late eighteenth-century Americans "universally defined establishment of religion as government preference for one religion" and therefore rejected only that scheme in the First Amendment.[97] Regardless of the correct understanding, each new American state clearly rejected, at the very least, the European model of church-state relations wherein the state preferred one

94. Curry, *The First Freedoms*, 215. Indeed, Curry continued, "Because it was making explicit the non-existence of a power, not regulating or curbing one that existed, Congress approached the subject in a somewhat hasty and absentminded manner. To examine the two clauses of the amendment as a carefully worded analysis of Church-State relations would be to overburden them" (216).

95. Thomas J. Curry, *Farewell to Christendom: The Future of Church and State in America* (New York: Oxford University Press, 2001).

96. Levy, *The Establishment Clause*, xxi.

97. Curry, *Farewell to Christendom*, 37. The historical evidence for this limited understanding of establishment, Curry asserts, is "certain and unambiguous." By this definition, even Massachusetts's church-state arrangement through 1833 — often cited by scholars as the last remaining establishment in America — would not have been considered an "establishment."

religious group over all others. Massachusetts, the last holdout, abolished the last traces of its official establishment in 1833.

What also remained transparently clear was that, despite official disestablishment, religion's central place in America's national life still seemed secure. Alexis de Tocqueville, visiting from Europe in 1830, observed that in the United States, "From the start politics and religion agreed, and they have not since ceased to do so." Although religion exercises no direct influence on government, the Frenchman discerned, "America is still the place where the Christian religion has kept the greatest power over men's souls." Though not an official religion, Christianity in the United States "does direct mores, and by regulating domestic life it helps to regulate the state."[98] Few American citizens would have been displeased with Tocqueville's perceptions. Curry has shown that Americans both before and just after the Revolution "habitually viewed Church-State relations within the framework of a Christian or Protestant society."[99] Even as state establishments disappeared, state and local laws, both formally and informally, continued to favor religion, especially in its Protestant forms. Since other American religious groups only slowly found (or were allowed to find) their public voices, a general Protestant consensus ruled American public life with little audible grumbling or legal objections.

This religiously homogenous public environment, coupled with the federal government's restricted jurisdiction in matters of religion, meant that the United States Supreme Court ruled infrequently on religious freedom issues during the first century of the new nation's life.[100] However, this situation changed dramatically in the middle of the twentieth century, when the Court affirmed that the Bill of Rights — including the First Amendment — applied to the states. Relying upon the Fourteenth Amendment (passed during Reconstruction to ensure that freed slaves received equal rights in the South), the Supreme Court "incorporated" the Bill of Rights into the body of laws by which the states must abide.[101] In terms of

98. Alexis de Tocqueville, *Democracy in America,* ed. J. P. Mayer, trans. George Lawrence (New York: Harper Perennial, 1988), 88, 291.

99. Curry, *The First Freedoms,* 196.

100. This does not mean that church-state issues did not make it into the courts at all, only that they did not appear very often in federal courts. The Mormon cases in the late nineteenth century represented the first significant exceptions to the Supreme Court's general silence on church-state matters, providing a harbinger of more juridical activity to come in the next century.

101. The Fourteenth Amendment, Section 1, reads: "All persons born or natural-

religion, the incorporation of the First Amendment occurred in pieces. In 1940 the Court in *Cantwell v. Connecticut* applied the free exercise clause to the states for the first time.[102] And in 1947, in *Everson v. Board of Education*, the Court ruled that the First Amendment prohibition against establishment also applied to the states.[103] An interpretive move little noticed at the time, the Supreme Court in *Cantwell* and *Everson* had expanded enormously the First Amendment's reach, ensuring that — especially in a country growing more religiously diverse by the day — more and more church-state cases would make their way into the federal courts.[104]

Although late twentieth-century religious conservatives viewed the Court's expansion of its own power as dangerous and fundamentally illegitimate, many church-state decisions nevertheless satisfied, and even occasionally delighted, them. For example, the Court allowed schoolchildren to receive religious instruction during school time if it took place off school grounds.[105] The justices allowed churches to remain exempt from

---

ized in the United States, and subject to the jurisdiction thereof, are citizens of the United States and of the State wherein they reside. No State shall make or enforce any law which shall abridge the privileges and immunities of citizens of the United States; nor shall any State deprive any person of life, liberty, or property, without due process of law; nor deny to any person within its jurisdiction the equal protection of the laws."

102. *Cantwell v. Connecticut*, 310 U.S. 296 (1940).

103. *Everson v. Board of Education*, 330 U.S. 1 (1947).

104. On the idea of incorporation and its consequences, see Michael J. Perry, *We the People: The Fourteenth Amendment and the Supreme Court* (New York: Oxford University Press, 1999); William E. Nelson, *The Fourteenth Amendment: From Political Principle to Judicial Doctrine* (Cambridge: Harvard University Press, 1988); and Raoul Berger, *Government by Judiciary: The Transformation of the Fourteenth Amendment*, 2nd ed. (Indianapolis: Liberty Fund, 1997). Although after half a century it seems fair to view incorporation as a fait accompli, the notion has received criticism. See, for example, Justice Clarence Thomas's concurring opinion in *Zelman v. Simmons-Harris*, 122 S. Ct. 2460 (2002), where he argued that "When rights are incorporated against the States through the Fourteenth Amendment they should advance, not constrain, individual liberty." This case, in which the Court ruled constitutional the city of Cleveland's school voucher scheme, provided an instance in which the vehicle of incorporation had in fact previously been an unfair tool to constrain liberty. Thomas continued: "Whatever the textual and historical merits of incorporating the Establishment Clause, . . . I cannot accept its use to oppose neutral programs of school choice. . . . There would be a tragic irony in converting the Fourteenth Amendment's guarantee of individual liberty into a prohibition on the exercise of educational choice" (at 2481-82).

105. *Zorach v. Clauson*, 343 U.S. 306 (1952). So-called released-time religious instruction was disallowed *on* school grounds in *McCollum v. Board of Education*, 333 U.S. 203 (1948).

taxes,[106] taxpayer-funded chaplains to begin legislative sessions with prayer,[107] and civic institutions to display crèches on public property.[108] As well, the Court guaranteed that religious groups have equal access to facilities at public universities[109] and primary and secondary schools.[110] It also ensured that religiously oriented student groups at public educational institutions would have equal access to student activity funds.[111] More recently, the Court indicated that taxpayer-funded school vouchers may be used at religious schools.[112]

These apparent victories notwithstanding, conservative Christians grew alarmed by what they viewed as an attempt by the Supreme Court to unfairly bulldoze religion off of the public square. Two cases in particular caused immediate controversy and continued to loom large in conservative complaints through subsequent decades. In 1962, in *Engel v. Vitale,* the Supreme Court ruled unconstitutional the practice of school-sponsored prayer. Then, less than a year later in a case brought by two churchgoing Unitarians, the Court outlawed the practice of school-sponsored devotional Bible reading.[113] For religious conservatives, these two cases signaled the beginning of a steady campaign, led by secularist

106. *Walz v. Tax Commission,* 397 U.S. 664 (1970).

107. *Marsh v. Chambers,* 463 U.S. 783 (1983).

108. *Lynch v. Donnelly,* 465 U.S. 668 (1984). Note, however, that the ruling in this case was limited, made in part because the crèche did not stand alone, sharing equal time with other holiday symbols, including a Christmas tree, a menorah, Santa Claus, and a "Season's Greetings" sign. For a thorough and persuasive critique of this decision, see Winnifred Fallers Sullivan, *Paying the Words Extra: Religious Discourse in the Supreme Court of the United States* (Cambridge: Harvard University Press, 1994). Other crèche cases have resulted in opposite outcomes; see, for example, *Allegheny County v. Greater Pittsburgh ACLU,* 492 U.S. 573 (1989).

109. *Widmar v. Vincent,* 454 U.S. 263 (1981).

110. *Board of Education v. Mergens,* 496 U.S. 226 (1990).

111. *Ronald W. Rosenberger, et al., Petitioners v. Rector and Visitors of the University of Virginia et al.,* 515 U.S. 819 (1995). The Court has not, however, allowed university students to withhold mandatory activity fees because they object (in this case on religious grounds) to certain groups receiving those monies. Provided the fees are distributed fairly, the majority ruled, the university can distribute money among different campus organizations in the service of facilitating free speech among students. See *Board of Regents v. Southworth,* 529 U.S. 217 (2000).

112. *Zelman v. Simmons-Harris,* 000 U.S. 00-1751 (2002).

113. *District of Abington Township v. Schempp,* 374 U.S. 203 (1963). For reaction to the decisions, see "Storm over the Supreme Court," CBS Reports television program, 1963.

elites and reinforced by secularist judges, against the forces of faith in American culture.

According to this narrative arc, more legal assaults upon religion and religious values soon followed those two decisions. In 1968 the Supreme Court struck down an Arkansas law that prohibited the teaching of evolution in public schools.[114] In 1971 the Court ruled unconstitutional Pennsylvania's practice of contracting with nonpublic schools to perform secular educational services.[115] Two years later the Supreme Court struck what

114. *Epperson v. Arkansas*, 399 U.S. 97 (1968). Since then the federal courts have also rejected various Christian attempts to soften what they see as the dogmatism of the public school science curricula. See, for example, *Freiler, et al. v. Tangipahoa Parish Board of Education*, 185 F. 3d 337 (1999), which rejected a Louisiana school board's attempt to mandate a disclaimer before science classes took up the subject of evolution. The disclaimer read: "It is hereby recognized by the Tangipahoa Board of Education, that the lesson to be presented, regarding the origin of life and matter, is known as the Scientific Theory of Evolution and should be presented to inform students of the scientific concept and not intended to influence or dissuade the Biblical version of Creation or any other concept." The statement continued: "It is further recognized by the Board of Education that it is the basic right and privilege of each student to form his/her own opinion and maintain beliefs taught by parents on this very important matter of the origin of life and matter. Students are urged to exercise critical thinking and gather all information possible and closely examine each alternative toward forming an opinion." The U.S. Supreme Court denied certiorari, allowing the appellate court's ruling against the statement to stand.

115. *Lemon v. Kurtzman*, 403 U.S. 602 (1971). This case recommended a tripartite test for laws to pass in order to satisfy the Constitution: the law must have "a secular legislative purpose"; its "primary effect" must neither advance nor inhibit religion; and it must not foster "an excessive entanglement" with religion. The "*Lemon* test" was variously deployed in subsequent cases, conveniently ignored in others. Initially hailed by some as a hermeneutical Holy Grail for religion-clause jurisprudence, the Court's *Lemon* test only shifted the scene of the same old interpretive battle. Instead of asking what "free exercise" and "establishment" meant, the Court began to ask what it meant by "primary effect" or "excessive entanglement."

Since its creation, the *Lemon* test has continued to bedevil First Amendment jurisprudence. Justice Scalia noted its inconsistent jurisprudential role in a 1993 decision: "like some ghoul in a late-night horror movie that repeatedly sits up in its grave and shuffles abroad after being repeatedly killed and buried, *Lemon* stalks our Establishment Clause jurisprudence once again. . . . Over the years . . . no fewer than five of the currently sitting Justices have, in their own opinions, personally driven pencils through the creature's heart (the author of today's opinion repeatedly), and a sixth has joined an opinion in doing so. . . . The secret of the *Lemon* test's survival, I think, is that it is so easy to kill. It is there to scare us (and our audience) when we wish it to do so, but we can command it to return to the tomb at will. . . . When we wish to strike down a practice it forbids, we invoke it, . . . when we wish to uphold a practice it forbids, we ignore it enwas perceived as an enormous blow when it legalized abortion in *Roe v. Wade.*[116] A Kentucky law mandating the posting of the Ten Commandments in public school classrooms ran afoul of the Court in 1980,[117] and subsequent attempts to sidestep this ruling customarily failed. In 1983 the Supreme Court upheld an earlier decision by the Internal Revenue Service to revoke the tax exemption for Bob Jones University — a bulwark of Christian fundamentalism — because of its racially discriminatory admissions policy.[118] In 1985 the Supreme Court ruled illegal the State of New York's use of Title I funds for remedial services in parochial schools.[119] Other, more recent cases confirmed conservative fears that the Supreme Court disdained religion, particularly conservative Protestantism. Trying to circumvent the Court's ban on school-sponsored prayer, Alabama passed a law in the early 1980s that provided for a period of "meditation or voluntary prayer" each school day; the Court tossed this out too.[120] And in 1992 the Court disallowed school-sponsored prayer at public school graduation ceremonies.[121] According to late twentieth-century conservative Christians, an imperious Supreme Court had Christianity on the run.

The chronology of these Court cases reveals that, far from developing on two separate tracks, defeats and victories intermingled and were often interrelated. The school-prayer and Bible-reading cases of the 1960s, and

---

tirely. . . . Sometimes, we take a middle course, calling its three prongs 'no more than helpful signposts.' . . . Such a docile and useful monster is worth keeping around, at least in a somnolent state; one never knows when one might need him"; *Lamb's Chapel v. Center Moriches School District,* 508 U.S. 384 (1993).

116. *Roe v. Wade,* 410 U.S. 113 (1973). Indeed, one scholar has argued that "For Christian conservatives, no other previous ruling of the Court so exemplified the almost complete triumph of secular humanism in America"; Brown, *Trumping Religion,* 21.

117. *Stone v. Graham,* 449 U.S. 39 (1980).

118. *Bob Jones University v. United States,* 461 U.S. 574 (1983). In response to increased public attention to the school after presidential candidate George W. Bush campaigned there in 2000, BJU reversed its long-standing policy against interracial dating.

119. *Aguilar v. Felton,* 473 U.S. 402 (1985). The Supreme Court changed its mind twelve years later in *Agostini v. Felton,* 000 U.S. 96-552 (1997), but the first decision formed part of the legal background in which these advocacy groups arose.

120. *Wallace v. Jaffree,* 472 U.S. 38 (1985). It should be noted that a public school "moment of silence" was not ruled entirely out of bounds by this decision; indeed, it was the legislature's declared intent to return voluntary prayer to public schools — and not the creation of a moment of silence itself — that seemed to have sealed its fate. Two justices, Powell and O'Connor, indicated that this was the decisive factor in their joining the six-member majority.

121. *Lee v. Weisman,* 505 U.S. 577 (1992).

the granting of abortion rights in 1973, catalyzed conservative Christian ef-
frontery, such that evangelicals and fundamentalists were fully engaged in
many subsequent church-state conflicts. By the 1980s, conservative Christian lawyers were organizing and offering amicus curiae briefs in relevant
cases before the Court. In upholding the revocation of Bob Jones University's tax exemption in 1983, the Supreme Court had attacked a member of
the family. By the late 1980s and early 1990s, religious conservatives had
begun actively participating in an increasing number of key cases, and had
even succeeded in directly winning some of them.[122] Not merely interested
bystanders, conservative Christians — alarmed, seemingly besieged by secularists on all sides — plunged themselves deeply into the ebb and flow of
church-state decisions after the 1960s.

Conservatives contended that the Supreme Court's apparently antireligious agenda was matched by the federal government's multiform attempts to weaken Christianity by invading once-sacrosanct areas of family
and community life. The nation's ruling apparatus indisputably grew by
leaps and bounds over the course of the twentieth century: from the New
Deal to the Great Society and even on to President Bill Clinton's New Covenant programs, the government's reach extended over more and more of
American life. This dramatically increased the government's contact with
previously autonomous areas of life such as education and the family —
spheres where religious conservatives adamantly insisted that the government did not belong. Sociologist Robert Wuthnow has located special-
purpose groups within the context of this phenomenon. "As the state has
expanded its functions," Wuthnow has observed, "particularly in the areas
of welfare, education, equal rights legislation and other kinds of regulation
that affect the day-to-day activities of citizens, special interest groups have
arisen for the express purpose of combating, restraining, or promoting certain types of government action."[123] Conservatives viewed these developments as a federal onslaught against Christian values, one that required a
vigorous response before secularists succeeded in completely erasing all
traces of America's true identity from public culture. To seek relief from
hostile courts and an overgrown federal government, religious conservatives grew more active not just in politics, but also in the legal arena. Chris-

---

122. Conservative Christian lawyers — though not those of TRI — were directly
responsible for victories in *Lamb's Chapel* (1993); *Rosenberger v. Virginia* (1995); and
Southworth (2000).

123. Wuthnow, *Restructuring*, 114.

tian legal advocacy organizations such as The Rutherford Institute represented one particular manifestation of a broad conservative counterattack.

4. Conclusion

The American histories of voluntary organizations, conservative Protestantism, and church-state jurisprudence all intersect at the location of
Christian legal activism. Though distinct, these stories also overlap in key
ways that informed the self-understanding of religious conservatives,
shaped their worldview, and molded their attitudes toward the larger culture. Despite frequent ambivalence, conservative Christians viewed themselves as custodians of American culture and identity. As the new millennium drew near, that core identity appeared threatened from many
powerful quarters. In response, conservative Christians shook off their previous public reticence and took action. Duty-bound as Americans and as
Christians to defend their nation from its enemies — especially internal
ones — the religious decided to turn litigious.[124]

The Rutherford Institute represented an important and illustrative
example of the religiously conservative turn to the courts. Chapter 2 examines why John W. Whitehead founded TRI. His complex understanding of
American history strongly influenced his decision to create a legal advocacy organization in the first place, and his frequent retelling of that history
revealed considerable anxiety about the disappearance of an American culture properly understood as Christian.

Chapter 3 surveys in detail the public materials generated by TRI
during its first two decades. Reflecting its founder's philosophy, TRI sought
to champion individual religious rights over against hostile agents of the
state. In addition to providing professional legal assistance, TRI also situated itself as a critical broker of information to a constituency newly awak-
ened to legal issues. Through books, newsletters, pamphlets, radio shows,
audiotapes, movies, and the Internet, Whitehead and TRI developed a
ready supply of resources for those who felt their religious rights were under attack. These materials also revealed an evolving understanding of religious freedom, a shift in thinking with practical consequences for TRI's
public visibility and success.

---

124. I first encountered this apt turn of phrase in Gerlin, "With Free Help, the Religious Turn Litigious."

Chapter 4 analyzes the specialized legal work performed by White-head and The Rutherford Institute in the federal courts. In dozens of cases TRI filed amicus curiae briefs that indicated how the organization's religiously tinged cultural perspective became incorporated into a legal hermeneutical framework. These briefs provide an occasion for considering the general efficacy of amicus advocacy, and more importantly, they offer critical evidence for evaluating the particular consequences of amicus advocacy for conservative Christians. By fighting an essentially cultural battle in a specialized legal realm, TRI revealed the possibilities and limitations of religiously motivated legal advocacy. In taking the fight directly to the perceived foe's home turf, legal special-interest groups like TRI may have chosen a strategy that relinquishes more than realizes coveted cultural goals.

Finally, chapter 5 uses The Rutherford Institute to evaluate the consequences of the conservative religious turn to legal advocacy. Many factors have contributed to this choice of strategy, including America's growing religious pluralism, the Supreme Court's own attempt to negotiate that pluralism in light of the First Amendment, and the enormous growth of government. Though it is a plausible strategy in light of who conservatives identify as enemies, legal activism has had several unintended consequences. In forming organizations such as The Rutherford Institute, conservative Protestants may have misplaced their energies, making unintended intellectual compromises and inadvertently feeding the bureaucratic monster they sought to fight.

∽ 2 ∾

Secular Humanism on the Loose:
John Whitehead and the Founding of
The Rutherford Institute

At one time Christians had command of the United States. Through toleration they receded until the non-Christians grew too strong to combat any longer. Once the non-Christians were in power they began eliminating Christianity from the system. . . .

This land can once again be a Christian nation. A reformation is at hand. All that is needed is the dominion-oriented Christian man.

John W. Whitehead, 1977[1]

The concept of neutrality . . . is a fallacy. All knowledge has a spiritual and religious base to it. One system enlightens, the other deceives.

John W. Whitehead, 1980[2]

The early story of The Rutherford Institute (TRI) is fairly straightforward. John Wayne Whitehead created his legal advocacy group in 1982. He later recalled to the *Wall Street Journal* that he incorporated his new organization with little more than his family address book, $200 in his pocket, and a missionary's zeal for defending religious rights. He quickly discovered that

---

1. John W. Whitehead, *The Separation Illusion: A Lawyer Examines the First Amendment* (Milford, Mich.: Mott Media, 1977), 35, 38.

2. John W. Whitehead and Jon Barton, *Schools on Fire* (Wheaton, Ill.: Tyndale House, 1980), 54-55.

a market for his services existed among religious citizens who needed legal aid. Within a decade the institute claimed to receive over two thousand requests for assistance each month at its headquarters in Charlottesville, Virginia. In ten years the organization's size increased in proportion to its busyness; by 1994 TRI employed ten full-time attorneys in six American offices and three overseas branches, with an annual budget of $8 million. In addition, scores of unpaid volunteers supported the institute's work, performing tasks from clerical filing to pro bono legal representation.[3] Whitehead's decision to assist Paula Jones in suing President Clinton in 1997 engendered even more attention to TRI's growing efforts. In a relatively short fifteen years, John Whitehead and his organization achieved considerable stability and public prominence.[4]

Though no longer a one-man show, The Rutherford Institute's identity cannot be separated from the biography and intellectual concerns of its originator. Especially in its infancy, The Rutherford Institute in every sense *was* John Whitehead. Indeed, TRI exhibited a fusion of founder and organization quite common in parachurch groups, especially conservative Christian ones.[5] Though many people executed duties in TRI's name, it was Whitehead — through books, movies, pamphlets, speeches, and legal opinions — who imbued TRI with its distinctive character. Therefore, gaining a sense of how Whitehead viewed his contemporary surroundings provides the best clues to what sparked the founding of his new organization. His voluminous writings and other public offerings presented most clearly the worldview that shaped his interest in legal activism. Whitehead believed strongly that Christianity belonged at the center of the American experience — historically, morally, and constitutionally. Near the end of the twentieth century he thought that secularist forces were deliberately seeking to supplant Christianity. Whitehead founded The Rutherford Institute in this

3. Andrea Gerlin, "With Free Help, the Religious Turn Litigious," *Wall Street Journal,* 17 Feb. 1994, B1.

4. The year 1997 probably marked the peak of TRI's success. In taking on the Jones case, Whitehead drew the attention of the mainstream press as never before; see, for example, Jay Branegan, "In Paula We Trust: With *Jones v. Clinton,* a Christian-Right Legal Group Makes Its Case," *Time,* 24 Nov. 1997, and Megan Rosenfeld, "On the Case for Paula Jones," *Washington Post,* 17 Jan. 1998, B1. However, the move repelled many once-reliable Christian donors, which in turn forced layoffs and contraction at TRI.

5. The history of conservative Christianity in twentieth-century America is dotted with religious leaders who created public organizations that directly reflected their own values and concerns. Prominent examples include Dwight Moody, William Bell Trollinger, Billy Graham, Jerry Falwell, and Pat Robertson.

context with two goals: to convince his fellow believers that secular humanism was indeed on the loose, and to enable Christian resistance to secularism to take successful legal form.

1. Christian Legal Activism: Whitehead's "Calling from God"[6]

In 1974 John Whitehead gained the two most indispensable credentials for his later work: he took his law degree from the University of Arkansas, and he converted to evangelical Christianity. He enrolled in law school following a stint in the army during which, having been relegated to home duty during the Vietnam War due to a physical defect, he often troubled his commanding officers by attending antiwar demonstrations and arriving on base with a peace symbol attached to his car's windshield. Following graduation from law school, where the self-described "left-wing radical" continued to protest the war and wrote for an underground campus newspaper, he joined a prosperous law practice. Religiously speaking, he remained far away from his eventual spiritual destination. Reflecting on those days, Whitehead later wrote that he was "almost an atheist" and "pretty stridently anti-Christian." According to an article in *Rutherford,* TRI's magazine, "back then he would not allow his wife, a Christian, even to discuss religion in their home."[7]

A visit to a local J. C. Penney diverted him from a more conventional career path and toward a religious awakening. Already a fan of science fiction, Whitehead found and purchased a book he thought belonged to the genre: Hal Lindsey's best-selling work, *The Late Great Planet Earth.*[8] The author's conjoining of biblical prediction and contemporary events immediately and profoundly impacted the young attorney: "it spooked me right into heaven," Whitehead later recalled.[9] Convinced that, through Lindsey,

6. Whitehead often described his legal advocacy work as his "calling from God"; see, for example, Branegan, "In Paula We Trust."

7. Jim Travisano, "Fighting for Religious Freedom," *Rutherford* 3, no. 1 (Jan. 1994): 3-11.

8. Hal Lindsey, *The Late Great Planet Earth* (Grand Rapids: Zondervan, 1970). Lindsey's apocalyptic work became the best-selling book of the 1970s.

9. Quoted in Ted Olsen, "The Dragon Slayer," *Christianity Today,* 7 Dec. 1998; Tim Stafford, "Move Over, ACLU: A Host of New Public-Interest Law Firms Are Helping American Christians Fight for Their Religious Liberties," *Christianity Today,* 25 Oct. 1993, is the one source in which Whitehead attributed his changing career priorities to having read Lindsey's best seller.

God had called him not to the law but to ministry, Whitehead quickly packed his family into their 1965 Dodge and moved to California so that he could attend Lindsey's Light and Power House Seminary.[10]

While Whitehead was there, a Los Angeles schoolteacher approached the new convert. Having explained to her students why she wore a crucifix, the teacher had landed herself in trouble with school administrators. Would Whitehead help her out? The lawyer-cum-seminarian stepped in at her request and succeeded in "persuading her principal to respect her constitutional rights." This, according to TRI materials, constituted only the first of many cries for help that Whitehead and — not much later — his new advocacy organization would faithfully answer.[11]

While in seminary, Whitehead later remembered, he deepened his understanding of church-state issues and "developed firsthand experience about how distorted legal views were hurting many religious people." He looked out at America and saw its conservative Christian subpopulation in need of a savior, one armed with the correct understanding of the Constitution and the courage to proclaim it and fight for it. As Whitehead explained in a 1994 pamphlet, "I discovered, in story after story, that a whole generation of religious people was being systematically disenfranchised from their rights in a free nation." Most of these people could not afford legal counsel: "Something had to be done."[12]

Few saviors accomplish their missions without deep personal sacrifices, and the organization's self-narrative made it clear that Whitehead was no exception. Time after time in TRI's materials, Whitehead emerged as a selfless visionary, a convert driven by his faith to assist his fellow believers and citizens at whatever the financial, professional, or familial cost. God's work, not creature comforts, remained his priority. ("It wasn't until 1986 that we had any living room furniture," readers of TRI's monthly magazine learned in 1994.)[13] Over the next several years, according to his official in-

10. Travisano, "Fighting for Religious Freedom."

11. *Justice for All: The Rutherford Institute Story* (Charlottesville, Va.: The Rutherford Institute, 1994).

12. *Justice for All*. This concern for the disenfranchised remained a consistent touchstone throughout the first two decades of TRI's existence. Though hardly above seeking publicity, Whitehead and TRI distinguished themselves from similar organizations by focusing upon grassroots concerns. Indeed, Whitehead's decision to take the case of Paula Jones could be viewed as fitting well into TRI's desire to help individuals too poor, too powerless, or too ill-informed to help themselves.

13. Travisano, "Fighting for Religious Freedom."

stitutional biography, Whitehead "steadily turned his newly found faith into action" by assisting those whose First Amendment rights required defending. This cost him a great deal of time and money, but even as "hard financial times ensued and threatened to discourage John and his growing family from their journey of faith," the dutiful pilgrim pressed forward with his dream of creating an advocacy organization.[14]

In 1979 the Whiteheads switched coasts again, moving to Washington, D.C., where he again practiced law. Soon unable to afford his office rent, Whitehead moved his practice into his home basement. The hero's sacrifice knew no boundaries for, despite obvious financial difficulties, he continued to accept pro bono religious cases. He nobly assisted the Nobels, homeschoolers who had been arrested for not enrolling their children in public school. Again, the costs were high: "John put more than $25,000 of his own money and hours of time into the case," and a friend even took over his house payments for a year. His eventual victory in the case, however, convinced him of the rightness of his cause.[15] The John Whitehead revealed in early institute materials was a selfless martyr on behalf of the politically weak and religiously oppressed, someone eschewing personal contentment so that he might pursue God's justice for others.

Even before he founded TRI, Whitehead was making a public case for the kind of legal activism to which he would soon devote his energies. After converting to Christianity in the mid-1970s, he emptied his thoughts into several rhetorical vessels. Through cultural critique, historical argumentation, and legal analysis, Whitehead sounded a tocsin to his fellow Americans, and most especially to his conservative Christian compatriots. Christianity once belonged at the center of American culture, Whitehead contended; this was in fact what the nation's founders intended. But contemporary America looks terribly disfigured when compared with the founders' original vision. For Whitehead the United States, when examined in light of its history and founding principles, was barely recognizable; it had become a fun house distortion of its original — and therefore purest — form. To restore the republic's true character, American Christians must awaken and trade in their cultural quietism for political activism. And, Whitehead insisted, that political activism must include entering the American courts.

Though his cultural analysis operated on multiple levels, Whitehead

14. *Justice for All.*
15. *Justice for All.*

most often framed his generalized jeremiad in legal terms. In his judgment the legal system formed a critical component of American democracy and identity. Indeed, he argued that it was largely through the courts that the founders' original plan for the nation had been overturned. In his writings Whitehead continually asserted that the misinterpretation and misapplication of the First Amendment's religion clauses — the distortion of the appropriate relationship between church and state — had caused the current American nightmare. Restoring the proper constitutional harmony between religion and republic, in other words, was the necessary and sufficient condition for arresting the country's disconcerting demise. This, generally speaking, served as the intellectual motivation for creating a legal advocacy organization.

2. Shattering *The Separation Illusion*

Three years after his conversion, in 1977, Whitehead published *The Separation Illusion: A Lawyer Examines the First Amendment*. Perhaps he thought the nation, fresh from a yearlong bicentennial celebration of America's birth, might be ready to rediscover the "real," original meaning of disestablishment. His first book, *The Separation Illusion* remained his most single-minded and complete examination of church and state in America. Indeed, with only subtle refinements he returned to the same themes again and again over the next two decades. In this work Whitehead began to lay the legal foundation upon which TRI would soon be erected. Anchored firmly in an understanding of America as a Christian nation, he sallied forth to critique the current shape of church-state relations and to call all (Christian) citizens to defeat the forces of secularism and to recapture the nation's original character.

Unlike the proverbial doctor who offers a patient both good news and bad news, John Whitehead the cultural physician had for his patient only bad news . . . and more bad news. The nation, once healthy, now ailed, and in *The Separation Illusion* the author diagnosed the malady and pointed toward the cure. He posed the guiding question early on: "If the United States was once so prosperous with Christianity as its foundation, then why have the people forsaken the Christian way to follow the dark path that is eating away at present-day America?"[16] In trying to build an ideal nation apart

---

16. Whitehead, *The Separation Illusion*, 13.

from God, humanity has been digging itself "a pit of no return."[17] As signaled by the book's title, Whitehead believed that the country's problems
stemmed from a common illusion concerning how church and state should
relate to each other. Only by recovering the proper understanding of the
First Amendment, Whitehead insisted, could the nation reverse its descent
into immorality (or worse). Dismal consequences awaited a nation whose
citizens refused to hear his prophetic word. Even the book's back cover set
an urgent, dire tone: "we must **ACT NOW**" before our basic freedoms, now
threatened, disappear altogether.[18] For the nation to restore itself to health
and prosperity, it must forgo the "illusion," the false belief, that the United
States can prosper apart from the divine.

The "separation illusion" of the title operated on two related but distinct levels for Whitehead. In purely legal terms, the illusion was that there
should be — in Thomas Jefferson's oft-quoted and even more often
misdeployed phrase — a "wall of separation between church and state."
According to the author, the nation's founders (including the third president himself) did not favor strict separationism, and the current judicial
preference for this church-state paradigm distorts their wishes. This misguided legal understanding reinforces and reflects a related, more general
"separation illusion," the erroneous belief that American society can sus-
tain itself without God. Whitehead argued that the Revolutionary War "established the greatest Christian nation this world has ever known," and ar-
rogantly forsaking that identity not only flouts the founders' intentions, it
may mean the very death of the republic.[19] The contemporary legal misunderstanding, then, both instantiated and exemplified the larger illusion, the
false assumption that the United States can thrive as a society without honoring God's will.

Though in his introduction Whitehead reassured his readers that his
"is not a book of utter despair," doom and gloom permeated *The Separation Illusion*. The narrative vacillated throughout between critique and
prescription, but the dreary emphasis remained upon the former. As such,
it had the lonely, plaintive feel of a classic jeremiad. By clinging to the separation illusion, he informed his readers again and again, America was
flirting with permanent ruin. The enemies of the nation are legion and

17. Whitehead, *The Separation Illusion*, 14.
18. In this book Whitehead often used capital letters and bold-face type to turn
up the rhetorical volume.
19. Whitehead, *The Separation Illusion*, 13.

well organized, the consequences of their godless attitudes and actions are dire, and time is quickly running out. Woe unto you, Americans; repent before it is too late.

2.1. America's Fall from Grace

Whitehead presented a distinctive historical narrative to explain to his audience how the nation had arrived at such a sorry state. In his view the story of America was the tale of a once-religious nation that had recently abandoned its originating ideals. Even before landing at Plymouth Rock, he insisted early in the book, the settlers of the new nation intended to live according to Christian precepts. The Mayflower Compact, which unnamed historians believe should properly be considered "the birth certificate of the American Republic," was clearly "based on biblical principles."[20] This spiritual centrism persisted throughout the colonial period and culminated in the creation of a new nation. For Whitehead, this religiously informed context represented the Eden from which the United States had since fallen.

In Whitehead's history of the American republic, in the beginning was the word, and the word was the United States Constitution. That and the Declaration of Independence were created by a collection of reverent men who intended for Christianity to reside at the new nation's cultural center. Relying entirely upon conservative Christian histories to make his case,[21] Whitehead argued that American laws both before and after the Constitution were thoroughly based in biblical religion. In the new nation, law was to reign supreme, and "the foundation of American law at that time was Christian theology, which was based on the Scriptures."[22] Indeed, Christian assumptions pervaded everything, everywhere. Whitehead contended that "the common presupposition base of that day was clearly taken from the Christian Bible," and that "the basic foundation of the govern-

---

20. Whitehead, *The Separation Illusion*, 39. Presumably the historians who hold this view are not those he earlier chastised for pretending to "objectivity." See below for a discussion of this critique.

21. Whitehead most frequently cited James C. Hefley, *America: One Nation under God* (Wheaton, Ill.: Victor, 1975); Rousas John Rushdoony, *The Institutes of Biblical Law*, 3 vols. (Nutley, N.J.: Craig Press, 1973), esp. vol. 1; and C. Gregg Singer, *A Theological View of American History* (1969).

22. Whitehead, *The Separation Illusion*, 45.

ment was Christian."[23] It simply cannot be denied, argued the author, that "Christianity and the holy Scriptures were the guiding lights" in drafting the Constitution.[24] In fact, though the document does not mention any deity, Whitehead nevertheless insisted that "the Christian influence was written into the Constitution in 1787."[25] How could it not have been? When the Constitution was adopted, the author claimed, 2 million of the 3.5 million citizens were Christian, with almost all of them subscribing to "basic Calvinistic beliefs."[26] From 1740 to 1789, "the great bulk of the people inhabiting the United States . . . were either Christian or living lives based on Christian presuppositions."[27] According to the author's interpretation of

23. Whitehead, *The Separation Illusion*, 18.

24. Whitehead, *The Separation Illusion*, 24. Whitehead circled around this point with varying degrees of credibility. For instance, he cited Winthrop Hudson's opinion that Calvinism was written directly into the Constitution — a judgment since echoed, or at least partially supported, by other American historians. Whitehead asserted that "the Christian view of government" is equivalent to the notion "that government is necessary to check the sinful propensities of men" (22). But this overlooked the way in which orthodox Christian anthropology intersected with the more secular political theories of influential authors like Montesquieu. This felicitous overlapping of theology and political theory undoubtedly helped the Constitution win passage: religious and secular alike could comfortably find their own worldviews reflected in the new charter. See Forrest McDonald, *Novus Ordo Seclorum: The Intellectual Origins of the Constitution* (Lawrence: University Press of Kansas, 1985); Mark A. Noll, *A History of Christianity in the United States and Canada* (Grand Rapids: Eerdmans, 1992), 114-19; and Sidney E. Mead, *The Lively Experiment: The Shaping of Christianity in America* (New York: Harper and Row, 1963), 38-54. So, although it is in some sense accurate to see Calvinism reflected in the American Constitution, it is an exaggeration to say, as Rousas John Rushdoony does in a quotation approved by Whitehead, "The Constitution was designed to perpetuate a Christian order" (24).

25. Whitehead, *The Separation Illusion*, 22. As mentioned in chapter 1, occasionally a desperate soul has pointed out that the Constitution in Article VII does refer to "the Year of Our Lord one thousand seven hundred and Eighty Seven," but most acknowledge that America's founding charter is, strictly speaking, a godless one. See, for example, R. Laurence Moore and Isaac Kramnick, *The Godless Constitution: The Case against Religious Correctness* (New York: Norton, 1996).

26. Whitehead, *The Separation Illusion*, 18. For a persuasive rebuttal, see Jon Butler, "Why Revolutionary America Wasn't a 'Christian Nation,'" in *Religion and the New Republic: Faith in the Founding of America*, ed. James H. Hutson (Lanham, Md.: Rowman and Littlefield, 2000). According to Butler, at least 80 percent of Revolutionary-era colonists did not belong to a church. "However politically useful in either the nineteenth century or our own times," he writes, "the concept of a 'Christian nation' does not resonate well with the facts of eighteenth-century colonial and American history" (197).

27. Whitehead, *The Separation Illusion*, 21.

American history, the Constitution clearly represented a Christian charter for a Christian people.[28]

Cognizant of historical evidence against his argument for an originally Christian America, Whitehead tried to face that evidence squarely. Many believe that Deists decisively influenced the new nation's character, he admitted. However, this is simply a lie foisted upon unwitting citizens by "non-Christian" historians.[29] Benjamin Franklin and Thomas Jefferson, he assured his readers, really did not fit the classic definition of a Deist. How can Franklin have been a Deist when he asked for a prayer at the Constitutional Convention on 28 June 1787?[30] Thanks to his pious gesture, the U.S. Congress has since opened its sessions with prayer. As well, Whitehead informed his readers, Franklin held the evangelist George Whitefield in high esteem, something that clearly indicates the Philadelphian's latent orthodoxy. Rehabilitating Jefferson proved a tougher task, but Whitehead attempted it anyway, claiming that the Virginian only half-heartedly dabbled in Deism. After all, Jefferson once wrote that "I tremble for my country, when I reflect that God is just." In doing so, argued Whitehead, the nation's third president was signaling his belief in something more than the impersonal and distant Deist deity. In the final analysis, Whitehead claimed, Deism may have slightly influenced these two men,

28. Though the U.S. Supreme Court plays the role of snake in this story of the nation's fall from grace, Whitehead did not hesitate to cite its rulings to prop up his argument that America has ever been a Christian nation. Citing rulings in 1892, 1931, and 1952, Whitehead detailed how at least some justices have examined the historical record and concluded — as he had — that the United States has been and always should be a thoroughly religious country. For example, the author approvingly cited Justice William O. Douglas from *Zorach v. Clauson* in 1952: "We are a religious people and our [*sic*] institutions presuppose a Supreme Being." For Whitehead, Justice Douglas stated an obvious truth more than two centuries old.

29. The author did not specify the identity of these villains.

30. The story of Franklin's call for prayer has long served as a common trope for those arguing for a United States founded on Christianity. The aged Philadelphian did in fact call for prayer during a particularly thorny period, but his proposal was voted down by his fellow delegates. This fact does not necessarily endow attendees with secularist credentials — it is likely they rejected Franklin's request because they did not want to pay a clergyman to deliver the prayer — but it does point out that the Constitutional Convention preoccupied itself far more with earthly, rather than spiritual, matters. On the facts and fictions surrounding Franklin's prayer, see Mark A. Noll, "Evangelicals in the American Founding and Evangelical Political Mobilization Today," in *Religion and the New Republic,* 137-39.

but "to call Franklin and Jefferson true deists is as erroneous as to call Karl Barth an evangelical Christian."[31]

If both the nation's key founders and its people were Christian and they so obviously intended for religion to have a decisive influence in American culture, how was it that contemporary Americans had come to believe in the separation of church and state? Whitehead had little trouble identifying the perpetrators of the separation illusion, those who had brought America to the brink of political and cultural ruin. Several culprits constituted a dark pantheon of cultural usurpers who conspired to drive Christianity from public life. Only by naming, refuting, and actively opposing these enemies could good Christians hope to restore America to its former integrity.

2.2. Enemies among Us: Secular Historians

To account for America's decline into secularism, Whitehead first claimed that the nation's narrative had been surreptitiously and deliberately hijacked. "Secular historians," he wrote, "have eradicated as much Christian influence as possible from history."[32] By suppressing America's religious roots, these historians have pretended to write "objective" history. In fact, Whitehead argued, there is no such thing: all stories and claims reflect a particular worldview. The question then becomes, Which worldview will be privileged? Which historical interpretation should be definitive? By removing religion from the American story, secular historians had not achieved "objectivity" or "neutrality" but instead had maliciously distorted history, replacing a true narrative with a false and damaging one.

In *The Separation Illusion* and subsequent works, Whitehead extended this critique to various enemies: those who aspire to objectivity are invariably tilting at windmills, for there is no such thing. According to the author, everyone, whether atheist or Christian, is religious. The choice, then, is not between subjectivity and objectivity, but between true faith and corrupt religion. Secular historians have chosen to propagate a false faith by telling a fallacious American story, one that excludes religion. Whitehead named no

31. Whitehead, *The Separation Illusion,* 21.

32. Whitehead, *The Separation Illusion,* 17. Others have lodged a similar complaint. See, for example, Warren A. Nord, *Religion and American Education: Rethinking a National Dilemma* (Chapel Hill: University of North Carolina Press, 1995), esp. 138-59.

names, but given the importance of history for both his cultural and legal critique, secular historians naturally appeared on his enemies list.

2.3. Enemies among Us: "The State"

Throughout *The Separation Illusion* Whitehead employed "the state" as a catchall category under which a vast menagerie of villains could be found. "The state" and "bureaucracy" served as authorial tropes that included a sundry cast of characters who had somehow insinuated themselves into the corridors of elite power. In the contemporary period, the attorney argued, "the state" had turned against the very constitutional system that created it and the very people who supposedly sustained it.

Echoing a theme common in late twentieth-century conservative politics,[33] Whitehead relentlessly complained of an ever growing and increasingly powerful government that disdained — and even destroyed — the rights of individual citizens. The "welfare state," the "Great Society," "big government" — all were programmatic manifestations of the quixotic goal of political utopia. Americans who attempted to create this perfect society were merely pursuing a civilization without God, and such a goal was both unchristian and un-American. Under a properly "scriptural" system of government — unlike the late twentieth-century version he found himself critiquing — the individual remained virtually autonomous. "Forsaking

33. See, for example, Charles Peters and Michael Nelson, eds., *The Culture of Bureaucracy* (New York: Holt, Rinehart and Winston, 1979); Linda L. M. Bennett, *Living with Leviathan: Americans Coming to Terms with Big Government* (Lawrence: University Press of Kansas, 1990); Harold G. Vatter and John F. Walker, *The Inevitability of Government Growth* (New York: Columbia University Press, 1990); Richard K. Armey, *The Freedom Revolution: The Republican House Majority Leader Tells Why Big Government Failed, Why Freedom Works, and How We Will Rebuild America* (Washington, D.C.: Regnery, 1995); James R. Kennedy and Walter D. Kennedy, *Why Not Freedom! America's Revolt against Big Government* (Gretna, La.: Pelican Publishing, 1995); Gregg Vanourek, Scott W. Hamilton, and Chester E. Finn, Jr., *Is There Life after Big Government? The Potential of Civil Society* (Indianapolis: Hudson Institute, 1996); Scott A. Hedge, ed., *Balancing America's Budget: Ending the Era of Big Government* (Washington, D.C.: Heritage Foundation, 1997); and John F. Walker and Harold G. Vatter, eds., *The Rise of Big Government in the United States* (Armonk, N.Y.: M. E. Sharpe, 1997) (a representative essay: "Bureaucracy: The Biggest Crisis of All"). Similar appraisals began almost as soon as New Deal programs were proposed. For an early comprehensive critique of Franklin Roosevelt's policies, see Merlo J. Pusey, *Big Government: Can We Control It?* (New York: Harper and Brothers, 1945).

the Scriptures as a guide for all things," on the other hand, "leads not only to chaos but also . . . to the totalitarian state — a government that totally controls its citizens."[34]

Regardless of which particular "statists" or "bureaucrats" Whitehead intended to identify, these agents of the state always represented opponents who must be resisted if the separation illusion would be shattered. Sometimes Whitehead aimed his criticisms particularly at lawmakers in Congress, those responsible for extending the state's unwelcome regulatory tentacles into the spheres of education and family. Most frequently "the state" indicated the judicial branch of government. Whitehead complained, for example, that federal judges had too often usurped the constitutional order in rigorously enforcing, and occasionally extending, the government's invasive regulatory regime. Specifically, the author reserved his most relentless and blistering attacks for the United States Supreme Court. Since the Civil War, Whitehead contended, the Court more than any institution had been responsible for denuding American identity of its essential Christian character. The relentless antipathy toward the Court expressed in *The Separation Illusion* indicated just how fervently Whitehead believed the contemporary American crisis to be substantially a *legal* one. Given that (il)legal machinations had created this mess, it was not surprising to find Whitehead soon proposing legal activism as a means of cleaning it up.

2.4. Enemies among Us: "Pure Democrats"

Though Whitehead often overlapped this category with others,[35] "pure democrats" loomed as particularly important enemies of "true" America. In his intellectual world "democracy" equaled the godless and tyrannical form of government identified with the French Revolution. He argued in *The Separation Illusion* that the United States is not really a "democracy" in the pure sense, nor should it be. The Puritans, the Pilgrims, and the founding fathers themselves were all aristocratically inclined, much more predisposed to hierarchy than to pure political equality. In fact, Whitehead in-

34. Whitehead, *The Separation Illusion*, 13.

35. It should be noted that this matrix of enemies is mine, not Whitehead's. Usually Whitehead described his enemies in terms of political vocation (such as federal judges or IRS bureaucrats), but he also believed firmly that ideas matter. "Pure democrats" can be found among many kinds of people, but wherever they are discovered, they should be resisted.

sisted, the "Calvinistic theology" they all shared "is directly opposed to
pure democracy."[36] The will of the people in fact was *not* the will of God.
Indeed, the popular will can cause all kinds of trouble; after all, "the crucifixion," he contended, "was a democratic event."[37] "Pure democrats" had
killed the Christian savior, and they now threatened to kill the most faithful national representation of his ideals.

Whitehead was decidedly queasy with the leveling implied by democracy not just because he equated it with tyranny and crucifixion, but also
because of its implications for the family as an autonomous social institution. Pure democrats, those who would make everyone equal to each other
in all things, have destroyed the American family. Why would democrats
target the family? "The family is the fundamental enemy of democracy," he
explained, because it is hierarchical, not egalitarian. Democracy requires
total brotherhood and, Whitehead warned, this "eventually eliminates fa-
therhood."[38] Unfortunately we can see the effects of democracy all around
us, and the consequences are dire: "As an institution, the family is passing
away. Only within Christendom has it thrived, but even there it is suffering
from democratization. The public school has largely emerged as a substi-
tute for the disappearing family in modern society. State control of education, as history instructs us, declares the death of the biblical family. . . .
The death of the family is sure to lead to the death of culture."[39] Democracy
means the razing of traditional family structures, the replacement of fathers
and mothers with governmental nannies more interested in perpetuating
government than caring for its charges.[40]

Not only is the family in trouble under a rigorously egalitarian regime,
Whitehead continued, but also individual rights are no longer secure. The
political and social freedom offered by democracy to its citizens sounds
tempting, the author admitted, but this really represents a diabolical trap by
which the government threatens to enslave its people. Rather than rooting
fundamental individual rights in God, as is proper, a democratic govern-

36. Whitehead, *The Separation Illusion*, 46.
37. Whitehead, *The Separation Illusion*, 48.
38. Whitehead, *The Separation Illusion*, 48.
39. Whitehead, *The Separation Illusion*, 50.
40. Whitehead was not the first to propose this revised political understanding. In
the 1960s, some supporters of Barry Goldwater's presidential candidacy — many of them
members of the John Birch Society — made a similar claim: "this is a Republic, not a Democracy!" See Lisa McGirr, *Suburban Warriors: The Origins of the New American Right*
(Princeton: Princeton University Press, 2001), 131.

ment guarantees individual rights by virtue of its own power. As the state grants individuals their freedoms, "it has to enlarge to enforce the rights it grants." Once granted this control, the state is poised to enslave the people.[41] This is inevitable, Whitehead warned. Totalitarianism is the only logical result of a government bent on equality. "Perfect equality . . . is only possible in a governmental system of total slavery." If you want to see an example of pure democracy in action, Whitehead suggested, take a look at the Soviet Union.[42] Democrats actually should be viewed not as patriots but as wolves in sheep's clothing, determined to transform the American republic not into the image of God but into that of its sworn enemy.

Democracy not only harms the family and the individual, but it also threatens the health of the church. "A government that operates on democratic principles," Whitehead continued, "will seek to reduce the church to nothing but a formal institution with no real significance."[43] A thoroughly egalitarian society, in fact, denies both Christianity and the Bible. Whitehead argued that "a truly godly people cannot establish a democracy since it is an unscriptural form of government."[44] After the fall, God established monarchy — not democracy — as the appropriate form of political organization. And what is so bad about hierarchical rule, anyway? Monarchies, his readers learned, "can be just as effective and benevolent as any other form of government." All depends on who holds the reins of power, regenerate or unregenerate people. "Basically, an ungodly people will find themselves under a tyranny," the author opined. "As the godly retain control, the tyranny recedes and freedom returns."[45] Having depicted egalitarian democracy as government with "a satanic flavor,"[46] Whitehead cast monarchy in a divine, and authentically American, light. The church would thrive under no other kind of regime.

2.5. The "Second American Revolution": Phase One

Whitehead asserted that the United States would still have this kind of regime — a hierarchical arrangement with God at the top — had not a "sec-

41. Whitehead, *The Separation Illusion,* 52.
42. Whitehead, *The Separation Illusion,* 53-54.
43. Whitehead, *The Separation Illusion,* 52.
44. Whitehead, *The Separation Illusion,* 57.
45. Whitehead, *The Separation Illusion,* 56.
46. Whitehead, *The Separation Illusion,* 51.

ond American revolution" occurred. The author sought to explain why, if the founders had designed an ideal, undemocratic republic intentionally suffused with Christian ideals, the nation no longer reflected that original design. For this he turned to the notion of a second revolution, one that reversed the results of the first. It originated in the legal realm but soon spread far and wide throughout American society. Trouble began during and right after the Civil War, an event reconfigured in *The Separation Illusion* as a conflict centrally between radical egalitarians in the North and aristocrats in the South — between demonic democrats and divinely favored monarchists. Having already rhetorically spat upon "pure democrats" and their radical egalitarianism, not surprisingly Whitehead accused Northern abolitionists of being the real villains in America's sectional conflict. Though Calvinism still reigned supreme in the South, Whitehead wrote, by the mid–nineteenth century Unitarianism and transcendentalism had taken over the North. This was not a happy development for America: "the Unitarian-abolitionist drive was fundamentally a move against its spiritual enemy, Calvinism."[47] Guilty of "idealizing the Negro," these Northerners sought to usher in a "utopian millennium" of equality.[48] Calling the Constitution an agreement with hell, abolitionists struck at the heart of America's identity and brought the country to the edge of anarchy. Radical egalitarians, social and political idealists, Unitarians, anti-Constitutionalists — Northerners embodied all the qualities Whitehead previously denounced.

But these accusations did not include the Northerners' greatest offense: to extend their ideas of radical equality, they had to increase the federal government's power over the states. The North's anti-Calvinist utopians sought to centralize the federal government in order to impose social and political egalitarianism upon the South. To do so, they upended the constitutional order: in other words, "This meant coercion."[49] The South, "with its emphasis on states' rights and the legality of the Constitution," served as an admirable "stumblingblock to the abolitionist drive."[50] But the North, having won the war, set out to bring down the Southern aristocracy and eliminate its preference for local autonomy. The North's diabolical tool

---

47. Whitehead, *The Separation Illusion*, 70.
48. John W. Whitehead, *The Second American Revolution* (Elgin, Ill.: Cook, 1982), 68.
49. Whitehead, *The Second American Revolution*, 68.
50. Whitehead, *The Separation Illusion*, 71.

for accomplishing this transformation, according to the author, was the Fourteenth Amendment.

The "radical," even "libertine" postwar Congress — one that unfairly lacked Southern representation — illegally ratified the Fourteenth Amendment.[51] The Northern-controlled Congress coercively imposed Reconstruction upon the defeated South, and though the vanquished eventually wrested back control of state governments from the black "puppet governments" established by their battle betters, the damage had already been done. "The federal government had established its power to intervene in state politics," Whitehead explained, "thereby dissolving state autonomy."[52] The North, by illegally manipulating the Constitution, had reconfigured the country. After the Civil War, "Americans found themselves living in a different nation, a nation enveloped by godless sentiments of hate and revenge, a land to which the Founding Fathers would have found themselves strangers."[53] According to Whitehead's understanding of history, the United States experienced a mere sixty years of Christ-centered, aristocratic political bliss before the democratic, utopian barbarians sacked the republic.

Clearly distressed by this blatant disregard for American principles and its repercussions, Whitehead circumambulated this point like a moth flitting about a bright light. Self-aware, he suggested to his readers that repeating this point was necessary because misunderstanding had persisted for so long. Life does not have to be as it is, Whitehead seemed to be urging: look at the history, there was a time when all was jurisdictionally right with the world. The Fourteenth Amendment may have "become a tool for furthering centralization of all governmental power in Washington, D.C.," but this should never have happened. This transformation "has been accomplished by misinterpretation and illusion."[54] If only enough American citizens would awaken to this horrible mistake, Whitehead implied, we might return to the halcyon antebellum days of Christian-flavored aristocracy and states' rights.

Whitehead intended to demonstrate the terrible consequences of this legal sleight of hand. By the end of the nineteenth century, "Calvinism was . . . nearly extinct, and humanistic man no longer was Unitarian or tran-

---

51. Whitehead, *The Separation Illusion*, 74-75.
52. Whitehead, *The Separation Illusion*, 75.
53. Whitehead, *The Separation Illusion*, 71.
54. Whitehead, *The Separation Illusion*, 77.

scendentalist but receded farther into illusion and became an evolutionist. He had found a way to separate himself even farther from God."[55] At this point, "phase one of the lie" had come to an end. Whitehead summarized what had happened: "Before the Civil War, the country was administered by a constitutional form of government which emphasized state and local government rather than national control and intervention. . . . The three postbellum amendments . . . ended the constitutional form of government and substituted a national government octopean in nature."[56] The octopus then prepared to spread out its tentacles.

2.6. The "Second American Revolution": Phase Two

With political power illegally relocated from the states to the federal government, "the country was now ripe for phase two" of the second American revolution. Whitehead contended that the revolution's chief agent was the United States Supreme Court. Upending constitutional norms through decisions cloaked in a smoke screen of neutrality, the Court had reconfigured the intended relationship between church and state. The hopes of the nation "now grew dim under the oppression of a strange and foreign government in Washington."[57] In pushing religion toward the sidelines of American life, Whitehead argued, the federal judiciary arbitrarily reconstituted the very substance of national identity. Indeed, as the United States entered the twentieth century, it no longer retained its original character: America was on the road to "post-America."

The U.S. Supreme Court accomplished phase two of the second American revolution through a deliberate, malicious program of hermeneutical sabotage — a program with tangibly disastrous consequences. Rather than remaining friendly to religious faith, as the founders had clearly intended, the Court continually misinterpreted the U.S. Constitution in a manner hostile to traditional religion. Moreover, the Court rejected the secure, religious — meaning Christian — foundations of the law in favor of a secularist, relativist moral ethic. The Court's claim to objectivity and neutrality was mere artifice. "Law has its origins in religion," Whitehead matter-of-factly stated, and any legal determination necessarily

55. Whitehead, *The Separation Illusion*, 76.
56. Whitehead, *The Separation Illusion*, 78.
57. Whitehead, *The Separation Illusion*, 76.

represented a "religious" decision: "The Supreme Court . . . makes a religious determination when it decides a case." The problem, of course, was that the Court no longer relied upon the correct religion: "Being humanists, the justices decide what is right or wrong on the basis of what their religion holds. The religion of humanity, however, is a relativistic religion; it merely depends on each circumstance whether a particular act is right or wrong."[58] Capricious judicial whim had replaced Christian certainty as the basis for judicial action.

Devoid of absolutes, the Court has been left with only its own determinative fancy. Free to vote for outcomes without feeling restrained by the absolute strictures of tradition, adrift on the sea of personal preferences, the justices practiced a form of democracy even more reprehensible than the pure democracy Whitehead previously critiqued. Since the 1940s, Whitehead claimed, the Court "has been deciding cases in the pure democratic and humanist terms of Rousseau's general will. But with this difference. The Court is deciding cases not by the general will of the majority, but by the general will of the minority (or interest groups)."[59] The Supreme Court justices were radical democrats; even worse, Whitehead charged, they were not even good ones.

For the author, this judicial behavior amounted to a veritable repeal of the Constitution. "When the Constitution is utilized by interpretation to accomplish the wishes of the presiding justices it then renders the Constitution worthless. No longer is it law; it is relativism. There is no morality because morality deals with *absolute* right and wrong. If there is no morality then an institution like the Supreme Court can adulterate the basic document of its country without thinking twice."[60] By ignoring the nation's religious roots and pushing religion out of the culture's center, the Court accelerated the country's ruinous transition from America to something else. "If Christianity is separated from America," he wrote, "then America no longer exists, and instead, something foreign comes to the forefront — Post-America."[61] In Whitehead's nightmarish perspective, five capricious humanists can determine — and have determined — the fate of a once-godly nation. The founders would hardly be able to recognize the nation they had long ago created.

58. Vatter and Walker, *Inevitability of Government Growth,* 59.
59. Vatter and Walker, *Inevitability of Government Growth,* 59.
60. Vatter and Walker, *Inevitability of Government Growth,* 59-60.
61. Vatter and Walker, *Inevitability of Government Growth,* 62.

Whitehead contended that hermeneutical legerdemain reached its apotheosis during Earl Warren's tenure as chief justice of the Supreme Court from 1953 to 1969. During this era the Court handed down two decisions integral to Whitehead's mythology of America's decline. In 1962 and 1963, the Supreme Court ruled unconstitutional the public-school practices of officially led prayer and Bible reading.[62] To reach those decisions, argued Whitehead, the Court had to ignore history. Instead of honoring American tradition, it invented law "out of nothing" in an "unethical and illegal" manner.[63] With these two "momentous" decisions, he claimed, "the Supreme Court declared death to God in the public schools of this country. . . . God somehow had become unconstitutional."[64] More than any others, argued Whitehead, those decisions "illustrate our move from 'One Nation Under God' to 'One Nation Under the Supreme Court.'"[65]

The author claimed that the Supreme Court in general and the Warren Court in particular stood "guilty beyond a reasonable doubt of willfully substituting fantasy for fact and for failing to investigate history." Having pushed official religious observances out of the public schools, the Court had deliberately twisted the meaning of the First Amendment so as to deprive the framers' original intentions of all significance. It continued to misinterpret the Fourteenth Amendment in order to impose its will upon the states. "Exercising a god-function," Whitehead proclaimed, "the Court radically altered the course of this country's government which, in turn, restricted our liberty that is so dear." The Court had transformed the Bill of Rights into a "Bill of Chains" to the state governments.[66]

The Supreme Court's "liberal, relativistic interpretation" has caused America to disappear, Whitehead wrote, for now we are living in "post-America."[67] This turn of events has been nothing short of a "fiasco."[68] Citizens now live under the ever-watchful eye of a tyrannical government: "The tentacles of control now extend from the District of Columbia to the smallest town in the United States."[69] Whitehead's narrative built to a crescendo:

---

62. *Engel v. Vitale*, 370 U.S. 421 (1962); *District of Abington Township v. Schempp*, 374 U.S. 203 (1963).

63. Whitehead, *The Separation Illusion*, 81.

64. Whitehead, *The Separation Illusion*, 88.

65. Whitehead, *The Separation Illusion*, 14.

66. Whitehead, *The Separation Illusion*, 66.

67. Whitehead, *The Separation Illusion*, 82-83.

68. Whitehead, *The Separation Illusion*, 66.

69. Whitehead, *The Separation Illusion*, 66.

It is conceded by most that this was once a Christian nation. The Constitution was written to reflect the Christian conscience of America. The First Amendment was to ensure noninterference with the Christian religious freedom of the States. The Supreme Court, by ruling that state-directed prayer and Bible reading in the public schools are unconstitutional, has violated that amendment. The Court, by patent misinterpretation of the Constitution, acted illegally. The appropriate question is: If the very judicial representatives of the government fail to uphold the law, how can they, in turn, expect the citizens to respect the law?[70]

The bureaucratic octopus had become insatiable in its desire to devour America's historical identity.

Such comments — rife throughout the book — clearly signaled that Whitehead inhabited a Manichean world of absolutes. In the author's interpretive universe, "constitutional" government is opposed to "centralized" government, states' rights are opposed to tyranny and totalitarianism, proper constitutional interpretation is opposed to "liberal," "relativistic," or ahistorical interpretation. In ignoring the good and embracing the evil, the Supreme Court had destroyed the Constitution ("once worshipped as a treasury of freedoms") in the interest of supporting "a highly centralized, octopean, bureaucratic system" of government.[71] For John Whitehead, twentieth-century America was a world turned upside down; his audience, despite geographical appearances, now lived behind enemy lines.

2.7. From "Post-America" to "America": Back to the Future

Given Whitehead's understanding of American history and his concomitant sacralization of the old over the new, he predictably prescribed a return to American roots as the only means of remediation. To dispel the "separation illusion," the author wrote, the nation must return to its original documents, both the Christian Scriptures and the Constitution. "The true hope . . . is the return to the holy Scriptures as man's guide," Whitehead opined early in the book. "Christ, and only Christ, provides the answer to modern

70. Whitehead, *The Separation Illusion*, 94.
71. Whitehead, *The Separation Illusion*, 83.

man's dilemma."[72] For the author, this was not only spiritual but also political advice.

To accomplish the desired turnaround, the Christian community must acknowledge its own role in allowing America to fall from grace. Although he hurled his most vitriolic critiques outward, Whitehead did spend considerable space in *The Separation Illusion* censuring his own Christian community. The present generation, he suggested, remains under a curse because it has turned away from God, and it must turn back toward the divine before it is too late. Christians get the government they deserve, and their inattentiveness to the republic's health has had terrible consequences. Partly because of the church's lassitude, Whitehead claimed, "the time is nearly ripe for a youth fuehrer."[73] In his opinion, the contemporary church has turned drastically inward, focusing on the individual and the personal psyche instead of Jesus Christ. How can a navel-gazing church be known by its fruits? Christians have become too "caught up in their own problems" while troubling events surround them. The church has "an existential, experience-oriented mentality" and relies more on psychoanalysis than on Scripture. It has, to his disgust, become "The Freudian Church."[74] The church should know better: "Salvation, not psychoanalysis, is the only answer."[75]

Not only has the church become unnaturally attracted to Freudian thinking, Whitehead continued, but there is an "overemphasis on God's love" these days.[76] The church has grown too generous, too willing to laugh and play games, too caught up in sensuality and self-determination. All of this has resulted from man thinking he can determine for himself what is good and what is evil. This clearly is the path to ruin; only the "pure, clean truth" of the Bible can properly serve as the church's compass.[77]

Too busy focusing upon their own personal peccadilloes, Christians have failed in their solemn duty to preserve American culture. Distracted and reticent, the church "has literally let down not only God but also the American people by failing to keep the faith intact." Whitehead again in-

72. Whitehead, *The Separation Illusion*, 15.
73. Whitehead, *The Separation Illusion*, 129. And lest any readers miss the allusion, Whitehead concluded the book with a horrific image of skeletons spilling from a gas chamber.
74. Whitehead, *The Separation Illusion*, 29-30.
75. Whitehead, *The Separation Illusion*, 34.
76. Whitehead, *The Separation Illusion*, 31.
77. Whitehead, *The Separation Illusion*, 33.

sisted that "the United States was once a Christian nation." If it is no longer, then the church bears a good portion of the responsibility. "The church
has stepped back much too long," Whitehead complained. "God created
man to act and to rule . . . not to hide within the institutional church."[78]

These comments reflected the author's strong affinity for a peculiar
branch of conservative Christian theology called Reconstructionism. Often
called "dominion theology" or "theonomy," Reconstructionism insists that
for Christians to prepare the way for God's millennial kingdom, they must
establish theocratic republics. Rousas John Rushdoony, the seminal thinker
behind this theology, published the movement's charter, *The Institutes of
Biblical Law,* in 1973.[79] There Rushdoony argued that the Ten Commandments and the Levitical codes (including the death penalty for all manner
of offenses, including heresy, blasphemy, and adultery) constituted the best
moral and legal foundation for constructing society.

Rushdoony provided an enthusiastic foreword to *The Separation Illusion.* In recommending his theological protégé's book — Whitehead likely
did his research in Rushdoony's library — the father of Reconstructionism
wrote that the U.S. Constitution had been created "not to express Christian
faith but to allow such faith freedom from the state in order to dominate society, law, and education."[80] Whitehead usually provided a more subtle
analysis, but Rushdoony's theological influence constantly lurked near the
surface. Indeed, Reconstructionist language occasionally pushed forward
in *The Separation Illusion,* as when Whitehead called for Christians to
"rule" and to "dominate" society.[81]

This connection with Reconstructionism, so clear and tangible in his
earliest writings, haunted John Whitehead as he and The Rutherford Institute drew more attention and aspired to wider acceptance. While never denying Rushdoony's formative influence upon him, Whitehead later sought
to distance himself from the more militant and exclusivist Christian claims
of Reconstructionists and their theological fellow travelers. Whether or not

---

78. Whitehead, *The Separation Illusion,* 30.

79. Rushdoony, *The Institutes of Biblical Law,* vol. 1 (Nutley, N.J.: Craig Press,
1973); vol. 2, *Law and Society* (Vallecito, Calif.: Ross Book House, 1982); vol. 3, *Intent of
the Law* (Vallecito, Calif.: Ross Book House, 1999).

80. Whitehead, *The Separation Illusion,* 9.

81. Frederick Clarkson, "Radical Reconstruction," *In These Times* 22, no. 7
(1998): 16, is useful on the relationship between Whitehead and Rushdoony. Clarkson
claims that Whitehead's later attempt to distance himself from his mentor was "a dissoci-
ation of convenience," not principle.

the Christian lawyer "evolved" away from Reconstructionist particularism later in his career, during the seventies and early eighties Whitehead clearly found Reconstructionism useful as a framework in which to locate his specific church-state analysis. Reconstructionists, like the "early Whitehead," emphasized the importance of biblical law for constructing and ordering society. As well, they offered a systematic critique of contemporary America that dovetailed well with Whitehead's own sense of a world turned upside down. Whitehead strongly believed that the nation would be much better off if Christians were in charge, and Reconstructionism offered him a comprehensive theological justification for advocating this belief. Whitehead and Reconstructionists like Rushdoony, if not officially members of the same club, coalesced effortlessly around the goal of Christianizing — or, through their historical eyes, re-Christianizing — the nation.

3. The End Is Near: The Establishment of Secular Humanism

Though often descending into technical legal and historical argumentation, Whitehead clearly aimed *The Separation Illusion* at a nonspecialized Christian audience.[82] But a year after this book, in 1978, Whitehead and a coauthor, former United States Representative John Conlan of Arizona,[83] published a lengthy article in the *Texas Tech Law Review* entitled "The Establishment of the Religion of Secular Humanism and Its First Amendment Implications." Addressed to a more specialized audience of legal professionals, this article picked up and amplified themes touched upon in his earlier work. Here the authors retold the story of a Christian America supplanted by usurping secularists, this time with careful attention to the critical role the law played in accomplishing and sustaining this "second American revolution." In this article Whitehead provided the fullest, most legally technical explication of a theme he would return to again and again: there is no such thing as neutrality, and those judges who claim to

---

82. The lack of concrete references is perhaps the best evidence for this. Whitehead happily inundated readers with footnotes — some serving little purpose other than to illustrate the author's breadth of knowledge — in other works. In addition to his article in the *Texas Tech Law Review* discussed here, see John W. Whitehead, *The Freedom of Religious Expression in Public Universities and High Schools*, 2nd ed., TRI Report 1 (Westchester, Ill.: Crossway, 1986), for an example of another reference-laden work.

83. John Conlan served two terms in the U.S. House of Representatives, from 1973 until 1976. He unsuccessfully sought nomination to the U.S. Senate in 1976.

act in its name are really seeking the un-American goal of replacing Christianity with a worldview hostile to it.

The argument developed in three parts. First, Whitehead and Conlan contended that in the twentieth century the United States Supreme Court completed a process by which the meaning of "religion" had been entirely transformed. For the first century of American history, when the Court invoked "religion," it meant traditional theism, particularly Christianity. This is "the historical and traditional definition of religion" and — given Whitehead's privileging of original intent in legal interpretation — the correct one.

Trouble began, however, with the Supreme Court's cases concerning Mormons in the late nineteenth century. Having touched upon this before in *The Separation Illusion,*[84] Whitehead elaborated here. In *Reynolds v. United States* (1879), which ruled constitutional Congress's authority to ban polygamy, the Court made a critical distinction. Referring to federal laws, the Court said that, "while they cannot interfere with mere religious belief and opinions, they may with practices." Congress was free to restrict "actions which were in violation of social duties or subversive of good order." To allow all practices justified for religious reasons would be "to make the professed doctrines of religious belief superior to the law of the land, and in effect to permit every citizen to become a law unto himself. Government could exist only in name under such circumstances."[85]

According to Conlan and Whitehead, this distinction between belief and action "laid the seed" for later troubles. Though little understood then, the Court's reasoning had far-reaching implications. "The traditional theistic religious practices that the *Reynolds* Court presupposed," the authors wrote, which "were entitled to first amendment protection have now judicially been reduced to 'mere opinion' or belief." Therefore, "Essentially, traditional theism, and, in particular, Christianity, has lost its historically-preferred position."[86] Reducing Christianity to "mere belief"

---

84. See Whitehead, *The Separation Illusion,* 98-100.

85. *Reynolds v. United States,* 98 U.S. 145, 166, 67 (1878). In determining when it is appropriate for the state to restrict religiously motivated actions, the majority relied upon the preamble to Thomas Jefferson's Bill for Establishing Religious Freedom: "it is time enough for the rightful purposes of civil government for its officers to interfere when principles break out into overt acts against peace and good order" (at 164). The distinction between belief and action employed by the Court reaches at least as far back as John Locke, *A Letter concerning Toleration.* Locke argued that the magistrate could intervene if religious opinions are "contrary to human society."

86. John W. Whitehead and John Conlan, "The Establishment of the Religion of

meant that it was no longer, constitutionally speaking, *the* belief, but something that prepared the way for it to stand before the law as just one among many religions.

Decades later, Whitehead and Conlan argued, the difficulties caused by this line of thinking emerged as the Supreme Court considered the beliefs of conscientious objectors. In a series of complicated cases beginning in the 1930s,[87] the Court — aided by changing Congressional laws on conscientious objection — steadily expanded the definition of religion. Though the Court's efforts could be viewed as a thoughtful (if often awkward) attempt to grapple with the nation's growing metaphysical pluralism, Whitehead and Conlan assessed this trend less charitably. In the 1940s, they argued, "traditional theism came under increasing attack"; and by the end of the 1960s the Court had reduced religious belief to mere sincerity of opinion.[88] The nature of this transformation was radical, nothing less than a shift away from the original presuppositions of the American experiment.

That by itself provides occasion for lament, in the authors' estimation. But treating Christianity as one among many religions, constitutionally speaking, did not simply move First Amendment jurisprudence toward neutrality. In fact, by reducing religion to mere sincere belief, the Court "has adopted a concept of religion which is tantamount to Secular Humanism's position of the centrality of man, because the basis of both is the deification of man's reason."[89] Despite claims to the contrary, the Supreme Court had not leveled the constitutional playing field; instead, it had transferred Christianity's privileged legal status to that of another competing worldview.

It was no coincidence, said the authors in making this case, that the expansion of religion's definition occurred during an era "in which humanism was on the verge of making a tremendous onslaught on the culture through the public education system."[90] Indeed, this "judicial transformation" — what Whitehead identified in *The Separation Illusion* as the second phase of the "second American revolution" — mirrored and augmented cultural developments. The American people were becoming increasingly

---

Secular Humanism and Its First Amendment Implications," *Texas Tech Law Review* 10, no. 1 (1978): 7.

87. For Whitehead the bookends to this transformation were *United States v. Macintosh* (1931) and *United States v. Seeger* (1965).

88. Whitehead and Conlan, "Establishment," 10.

89. Whitehead and Conlan, "Establishment," 12.

90. Whitehead and Conlan, "Establishment," 9.

secularized in the twentieth century, more and more willing to lead lives without fulfilling their obligations to their Creator. "Society's basis of truth" had shifted "from traditional theism's emphasis on God-centeredness to Secular Humanism's emphasis on man-centeredness."[91]

For Whitehead and Conlan, the Supreme Court's ratification of this tragic cultural transition occurred in *Torcaso v. Watkins*. Speaking unanimously in 1961, the justices ruled unconstitutional the state of Maryland's requirement of belief in God for public officeholders. In so doing, the Court asserted that the First Amendment required the state to remain completely neutral among all belief systems, theistic or nontheistic. In this case the Court for the first time identified "Secular Humanism" as one of those belief systems.[92] Though buried in a footnote, this signified for Whitehead and Conlan the "stark turnabout" in First Amendment understanding that had been under way since the late nineteenth century, part of a long period of the "continual dilution and dichotomization" of the concept of religion. By the end of the 1960s, then, according to this version of American legal history, the Court's definition of religion included traditional theists, agnostics, atheists, and just about anyone else who claimed a sincere belief in just about anything.[93]

Once the Court equated belief with religion in this way, Whitehead and Conlan contended, the establishment clause required the state to refrain from preferring *any* metaphysical system — including secular humanism. In an earlier decision the Court embraced this understanding. Writing in *Abington v. Schempp* in 1963, Justice Tom Clark tried to reassure those disturbed by the Court's decision outlawing the public school practice of officially sanctioned devotional Bible reading. The Court, and the First Amendment's prohibition on establishment, did not reflect an antipathy toward traditional religion, Clark suggested. In fact, the law still held that the state "may not establish a 'religion of secularism' in the sense of affirmatively opposing or showing hostility toward religion."[94]

In reality, Conlan and Whitehead averred, Justice Clark's reassurances accomplished nothing. In fact, legal neutrality among religions cannot exist. No matter how much the justices may cling to that idea, White-

91. Whitehead and Conlan, "Establishment," 10.

92. *Torcaso v. Watkins,* note 11 (1961), which reads in part: "Among religions in this country that do not teach what would generally be considered a belief in God are Buddhism, Taoism, Ethical Culture, *Secular Humanism,* and others" (my emphasis).

93. Whitehead and Conlan, "Establishment," 15.

94. *District of Abington Township v. Schempp,* 374 U.S. 203, 225 (1963).

head and Conlan argue, it is a logical impossibility: "The Supreme Court's theory of neutrality by the state is merely a hopeful illusion."[95] The legal system is in fact "inescapably religious." It represents, and is undergirded by, a particular worldview. In Tillichian terms, the law "establishes in practical fashion the ultimate *concern* of a culture." The only question that remains, then, is which concern, which belief system, which *religion* will be privileged. The state must always privilege one understanding over others, and if Christianity has been removed from public culture, something else must necessarily have taken its place. The Supreme Court, by advancing "the myth of neutrality,"[96] had really only exchanged one religion for another. In sum, Conlan and Whitehead concluded, "Traditional theism, particularly Christianity, has been disestablished as the State's presuppositional base in exchange for the religion of Secular Humanism."[97]

Having argued this point, the authors turned to examine the emergence and content of secular humanism — the new established religion. As before in *The Separation Illusion,* their story was a declension narrative, one of the fall of "biblical theism" from its rightful place as the foundation of American culture and law. Christianity was "clearly expressed" in both the Declaration of Independence and William Blackstone's *Commentaries,* from which American law was directly derived; both reflected the notion that "God was the source of all laws."[98] After the Civil War, however, an "onslaught of aggressive humanistic thought" emerged and began to supplant this original understanding.[99] Accelerated by the Darwinian theory of evolution, a system of "arbitrary absolutes" began to replace past moral and legal certainties.[100] By the twentieth century this movement culminated in "the establishment of Secular Humanism in contemporary American society."[101]

The authors expended a great deal of energy defining "secular humanism," chiefly to prove the hostility of this new and dominant religion

95. Whitehead and Conlan, "Establishment," 22.
96. Whitehead and Conlan, "Establishment," 22.
97. Whitehead and Conlan, "Establishment," 23.
98. Whitehead and Conlan, "Establishment," 26.
99. Whitehead and Conlan, "Establishment," 27. To tell this story, the authors relied heavily on two sources: Rousas John Rushdoony, *The Nature of the American System* (Nutley, N.J.: Craig Press, 1965), and Francis A. Schaeffer, *How Should We Then Live? The Rise and Decline of Western Thought and Culture* (Old Tappan, N.J.: Revell, 1976).
100. Whitehead and Conlan, "Establishment," 28.
101. Whitehead and Conlan, "Establishment," 29.

toward traditional Christianity. In doing so they relied upon a wide range of secularist writings, quoting liberally from, for example, Humanist Manifestos I and II.[102] The primary difference between Christianity and this new metaphysical usurper resided in the different objects of worship in each system. Whereas traditional theists derive everything from God, the secular humanist "worships Man as the source of all knowledge and truth."[103] Secular humanism "affirmatively rejects all supernatural religions," "denies the relevance of Deity or supernatural agencies," holds to "the supremacy of 'human reason,'" and believes fervently in "the inevitability of progress."[104] By definition secular humanism can thrive, the authors contended, only in the absence of its theistic alternatives.

Whitehead and Conlan appeared most alarmed that, under the paradigm of secular humanism, morals become arbitrary. Because it "clearly rejects . . . biblical absolutes" or "any form of absolute standards," ethics become determined by the whims of a particular situation.[105] Evolution is the linchpin of this worldview: by divorcing human origins from the divine, nothing is left for humanity but to worship itself and invent its own ethical system out of whole cloth.[106] "If there are not absolutes," the authors warned, "then each individual is absolute and the sole judge of his own actions." This makes it impossible for the secular humanist to criticize the crimes of Hitler and Stalin; for the humanist, for whom morals are purely a matter of preference, "such condemnation would be hypocrisy."[107] With such a relativist system embedded in American life, the authors contended, totalitarianism cannot be far behind.

A legal correlate to this amoral worldview exists, the authors noted, and can be found in a famous dictum from Justice Oliver Wendell Holmes. In *The Common Law* Holmes wrote that "The life of the law has not been logic; it has been experience." In the view of Conlan and Whitehead, this kind of context-based application of the law commits the same sin in the legal realm that secular humanism does in the wider culture. Gone are the

---

102. Humanist Manifesto I was issued in 1933, and Humanist Manifesto II appeared forty years later. Paul Blanshard and the *Humanist,* a journal, also provided much ammunition.

103. Whitehead and Conlan, "Establishment," 30-31.

104. Whitehead and Conlan, "Establishment," 34, 37, 38, 39.

105. Whitehead and Conlan, "Establishment," 34, 36.

106. Whitehead and Conlan, "Establishment," 47-54. The authors spent an entire section detailing the consequences of evolution and its centrality for secular humanism.

107. Whitehead and Conlan, "Establishment," 45.

eternal absolutes referenced by the Declaration of Independence and reflected in the Constitution, and gone is the proper judicial obeisance to
those absolutes reflected in a hermeneutical privileging of original intent.
Holmes and his ilk[108] have replaced those absolutes with arbitrariness. As
Chief Justice Fred Vinson, quoted to damning effect in this article, wrote in
1951: "Nothing is more certain in modern society than the principle that
there are no absolutes. . . . All concepts are relative."[109] Under the humanist
scheme, the law becomes merely what the state says it is.[110] The end result:
"Secular Humanism in effect eradicates the entire basis of American
law."[111] Relativism runs amok and totalitarian darkness is just around the
corner.

As in *The Separation Illusion,* this essay contained myriad Chicken
Little–like warnings that the American sky is falling and relatively few prescriptions for averting the impending cataclysm. Confident that they have
proven that secular humanism in fact constitutes a religious ideology, that
it has replaced Christianity as America's established religion, and that it vi-
olates everything good and true about American life, Whitehead and
Conlan seemed to assume that all right-thinking jurists and outraged
Americans would join hands and immediately set about "recovering the
dignity of Man based in the creature-Creator relationship."[112] Having
spilled a full sixty-six pages of law-journal ink in exhaustively making their
case, the authors trusted that the restoration would soon commence. As assumed in *The Separation Illusion,* knowledge is power and would naturally
lead to rebellion.

4. Schools on Fire

For John Whitehead in the late 1970s, nowhere had the separation illusion
become so prominent, or the disastrous consequences of the illusion so evi-

---

108. The authors also made much of Harvard Law School dean Roscoe Pound and
his move toward a "sociological jurisprudence." According to them, Pound once confessed that "I am skeptical as to the possibility of an absolute judgment"; Whitehead and
Conlan, "Establishment," 57.
109. Whitehead and Conlan, "Establishment," 60; Vinson quoted from *Barron's,*
18 June 1951.
110. See Whitehead and Conlan, "Establishment," 58-59.
111. Whitehead and Conlan, "Establishment," 61.
112. Whitehead and Conlan, "Establishment," 65.

dent, than in the nation's public schools. With coauthor Jon Barton,[113] Whitehead turned his attention to the educational aspects of the "separation illusion" in a book entitled *Schools on Fire*, published three years after his first work and two years before founding his advocacy organization. In a narrative reflecting the subtlety of its title, Whitehead and his coauthor revisited the themes of *The Separation Illusion* and applied them specifically to education. Indeed, the narrative outlines were strikingly similar: a diagnosis of moral crisis, a historical explanation of how that crisis came about, an identification of enemies, and a call to action.

The nation faces a "moral crisis in the blackboard jungle," the authors observed. The schools are increasingly full of violence and sex, abortions and venereal disease, drugs and alcohol. American students are growing dumber, not smarter. There is "TERROR IN THE SCHOOLS," shouted one capitalized subheading, terror that has spread to the streets: teenage ruffians not only disrupt the educational process, they are now responsible for over half of all violent crimes nationwide. And all of this is happening at a time when a God-centered school experience has been replaced by a values-clarification curriculum, one that encourages a "do-your-own-thing" mentality. The schools, in other words, are on fire.[114]

This conflagration, Barton and Whitehead contended, can be blamed on the infiltration of secular humanism into the public schools. The authors pulled no punches: the current educational philosophy "which has seemed right to so many but which has nonetheless led our educational system 'to the valley of the shadow of death' is *humanism*" (24). Whereas education once had a "Christian undergirding" that provided for "such things as absolute right and wrong," this is no longer true (11). American education, like the entire nation, has fallen from paradisiacal bliss into the darkness of the present godless age, one in which humanism predominates. The contrast could not be more stark: humanism, the authors write, "takes the position that there is no God and therefore no absolutes." Humanism means that education is no longer scripturally centered, and "once biblical foundations are discarded, the ultimate consequence is a loss of standards" (11-12). Instead of promoting traditional values, the public schools con-

---

113. Barton, a former English teacher, developed a course entitled "The Bible as Literature" at Santa Monica (Calif.) High School. Whitehead called Barton as an expert witness in *Wiley v. Chattanooga*, a case decided in favor of allowing a private civic organization to fund an elective Bible class for public school students.

114. Whitehead and Barton, *Schools on Fire*, 1-20. The parenthetical page numbers in this section refer to *Schools on Fire*.

done "adultery, trial marriages, wife-swapping, infanticide, killing of the elderly, and even cannibalism" (21).[115] This is the environment in which contemporary students find themselves. With humanism and its "situation ethics" pervading the public schools, the authors offered, it is little wonder that moral chaos reigns.

Barton and Whitehead provided specific examples of humanism and humanists in American society as a way of giving flesh to this relentlessly disparaged intellectual category. Readers learned the basics about self-identified humanists like Paul Blanshard, who in the *Humanist* raised up "three cheers for our secular state" in part because, through the educational system, it had been so effective in making Americans less religious. Short sections on Humanist Manifestos I and II attempted to bolster the authors' case that "humanism — by the very definition given to it by its major adherents — seeks to undermine the moral and spiritual fabric not only of education but of our entire cultural heritage by eliminating the principal tenets of Judeo-Christian thought" (70-71). Humanist designs have been directly reinforced, the authors argued, by the United States Supreme Court. American schools, and society in general, have seen "constant deterioration since 1963 — the same year that the Supreme Court ruled both prayer and devotional Bible reading unconstitutional in our public schools" (25). Thanks especially to well-organized and articulate humanists, as well as Supreme Court justices sympathetic to secularists, the schools have become enflamed with relativism. This "anti-God constituency" (26), though numerically small, continues to be culturally ascendant.

As a key theme, the myth of neutrality echoed throughout Whitehead's corpus, and he and Barton emphasized it in *Schools on Fire*. Secularists purport to replace an education leavened by Christianity with one that is neutral. But "secular" is not equivalent to neutral, the authors insisted; this is a "fallacy." They urged that "the 'secular' teacher who claims neutrality in the matter of religion is either being misled or is intentionally deceiving students. No one can be neutral concerning God and his teachings" (54). Everyone has faith, even atheists. The question, therefore, is not one of deciding between a preferred worldview and neutrality, but one of deciding which

---

115. Here the authors relied upon James Dobson's description of *Man: A Course of Study* (MACOS). A curriculum for middle and upper elementary school grades first issued by the Education Development Center and the National Science Foundation in 1970, it quickly became a target for religious conservatives. Though not the diabolical humanist plan it was often accused of being, MACOS by its very name inevitably engendered criticism from religionists suspicious of any system not centered on the divine.

worldview to prefer. Once readers recognize this fact, reasoned the authors, the correct choice becomes obvious: "All knowledge has a spiritual and religious base to it. One system enlightens, the other deceives" (54-55).

One way to understand how secularism has perverted public education, according to Barton and Whitehead, is to think of what really stands at the center of the curriculum. Is it God, as it once was and properly should be, or is it "man"? Repeating another common theme, the authors noted how the proper focus has been subverted: "At one time children in America learned of God and moral absolutes in the public schools, but no more. Now the God of their fathers is mocked and ignored, and the moral absolutes have been replaced with the relativistic values of secular humanism. In both instances man — and not God — 'becomes the measure'" (52). For the authors, an education centered on humanity improperly directs attention away from God, the only true object of human endeavor.

If the nation does not rise up and reclaim its God-centeredness, there will be further consequences: "By denigrating the God under whom this republic is supposed to stand 'indivisible' (as affirmed in our Pledge of Allegiance) and in whom this nation is supposed to have its 'trust' (as engraved on our coinage), we have deceived, deluded, and misled ourselves as a democracy. We cannot fool, cheat, or ignore our Creator (a characteristic of God acknowledged in our Declaration of Independence) without paying a severe penalty" (26). In fact, wrote Whitehead and Barton, those with the eyes to see can already perceive signs of God's displeasure with public education. Both tax revolt and the growth of Christian schools, the authors suggested, reveal that God is even now "purging our public schools" (29).[116]

Extinguishing the educational fire, Whitehead and Barton not surprisingly argued, requires rejecting public education's current moral desue-

---

116. As the authors wrote *Schools on Fire*, a tax revolt was under way in California. On 6 June 1978 a majority of Californians passed Proposition 13, which capped the amount of taxes the state could levy in support of public schools. The authors claimed divine sanction for the ensuing protest, likening it to the Boston Tea Party. California, as "the state which has for many years led the nation in practically every major category of immoral conduct," was a logical place for God to have joined the battle (43). And though God may not have directly caused this revolt, suggested the authors, "it has been permitted by him!" They "believe that God will allow a monetary crisis to continue in our schools until American education's sandy, moral foundation is eroded away." Then, at the crisis point, citizens may shore up public education upon a proper moral, God-centered foundation (29).

tude and returning curricula to the rock of biblical truth. "We believe that the moral dilemma in our public schools can only be overcome by moving toward — not away from — these absolutes" (23). How is this accomplished? Good Christians alarmed by the current state of affairs are not bereft of options: "We can pray for, work for, and — with proper direction — even fight for a system of public education in this country that honors God and at the same time respects the law" (29). Moreover, Christians should treat public education as "one of the greatest mission fields today" (58). Christians, under the dictates of the Great Commission, are obliged to bring their religious truths to bear in whatever arenas they find themselves. Power resides in their witness: "If Christianity were to have a greater impact in education, the course of history could be changed" (59). Quit whining, the authors advised, and do something: "Rather than continue to bemoan the demise of public education in this country, *each of us* as Christians should 'gird up our loins' and utilize the power and odds which God has so abundantly made available to us" (145).

In practical terms, what forms would this Christian activism take? As in *The Separation Illusion,* the book remained short on specific advice. Know the law, the authors urged, and one can effectively channel Christian resistance. Parents should remain alert to the multiple ways in which religion can appropriately appear within the public school context, and they should make sure that administrators and teachers support those expressions. Each Christian teacher also has a role to play, for he "is not only in a good position for winning the souls of his students," but he can also be a witness to fellow teachers (106). Trying to persuade, frighten, and goad the audience to action, *Schools on Fire* — much like *The Separation Illusion,* its literary predecessor — constituted less a how-to manual for resistance and more a contentious cultural critique. At this point Whitehead was still trying to mobilize a lethargic multitude by arming them with information; only later would he provide more specific battle plans and lead the charge himself.

5. The New Tyranny

Whitehead again focused on the arena of education in a shorter book called *The New Tyranny: The Ominous Threat of State Authority over the Church.* Published in 1982, the year he founded The Rutherford Institute, this pamphlet-sized work issued from Coral Ridge Ministries, the organizational home for conservative Christian evangelist D. James Kennedy.[117] In *The New Tyranny* the author argued that the recent rise in the popularity of Christian schooling can be directly attributed to the contemporary triumph of secularism in public education. Unhappy with the amoral and antireligious cast of contemporary public schools, Christians have begun to create their own educational alternatives as a means of reasserting parental control over children. However, Whitehead warned, the authoritarian secular government seeks control over all children within its boundaries, Christian or not. Whether or not they realize it, American Christians and the state are engaged in nothing less than "a battle for the child's mind" (3). Whitehead sounded this literary tocsin in the hope that Christians, armed with true knowledge of the situation, will be able to stamp out this "new tyranny" and defend their basic rights.

Whitehead trotted out his best inflammatory rhetoric, beginning *The New Tyranny* with an epigraph from George Orwell: "If you want a picture of the future, imagine a boot stamping on a human face — forever" (3). Godless Nietzsche, evil Hitler (whose philosophy of education closely matches that of America's current humanist regime), humanist Dewey (who, Whitehead cleverly noted, was born the year *Origin of Species* was first published), the invasive Internal Revenue Service — these villains, relativists and humanists all, form part of a conspiracy to subvert the Christian foundation of Western, and especially American, culture.

The problem with the philosophy espoused by this collect of infamy, according to Whitehead, lies in its deceptive nature. First of all, Americans have too often assumed that humanism is confined to a few eggheads in the academy. On the contrary, Whitehead insists, "It is a crusade — a crusade, in part, carried out through the public school system" (7). And humanists have high aspirations: these crusaders "are determined that humanism is going to become the universal system of thought and action" (8). Second, humanism's disciples often present themselves as advocates of mere neutrality, but, reiterating a theme present in almost all his writings, Whitehead contends that there is no such thing as neutrality. All metaphysical or philosophical positions presuppose a particular worldview. Neutrality in education, as in the law, is a myth: "there is no neutrality" (19). The question, then, is not how to be neutral among competing metaphysical claims; such a quest is by its very

117. John W. Whitehead, *The New Tyranny: The Ominous Threat of State Authority over the Church* (Ft. Lauderdale, Fla.: Coral Ridge Ministries, 1982). Due to its small size and inexpensive cost, this book seemed to have been aimed at bulk-buying church audiences — most of whom would have heard of it through promotion on Kennedy's television show. The parenthetical page numbers in this section refer to *The New Tyranny.*

nature quixotic. The question, rather, is which worldview, Judeo-Christian theism or secular humanism, should be privileged in education.

Having portrayed the alternatives in this fashion, Whitehead presented the reader with the obviously correct choice. Humanism, after all, equals total relativism. Humanists practice "*situational ethics* which means that, in the end, anything goes" (6-7). Contrast this metaphysical option with Christian theism, which, as all his readers must know, provides moral absolutes and standards to guide children's education.

Those who have left the public schools to ensure the proper Christian foundation for educating their children, Whitehead continued, should not delude themselves into thinking they have reached the educational promised land. For this humanist crusade to control American hearts and minds knows no boundaries. The state most clearly manifests its totalitarian intentions in seeking to regulate private religious schools. Since schooling children is something with which only parents are charged, they alone should have the right to delegate part of that schooling to other institutions of their choosing. In meddling in Christian schools, the state has created the "new tyranny" of the book's title, attempting to usurp the responsibility of parents to provide their children with biblically based education. Whether by mandating public education or by regulating the curriculum of private schools, the state attempts to enforce its "new tyranny" upon the American people (18-25).

Whitehead argued that this parentally controlled conception of education not only matches up with the Bible, but it also reflects early American understanding and experience. From the first Puritan schoolbooks to McGuffey's Readers, American education concerned itself with teaching children a scriptural worldview. The disappearance of real men of substance from American public life can be linked directly to the removal of this backbone from primary and secondary education. "The great men who built this country from the ground up sat under the McGuffey-type of Judeo-Christian teaching. Many lament that since those days have passed, so have the days of great men" (30).

Whitehead warned that if the state's attempt to control education is not thwarted, other freedoms will soon be at risk. The dire future predicted by George Orwell in *1984* will be upon us. Christians must respond with "whatever sacrifice is necessary." The only alternative, Whitehead intoned ominously, "is the relentless, progressive encroachment of state authority — and ultimate enslavement to the humanistic superstate" (32).

The doctrine of the separation of church and state is simply part of the humanist master plan. It is "a *false political doctrine* used to restrict the emergence of Christian ideas and lifestyles" (33). In the contemporary — and false — understanding, the civil government and theistic religion are kept apart from one another. Properly understood, the author contended, the separation of church and state supports those who want to keep the government away from private religious schools. The biblical understanding of separation provides for distinct religious and civil spheres, but with the presupposition that the church remains autonomous within a unified world sustained by a providential God (33-41).

The government's ongoing attempt to require private schools to be licensed, Whitehead urged, is at bottom "a question of lordship." Who is properly sovereign, Jesus Christ or the state? Whether requiring license, accreditation, or certification from religious schools, the state is asserting its lordship over education. This is beyond the government's jurisdiction, Whitehead argued; only God properly has the all-encompassing sovereignty the state seeks for itself (42-51). The modern state has become "Baal," claiming for itself an authority it does not rightfully have (56).

It is time to prepare for battle, Whitehead concluded: "true biblical Christianity is moving toward a head-on collision with the modern humanist state." One must either choose the side of Caesar or choose the side of Christ. "We are at war, and there are no neutrals in the struggle" (60-61). It is time to "make our stand at the spiritual and legal barricades" (66). Our biblically based freedoms are at stake.

6. *The Second American Revolution*

In the same year *The New Tyranny* appeared, Whitehead also published *The Second American Revolution,* a book that would become his most commercially successful work, reportedly selling over 100,000 copies. In this work Whitehead traversed much the same territory covered by his previous writings, providing a familiar narrative of a once-Christian America grown secular thanks to the U.S. Supreme Court's hermeneutical sleight of hand and an acquiescent culture. Though many of his themes were familiar, Whitehead did deepen and amplify previous themes in significant ways. As his most successful publication in terms of sales, *The Second American Revolution* revealed the intellectual credentials Whitehead first presented to those who would help establish TRI and contribute the money, time, and attention needed for its success.

In general, *The Second American Revolution* contained a much richer bibliography than *The Separation Illusion*,[118] and Whitehead provided more evidence to support the claims he and John Conlan made in their coauthored article. With livelier and more inviting prose, a more coherent narrative structure, and a text peppered with editorial cartoons by Pulitzer Prize–winner Wayne Stayskal of the *Chicago Tribune*, this book seemed geared toward a more popular audience. In retrospect, Whitehead seemed more proud of this work than of all his others — the cover of almost every subsequent book referred to TRI's founder as "author of *The Second American Revolution*."

This time Whitehead emphasized the Reformation as the fountainhead of a scripturally based United States. By shifting authority to the Bible, the reformers demonstrated that "whenever a culture establishes its institutions upon the teaching of the Bible, it is able to have freedom in society and government."[119] This was the legacy bequeathed to the West, that the Bible provides the best foundation for civilized society. Though fallen humanity can never carry them out perfectly, "when biblical principles have been administered with some consistency, they have brought about positive results."[120] Whitehead asserted that "Christians are called to apply God's revelation to all areas of life and to all disciplines."[121]

Whitehead sounded distinctive riffs on biblical history as well. Adam, readers might have been surprised to learn, was confronted in the Garden of Eden with what was essentially a legal dilemma. The attorney suggested that the first man had a choice between legal systems. He could have chosen to honor God and keep God's law, or to "assume an autonomous attitude and thus formulate his own laws without reference to God." Adam opted for the latter option. By choosing wrongly, Whitehead wrote, Adam became "the first humanist."[122]

It is in *The Second American Revolution* that Whitehead first brought

---

118. Compare his eighteen-page bibliography — with bigger pages and smaller print — to the seven-page list of sources in *The Separation Illusion*.

119. Whitehead, *The Second American Revolution*, 24.

120. Whitehead, *The Second American Revolution*, 26.

121. Whitehead, *The Second American Revolution*, 27. Though Rushdoony did not provide an introduction to this book (as he had for *The Separation Illusion*), Christian Reconstructionism still clearly retained its hold on Whitehead. In chapter 6, "What Is the Higher Law?" the author elaborated the content of the Ten Commandments and their appropriateness for structuring the contemporary political order.

122. Whitehead, *The Second American Revolution*, 27.

Samuel Rutherford on to the public narrative stage. Rutherford wrote *Lex, Rex; or, The Law and the Prince* in 1644. In this work, quickly banned in Scotland and soon burned in England, the Scottish divine challenged the common seventeenth-century presumption of the divine right of kings. Even the monarch, Rutherford insisted, must bow before the law — which was, of course, based upon the fundamental principles of the Bible.

Whitehead made extravagant claims about the Scotsman's influence on developments in America. According to the author, Rutherford's ideas were transferred to the American colonies "in substance and without significant alteration."[123] John Locke and John Witherspoon served as the most direct conduits. Witherspoon "brought the principles of *Lex, Rex* into the writing of the Constitution"[124] by applying Rutherford's idea of a covenant between ruler and God. "Taking their cue from Rutherford," Whitehead wrote, the colonists justified their rebellion by claiming that King George had violated their God-given rights. Moreover, he continued, it was Rutherford who "established the principle of equality and liberty among men," an idea that the founders later inscribed in the Declaration of Independence. To the extent that Jefferson and company relied upon Locke for their political ideas, Whitehead suggested, they were relying upon warmed-over Rutherfordian political philosophy.[125] In the author's intellectual history of America, Samuel Rutherford looked over the shoulders of Thomas Jefferson and James Madison as they designed the new republic.

In addition to introducing readers to Rutherford, Whitehead also made a subtle but significant linguistic shift in discussing American origins. Whereas earlier he referred simply to the Bible or Christianity as the nation's scaffolding, in this book he often invoked "Judeo-Christian theism" or "the Judeo-Christian tradition."[126] No longer just "Christian," the United States is "Judeo-Christian America."[127] Whitehead provided no explanation for this shift in terminology.

In this version of the country's fall from "Judeo-Christian" Eden, early nineteenth-century pietists share blame with Civil War agitators.

123. Whitehead, *The Second American Revolution*, 28.

124. Whitehead, *The Second American Revolution*, 28.

125. Whitehead seemed to rest these dubious claims upon Francis Schaeffer, who provided the foreword to this book.

126. Whitehead, *The Second American Revolution*, 32, and here and there throughout the rest of the book.

127. So, for example, chapter 3 is entitled "From a Judeo-Christian America to — ?"; Whitehead, *The Second American Revolution*, 32.

Whereas early pietists understood personal and social reform to be complementary Christian projects, a new wave of pietists in the antebellum period turned only inward for reform. This mistaken spiritual strategy "eventually led to a reduction of the Christian influence on the external world, leaving the field increasingly open to domination by those with non-Christian views."[128] After the enormous upheaval of the 1860s, humanism marched into this ever-larger spiritual vacuum and has been there ever since. No longer appealing to the Bible, humanists were and are autonomous, literally a law unto themselves — a notion far, far away from the country's "Judeo-Christian base."[129] Presently, he suggested, we are "locked into an age where humanism has come to full flower and is now confronting Christianity with a fierceness as never before."[130]

Whitehead expanded his treatment of this revolution in the legal realm, where an "aggressively humanistic legal elite" rules, spreading moral arbitrariness wherever and whenever decisions are handed down.[131] His by-now-familiar analysis of this situation took on a slightly different tone. Though still speaking of the regime of "sociological law" — first identified with Harvard law professor Roscoe Pound in the earlier *Texas Tech Law Review* article — he now described it in more political terms. Law, he claimed, has become a matter of mere majority vote. Whoever is in charge determines the meaning of the law. Now that God and the Bible have been excluded from the law, those belonging to the "Judeo-Christian tradition" have much to fear: "the legal profession and the courts and numerous agencies that intimately affect our daily lives become a more and more exclusive preserve for those who have political muscle to make their sociological ideas prevail. These ideas become, in effect, the world view forced upon the majority, willingly or unwillingly."[132] Having rejected biblical absolutes, "the courts have replaced law with politics."[133] And Christians are no longer allowed to vote; state institutions have usurped majority rule. Whitehead lamented: "We are now at the mercy of the nine people who sit on the Supreme Court. And as *Roe v. Wade* indicates they have power over life and death."[134]

128. Whitehead, *The Second American Revolution*, 35. Whitehead had been reading more Perry Miller and Ernest Tuveson.
129. Whitehead, *The Second American Revolution*, 36-37.
130. Whitehead, *The Second American Revolution*, 40.
131. Whitehead, *The Second American Revolution*, 46.
132. Whitehead, *The Second American Revolution*, 51.
133. Whitehead, *The Second American Revolution*, 52.
134. Whitehead, *The Second American Revolution*, 56.

For Whitehead, *Roe v. Wade* served as the most egregious example of what has gone wrong. In this 1973 decision upholding the constitutionality of abortion, he argued, the Supreme Court invented a right to privacy that has "no true constitutional basis."[135] More than any other case, *Roe* illustrated the present meaninglessness of the Constitution. Our founding document now "has little value except as a shibboleth used by the courts to justify their intrusions into the lives of the people."[136] The secular courts have instead decided to invent the laws and inflict them upon an unsuspecting populace.

This theme of intrusion emerged as the central thread of *The Second American Revolution*. Before, when complaining about the courts, Whitehead cast his critique in terms of amorality, lawlessness, the violence inflicted upon society in general. Despite his colorful comparison of the federal government to an octopus, the state's invasiveness played a much less prominent role than did cultural decay. In this work, however, the state — especially as embodied by the federal courts — loomed larger. It is aggressively extending its tentacles closer and closer to home. Growing increasingly drunk on its own power, the state has begun to consciously extend that power as far as it possibly can. The justices are no longer just reshaping American political culture in their own (godless) image; in fact, they are now actively expanding and redefining the boundaries of that culture so that all aspects of life come under its jurisdiction.

"Statism" became one way for Whitehead to name this by-now-familiar beast. "All authority has virtually been transferred to a state institution: the Supreme Court and its inferior federal courts," Whitehead asserted. The courts now "have power over every facet of our lives — even our life and death itself."[137] And they mean to exercise that power. White-

---

135. Whitehead devoted exhaustive chapters to this topic: "The Convenient 'Right to Privacy'" and "The Abortion Mentality"; see *The Second American Revolution*, 115-32. He hardly stood alone, or at the extreme, in criticizing the Supreme Court's decision in *Roe*. For example, constitutional scholar Laurence Tribe — someone not usually associated with conservative politics — chided the *Roe* Court for deploying a "somewhat obscure 'privacy' rationale" and for "reaching beyond the facts of the case"; see Laurence H. Tribe, "The Abortion Funding Conundrum: Inalienable Rights, Affirmative Duties, and the Dilemma of Dependence," *Harvard Law Review* 99 (1985). For a helpful schematization of critiques of *Roe*, see Susan Clement et al., "NOTE: The Evolution of the Right to Privacy after *Roe v. Wade*," *American Journal of Law and Medicine* 13 (1987): esp. 376-79.

136. Whitehead, *The Second American Revolution*, 58.

137. Whitehead, *The Second American Revolution*, 59.

head detailed the rise of "activists" to the bench, judges who happily "go beyond the situation" before them "and dictate new rules or law."[138] President Carter deserved much of the blame, having created a "sharp surge" in activist judges with his Omnibus Judgeship Act of 1978. The members of this "imperial judiciary" have done everything from ensuring the killing of fetuses to instructing schoolchildren how long to wear their hair. Judges no longer merely administer the law; they have become the self-appointed guardians of the national conscience, a "legiscourt" practicing "legisprudence," a "new oligarchy."[139] "There is no longer consent of the governed," Whitehead complained. "The governed don't have a chance to consent or even object."[140]

President Carter came in for particular criticism for appointing justices who cavalierly reject "the design of the biblical family."[141] Whitehead found antifamily attacks particularly alarming because, among other things, the family "has served as a buffer (a safety zone) between the individual and the state." As long as the traditional family remains intact, "it affords members of the family protection from total statist control." By seeking to break down the family, then, activist judges were destroying that critical buffer zone. "If this continues," Whitehead warned, "the individual will be left naked against the state."[142] With parents safely out of the way, "the state will become the parent, and all family members will be its creatures."[143] The courts have truly become, according to a chapter title, "A Law unto Themselves."

The lawlessness of judges is scandalous not just for these reasons, Whitehead reminded his readers, but also because their philosophy of secular humanism is fundamentally incompatible with Christian faith (or, as he was more likely to put it in this book, "the Judeo-Christian tradition"). The "religion of secular humanism" cannot tolerate any competitors, which means that the Supreme Court's purported attitude of "benevolent neutrality" toward all faiths really only amounts to "a posture of objectiv-

---

138. Whitehead, *The Second American Revolution*, 60.

139. Whitehead, *The Second American Revolution*, 66, 87, 71.

140. Whitehead, *The Second American Revolution*, 72.

141. Whitehead, *The Second American Revolution*, 62. In a footnote, Whitehead singled out future Supreme Court justice Ruth Bader Ginsburg for opprobrium, noting her "vocal antifamily sentiments" and her "penchant for government-imposed humanistic values"; see Whitehead and Conlan, "Establishment," 63 n. 19.

142. Whitehead, *The Second American Revolution*, 64.

143. Whitehead, *The Second American Revolution*, 65.

ity."[144] In fact, just like in ancient Rome, "all religions exist at the pleasure of the state."[145] Don't be duped, Whitehead warned, for the Supreme Court "uses this fiction of neutrality as a sugarcoating to make palatable to us the bitter pill of the abandonment of Christian values and of the moral order that accompanies them."[146]

Another significant advance from Whitehead's previous thinking can be seen in his relative universalizing of religious freedom. Here for the first time Whitehead linked the First Amendment rights of Christians with those of other religious groups. The logic bears rehearsing:

> We must be cognizant of the fact that . . . the rights of Christians are many times dependent upon the rights of other religious groups. For example, if the Supreme Court were to rule that it was illegal for the Hare Krishnas to evangelize in public places, then Christians and Jews would also be banned. Under the present judicial mentality, the constitutional principles will apply across the board. It is, therefore, incumbent upon the Christian community to defend the principle of free religious expression for all religious groups. Christians can be confident that "the truth of Christianity will prevail in an open marketplace of ideas."[147]

This rationale helps explain why The Rutherford Institute and other Christian legal advocacy groups, though reflexively identified by the media with "Christian Right" exclusivity, occasionally pressed cases on behalf of non-Christian groups. Against the secularist "octogovernment," people of faith could be at least temporary allies in service of the cause.

The last fresh aspect of *The Second American Revolution* arrived in the final chapters. As in earlier works, Whitehead chastised his Christian audience for assuming that this is not their problem. An entire chapter made this case. It is time, he wrote, "to discard the idea that Christians can simply go about their business" while wearing cultural blinders.[148] The church has failed to uphold its responsibilities, having "allowed the tide of humanism to roll over society and encompass it." This has been especially true in "the Christian community's silence and acquiescence to the ever growing

144. Whitehead, *The Second American Revolution*, 86.
145. Whitehead, *The Second American Revolution*, 87.
146. Whitehead, *The Second American Revolution*, 87.
147. Whitehead, *The Second American Revolution*, 113.
148. Whitehead, *The Second American Revolution*, 145.

power and unconstitutionality of the federal government." It is time for action, Whitehead urged, and compromise to avoid conflict is simply not an option: remember, "Christ said he came not to bring peace but a sword."[149] Christians must actively resist "state paganism."[150]

The difference from earlier works resided not in his now-familiar critique of lazy Christians, but in his offering a concrete program of action. Borrowing from Samuel Rutherford and *Lex, Rex,* Whitehead outlined three distinct kinds of appropriate resistance. The first option should be to defend oneself by protest; in contemporary society, the author explained, "this would usually be by legal action."[151] If this path fails, Christians should flee if possible. Finally, if protest is ineffective and flight impossible, persons may as a last resort use force. On Whitehead's understanding, Rutherford was careful to distinguish between lawless uprising and forceful self-defense, and only the latter option can be justified.

Armed revolution is simply not an option,[152] Whitehead insisted, and given the "immense power" of the modern state, there is hardly any place left to flee to. This leaves the contemporary Christian with protest as the best path of resistance. Though he dismissed the options of both proactive fight and flight, Whitehead deployed war imagery to make the case for Christian resistance. "We as Christians," the author exhorted, "must once again commit ourselves to the whole view of Christianity. We must influence all areas of life including law and politics. We can leave nothing untouched by the Bible. . . . We must prepare to be the warriors we should be." The church is at war, "the battle lines are drawn between humanism and Christianity."[153] If

149. Whitehead, *The Second American Revolution,* 146.
150. Whitehead, *The Second American Revolution,* 150.
151. Whitehead, *The Second American Revolution,* 156.
152. Whitehead was careful to insist that the Bible offers no examples of men who sought to violently overthrow the government; this simply is not an option. This relative reasonableness was not shared by all late twentieth-century Christian conservatives who similarly criticized judicial activism. See, for example, Richard John Neuhaus, ed., *The End of Democracy? The Judicial Usurpation of Politics; The Celebrated* First Things *Debate with Arguments Pro and Con* (Dallas: Spence Publishing, 1997), which collects essays and letters connected with an intellectual dustup over a *First Things* symposium of the same title in November 1996. The introductory editorial argued that "we may have reached . . . the point where conscientious citizens can no longer give moral assent to the existing regime." Some suggested that the tone of some essays was suggesting less-than-civil disobedience, and three members of the editorial board resigned in protest.
153. Whitehead, *The Second American Revolution,* 159.

Christians fail to "reclaim the world for Christ," they will soon find themselves saluting a "new fuhrer."[154]

So, what shape should this protest take? First, the author set before his readers several related intellectual tasks. As in his earlier works, Whitehead urged the church to remember, recover, and restore. First, Christians must return to the notion that their principles should be externalized: "The truths of the Bible must flow from the mind into the world."[155] Philosophy dictates how one should act, so getting one's mind right should result in the right actions. Next, Christians must remember that they have "a mandate from the Creator to be a dominant influence on the whole culture."[156] Personal evangelism is important, Whitehead granted, but it cannot be the sole focus of the Christian life: "To give a large section of the whole world over to paganism without a fight is to cheat God."[157] Third, Christians should be chary of pluralism. Respecting differences is fine, but accepting those differences as morally equivalent is both dangerous and wrong.

Whitehead concluded his prescriptions for recovery with more concrete suggestions. First, he advised, read some good books to reinforce his message; Whitehead provided a list of recommendations heavy on the Schaeffers — both Francis and his son Franky — and including a book by Rushdoony. Watch the video versions of both *The Second American Revolution* and *Whatever Happened to the Human Race?*, a companion film to the book of the same title by Francis Schaeffer and C. Everett Koop. Much more critical than this, Whitehead urged, is for Christians to become active in local politics. "If America is going to be revitalized in a Christian sense," he averred, "it will be done at the local level."[158] Lobby officials on legislation, work hard to have like-minded judges appointed to the bench, vote for Christian candidates, and run for office. Attend law school, where you should strive to make the curriculum cover the Christian foundations of law; practice not as a legal technocrat but as a thoroughly Christian attorney, for "the world needs the counsel of the godly lawyer."[159] And finally, Whitehead insisted, Christians should tend to their own families. Parents must spend time with their children, working diligently to counteract the multifarious secular influences around them. In sum, only Christians can

154. Whitehead, *The Second American Revolution*, 160.
155. Whitehead, *The Second American Revolution*, 162.
156. Whitehead, *The Second American Revolution*, 163.
157. Whitehead, *The Second American Revolution*, 164.
158. Whitehead, *The Second American Revolution*, 166.
159. Whitehead, *The Second American Revolution*, 172.

provide the right approach to important social and political issues and restore balance to our secularized culture — it is time to get busy.[160]

If Christians follow this plan of action, Whitehead argued, they can
achieve several specific goals. First, the faithful can help restore the proper
boundaries of the federal government by returning power to state and local
governments, where it properly belongs. The authority of the courts would
be circumscribed, and the national bureaucracy would be reduced. (The Internal Revenue Service is a good place to start this part of the program.) If
Congress refuses to exercise its power to accomplish this on the people's
behalf, Christians should protest by disavowing federal funds on the state
and local levels. The financial pain would be great, Whitehead admitted,
but the people's freedom would be regained.

Next, if other alternatives are foreclosed, Christians should sue like
crazy: "If legal action becomes feasible, it should be pursued aggressively."[161] Too often religious citizens have adopted a purely defensive posture while secular humanists set about clearing the culture of religion.
Whitehead suggested that it is time for Christians to take the offensive.
"There is an advantage to suing before being sued," Whitehead argued. The
one who sues can frame the issues and arguments to suit him, not his opponents: "the first man out of the chute has the jump on others involved in
the race."[162] The author offered an example from his own experience to
support his point.[163]

Third, Christians could consciously set out to ensure that "the entire
education structure" is "reinstilled with Judeo-Christian theism." If, as
seems more and more likely, public schooling cannot be reformed, Christians must opt out of the system altogether, working to ensure that their
taxes are diverted from institutions that teach "the materialistic world
view" and establishing their own schools.[164] And finally, the fourth specific
goal right-thinking Christians should pursue is making sure the church is

160. Whitehead, *The Second American Revolution*, 161-74.
161. Whitehead, *The Second American Revolution*, 176.
162. Whitehead, *The Second American Revolution*, 177.
163. As the lead attorney for a church sued for discrimination because it fired a
homosexual employee, Whitehead turned the tables, avoiding a trial by asking the court
for a summary judgment. The church won its case (*Walker v. First Orthodox Presbyterian
Church of San Francisco*), which Whitehead took as vindication of his activist approach:
"An entirely different outcome could have resulted if we had gone on the defensive." See
Whitehead, *The Second American Revolution*, 178.
164. Whitehead, *The Second American Revolution*, 178.

truly a servant church. If Christians will do as Christ instructs and care for the sick and needy, the need for governmentally administered welfare would disappear. Working toward all these concrete aims, Christians might at last begin to break down "the massive machine of government."[165]

7. Conclusion

In these five early works, John W. Whitehead erected the intellectual scaffolding that would undergird The Rutherford Institute's mission. First, he offered a thorough diagnosis of a contemporary crisis. Americans now live in a nation dominated by secularists, humanists, and secular humanists. They have seized control of the government, from the Internal Revenue Service to Congress to — most critically — the federal judiciary. From these official perches they have sought to impose their relativist, antireligious understanding of the world upon the rest of the nation. Nowhere have they been more aggressive, or more successful, than in the realm of public education. The result has been an American citizenry increasingly controlled by an "octopean" government. Individual rights — especially those of Christians — are fast disappearing. The time is ripe for a new Hitler to consummate this revolution in American identity; 1984 is approaching in more than mere chronological terms.

Whitehead's diagnosis of the crisis cannot be separated from his understanding of American history, and his sense that what once was, should always and forevermore be. Both the nation's founding documents and early American experience should be normative for social and political organization, Whitehead clearly believed; indeed, his definition of "crisis" is the absence of those standards. The trajectory of American history, generally speaking, is clear: the nation was created by Christian people for a Christian people, and it was to be ruled by a government friendly toward religion and hostile to interference in citizens' lives. In almost two hundred years those originating principles have been completely upended, such that contemporary Americans find themselves living in an increasingly secularist country intruded upon in multiple ways by a bloated, antireligious government.

Within that superficially simple story, Whitehead offered more complicated details that revealed a great deal about his political philosophy, his religious principles, and his motivations for legal activism. He disclosed his

---

165. Whitehead, *The Second American Revolution*, 180.

preference for hierarchy, order, and states' rights in his indictment of Northern abolitionists over against Southern aristocrats. Correspondingly, he greeted with distaste anything that smacks of egalitarianism, especially of the metaphysical variety. This attitude was reinforced by — or perhaps stemmed from — his Reconstructionist ideology, one that called him and his fellow Christians to achieve dominion over the political order and reconstruct it on a more biblical foundation.

Whitehead embedded within this historical framework some specific tenets that bore directly on his motivations for, and the shape of, his legal activism. The individual is almost always sovereign over against any judge or other agent of "the state." The original meaning of texts — as he understood that meaning, of course — should determine how to resolve contemporary issues. Perhaps most critically, neutrality — both as a philosophical principle and as a legal doctrine — is a mere ruse, a device to replace one worldview with another, less authentic one.

The late twentieth-century contemporary scene is marked by battle, in Whitehead's estimation, between Christians and secularists. This battle can and does take many forms, but at root the conflict is the same. In Whitehead's world there are fellow religionists and there are secularists, there are true Americans and there are subversives, there are biblically grounded moralists and there are morally indifferent relativists. His is a Manichean universe where one is either a child of the light or a child of the darkness. Christians must join the battle, on all fronts, before the darkness overwhelms them.

Taken together, these ideas constituted the intellectual structure upon which John Whitehead founded TRI. *The Second American Revolution* in particular, claimed TRI's official materials, "sparked a real revolution in public interest." It was this work that sent the lone prophet's word out among the people, and it provided the catalyst for creating TRI. "John's phone began ringing off the hook with inquiries," the official story related. "Hundreds of people who had suffered discrimination, but had kept silent for years, now read that something could be done to protect their freedoms. The Rutherford Institute was born."[166]

---

166. *Justice for All.*

~ 3 ~

Raising the Alarm: Whitehead and
The Rutherford Institute in Public

*The country, through a strange transmogrification, has developed
from a federation of constituent states and local governments to a
highly centralized, octopean, bureaucratic system. It is no longer
America, but post-America. The Constitution, once worshipped as
a treasury of freedoms, is now an instrument utilized to build a
godlike government. In consequence, the totalitarian state stands
beckoning for its curtain call, and Orwell's 1984 becomes more of a
reality moment by moment.*

John W. Whitehead, 1977[1]

John W. Whitehead founded The Rutherford Institute in 1982, deliberately
choosing its name to signal the values for which he and his new organization would stand. Whitehead christened TRI in honor of Samuel Rutherford, a seventeenth-century Scottish preacher who famously resisted the
idea of the divine right of kings. A professor at St. Andrews, Rutherford
penned *Lex, Rex: The Law and the Prince*, which contended that even roy-
alty must bow before the law.[2] The book soon attracted the attention of the
authorities. In 1661 monarchists burned *Lex, Rex* in Edinburgh, and King
Charles II eventually charged the Scotsman with high treason.[3] Resolute to

1. John W. Whitehead, *The Separation Illusion: A Lawyer Examines the First
Amendment* (Milford, Mich.: Mott Media, 1977), 83.
2. Samuel Rutherford, *Lex, Rex: The Law and the Prince* (London: John Field,
1644).
3. The king was unable to punish Rutherford, who received news of the monarch's
charge on his deathbed in 1661.

the end in resisting state oppression, Rutherford gave voice to Whitehead's aspirations three centuries later, providing inspiration for the attorney's late twentieth-century crusade. "What ultimately convinced me to use Rutherford's name," Whitehead explained, "was his idea that all men are subject to the law, and none are above it."[4] According to TRI's founder, Americans later integrated that principle into their new political experiment in response to another lawless monarch. "This same premise, that leaders are responsible to a law higher than themselves," he told a reporter, "was central to the formation of the US government."[5]

According to Whitehead, this founding ideal had recently come under withering attack. In the last half of the twentieth century, the nation's radically secularized political and legal authorities had steadily eroded civil liberties in general and religious freedom in particular. Faceless government bureaucrats had sought successfully to increase their own power at the expense of individual rights. The Rutherford Institute signified Whitehead's decision to enter this cultural and political battle on the side of the underdog. "It is my firm belief," he wrote on the cover of a TRI brochure, "that religious people should know there is a place they can go when they are oppressed and need active legal help."[6] TRI intended to empower the powerless, to defend individual citizens against a hostile and oppressive government, and to allow them to preserve their rights and freedoms. In resisting the state's tyranny through the law, Whitehead believed that TRI would not only preserve civil liberties, it could also help restore America's originating ideals.

In the first twenty years of its existence, the institute consistently sounded this central theme. Whether in books, pamphlets, newsletters, radio programs, audiotapes, Web pages, or movies, materials depicted the organization as the noble champion of American religious liberties over

4. John W. Whitehead, *Slaying Dragons: The Truth behind the Man Who Defended Paula Jones* (Nashville: Nelson, 1999), 195.

5. "Haunted by Scots Preacher," *Scotland on Sunday*, 25 Jan. 1998, 11. Whitehead later explained why he decided to help Paula Jones by appealing directly to this ideal. Critics claimed he was merely grandstanding, but Whitehead argued that this case fell squarely within TRI's original mission to defend ordinary citizens from abuse by those in power. It was the part of Rutherford's writings "which stated no one is above the law," he wrote, that "led me to take on the president of the United States many years later"; John Whitehead, *Slaying Dragons*, 195.

6. *Justice for All: The Rutherford Institute Story* (Charlottesville, Va.: The Rutherford Institute, 1994).

against a secularized political and legal system increasingly hostile to religion. Whitehead relentlessly disseminated this worldview, refining his ideas about culture and the law as his organization involved itself more and more in litigation. Marshaling multiple resources, Whitehead and TRI mounted a comprehensive informational campaign designed to rouse a sleepy, unwitting populace to the alarming disappearance of "true" American values. If Christians would only recognize the direness of their contemporary situation, Whitehead believed, then religious freedom — and, in fact, most other individual rights — could be successfully reclaimed and defended.

The public offerings from TRI and Whitehead, plentiful and diverse, took two general forms that reflected the dual nature of the perceived crisis.[7] First, Whitehead continued and expanded his cultural analysis in the hopes of spurring his audience to action. Metaphysically and culturally wide-ranging, these resources presented information and a call to action at the level of metanarrative. In books and movies especially, TRI's founder energetically sought to convince Christians that a cultural and spiritual crisis existed in contemporary America, a crisis that demanded their immediate response as both Christians and American citizens. Something has gone terribly wrong, and recent historical trends must be altered before the situation becomes irreversible. Second, Whitehead and TRI issued books and pamphlets of a more practical nature. Often such materials served as reference works, offering advice on subjects such as how to legally picket abortion clinics or which religious behaviors are constitutionally protected in the workplace. Shorter, portable, less heavily footnoted, these resources sought to empower Christians to actively assert and defend their constitutional rights.

These practical offerings were not bereft of intellectual argumentation, to be sure; in fact, ideas supplied their very raison d'être. For Whitehead, ideas mattered. Latent in all his arguments was the assumption that if only clarity of knowledge could be imparted, remedial action would then follow. Convert his audience to his understanding of the world, and they would help him set things right again. In both kinds of resources, Whitehead indicated his belief that Christians had remained dangerously ignorant of constitutional issues and their practical implications, not just for religious freedom in particular, but also for individual freedoms in general.

7. By "public offerings" I mean to distinguish materials intended for a general audience from more specialized legal materials, which will be discussed in chapter 4.

Seeking strenuously to fill this informational gap, Whitehead positioned himself and his organization as a trusted broker of intelligence for people unacquainted with or fearful of the American legal system.

1. The Long Arc of Cultural Decline

After founding The Rutherford Institute in 1982, Whitehead continued to develop themes first introduced in earlier works. *The Separation Illusion, Schools on Fire, The New Tyranny, The Second American Revolution* — all warned of the government's ominous encroachment upon religious freedom, and all urged Christians to stand up against the state before their constitutional rights disappeared altogether. TRI sought to enable religious people to resist the state's secularist designs, and in its youth the organization funneled its energies almost exclusively into religious freedom cases. However, at the same time, Whitehead constantly linked the free exercise of religion with a broader constellation of individual freedoms under threat in the contemporary world.

Merely suggested in his earlier writings, this interrelationship began to appear more often and more insistently in materials issuing from TRI. It was no accident that when Whitehead later developed a radio program, it was called *Freedom under Fire* and not *Religious Freedom under Fire.* In his estimation, the American government of the late twentieth century threatened not just one but *all* individual freedoms. As he more fully articulated the interrelationship of civil rights to his public audience, Whitehead led his organization in advocating for people and causes beyond his natural power base within the comfortable confines of Christian conservatism. In a variety of books, pamphlets, and movies, Whitehead explained, provoked, chastised, and cajoled in an attempt to bring his religious fellow travelers along with him into the public sphere. Justifying The Rutherford Institute's work became a critical part of his newly institutionalized vocation.

1.1. The Stealing of America

Although he began his literary career with a focus on religious freedom issues, by the early 1980s Whitehead had already begun to broaden the scope of his analysis to sound a general alarm about the American government's "dangerous direction." In 1983, a year after officially founding TRI, Whitehead published *The Stealing of America.* Repackaging themes from *The Separation Illusion* and his most successful book thus far, *The Second American Revolution,* he offered a broader — if shallower — treatment of them. Familiar American icons — the Statue of Liberty, the eagle seal, the Liberty Bell, George Washington, the blindfolded goddess of justice with scales in her hand — were arranged on the book's cover, but Whitehead's patriotism did not lead him to endorse the status quo. The state was acting "oppressively and lawlessly," and citizens must resist. He summarized the awful state of things in his preface: "The assertion of governmental authority over areas of life once considered to be under individual and private control means that the American state has become more than a government. It is making claims and is acting as if it possesses the attributes of deity. It is a state that now claims total ownership. As a result such areas as human life, the family, the church, the school, and private property have become more and more the province of state authorities."[8] For Whitehead, not just religious freedom but the very fabric of freedom itself was unraveling.

In customary fashion the lawyer loudly called his readers to arms, relying on familiar rhetoric to impress upon his audience the urgency of the contemporary situation. The country was "a broken reed," and "the old forms (the glue that bound society together) such as traditional religion and the family, that once predominated, have been shaken." No longer did any moral certainties exist to provide social cohesion: "The idea of absolutes is dead. All things are seen as relative, even the value of human life" (1). The fruit of relativism is all around you, Whitehead told his audience. Who can look out upon an America riddled with drug abuse, abortion, violence, and divorce and not see a crisis of epic proportions?

He suggested that the intellectual culprits responsible for the nation's deplorable plight could be easily identified: modern science, cultural indecision about what kind of future to pursue, moral relativists, technologists, and egalitarians who seek to break down the "natural" hierarchy in human society.[9] All had contributed to the rise of "cosmic secularism," a totalitarian worldview that is attempting to displace traditional religion at the center of American culture. "Those in leadership — government, media, edu-

8. John W. Whitehead, *The Stealing of America* (Westchester, Ill.: Crossway, 1983), xi. Parenthetical page references in the text of this discussion refer to *The Stealing of America.*

9. Modern science is "outrunning the human spirit," Whitehead wrote. "Man is becoming obsolete." He "has been defined away. . . . He has become unnecessary, a despoiler in an otherwise pristine 'nature'" (*The Stealing of America,* 2).

cation" — are especially responsible, for they are moving "toward greater control and manipulation of the individual" (5).[10] Particularly insidious is the influence of the electronic media, which "more than forms public opinion . . . *it alters the consciousness and world view of entire populations.*" Whitehead asked his audience to contemplate what Hitler could have accomplished with such sophisticated tools (5, author's emphasis).

References to Hitler and the Nazis ran throughout Whitehead's corpus in general and *The Stealing of America* in particular, suggesting with little subtlety the dire fate that might await the United States if the current crisis continued. Early on he wrote: "It is the thesis of this book that if the present trends of our government and society are not reversed, then the future hovers between an iron-fisted state and one that conceals the iron fist under a velvet glove" (xii). Whitehead deployed Holocaust imagery to alert his audience to imminent danger, to jolt his readers from their cultural slumber: the second chapter's title claimed the nation was even now "On the Road to Auschwitz." We cannot afford to think that the awful events of midcentury Germany could not happen here; remember, he admonished his audience, the Nazis were freely elected to office by the people under a constitutional government. Pre-Nazi German Christians forgot Reformation ideas in "much the same way the American church has failed to maintain these principles today" (10). Awake! Awake! Whitehead all but cried. Otherwise, Americans will find themselves in a nation turned upside down. "Off in the distance," Whitehead warned, "we can hear the stamping boot coming closer and closer" (7).[11]

In the next chapter he continued to detail the myriad ways in which contemporary America mirrored pre-Nazi Germany. Borrowing material and a title from Leonard Peikoff, Whitehead itemized, at chapter length, "Some Ominous Parallels." According to his sources and his own observations, the list of commonalities was extensive: economic destabilization; public loss of confidence in governmental institutions; a recent war defeat,

---

10. Although he occasionally named names, Whitehead typically inveighed against general categories of villains rather than specific individuals.

11. Though the schematic details differed, Hal Lindsey's influence upon Whitehead can be seen in the shadow each drew over the present historical age. TRI's founder entitled his first chapter "A Time of Parenthesis" — premillennial dispensationalists often spoke of the present age as a time of "parenthesis" between the sixth and final stages of God's master plan for human history. See especially Timothy P. Weber, *Living in the Shadow of the Second Coming: American Premillennialism, 1875-1925* (New York: Oxford University Press, 1979).

which destroys a culture's self-esteem; loss of traditional value structures; a concomitant devaluation of human life. Events spanning from Kennedy's assassination to Nixon's resignation and beyond, the author argued, "have left fragmentation, violence, and rejection of values" in their wake (24).

With frequent references to Hitler, fascism, and totalitarianism, Whitehead's worldview reflected the Cold War context in which he published. The black-and-white, good-versus-evil Manicheism commonly expressed during the tensions between the United States and the Soviet Union came through strongly in *The Stealing of America*. With a former adherent's intensity,[12] Whitehead cast a wary eye toward Communism. "The growth and power of the state," Whitehead wrote, "is the most significant political development of the twentieth century" (3). Communism's popularity indicated that many believed that government can be "a total, final solution to man's problems." Warning of a "monolithic sameness" on the contemporary ideological scene, Whitehead tried to convince his American audience that their nation was not immune to the red specter. The American public currently faced "an onslaught of totalitarian ideas and acts" (xi), he claimed. For the author, there could be little doubt that "the world" — including the United States — "is moving inexorably toward statism" (4).

Lest readers remain unpersuaded by his indictment of contemporary trends, Whitehead labored further to explain just why "statism" should be resisted with all possible energy. Most alarmingly, this kind of government robs people both of their worth and of their freedoms as individuals. Communists have "a very low view of people." They are "materialists," "tyrants and oppressors," and we should not be seduced by their claims (29). "As modern men look to the state as the source of rights and bread," Whitehead warned, "increasingly they too become slaves to the governmental elite" (7).

In *The Stealing of America*, Whitehead expanded his enemies list. B. F. Skinner and John Dewey made their obligatory appearances, and this time they were joined by Francis Crick. Whitehead quoted the geneticist to good effect in making his case: "As soon as we understand cell chemistry, we know that a metaphysical explanation of life becomes superfluous" (45). (Man reduced to a chemical reaction, Whitehead commented, is man reduced to "junk and a throwaway.") As in his other works, "the state"

---

12. Whitehead, reflecting on his college and immediate postcollege years, described himself in those years as a Marxist; see Ted Olsen, "The Dragon Slayer," *Christianity Today*, 7 Dec. 1998.

loomed as the most prominent foe, but here the author gave flesh to that category with specific examples. The Internal Revenue Service, with its high taxes and attempts to revoke tax-exempt status for religious groups, stood guilty of "oppressive tactics."[13] This and other "federal bureaucratic agencies" had subverted the representative process by exercising power without true accountability (27). Another agent of the state, the courts, ranked high on the enemies list, but this category came more alive for readers as Whitehead cited a few examples of egregious legal behavior.[14] "The

13. The IRS loomed large in Whitehead's sights as a particularly effective tool of state oppression. Many conservative Christians intensified their hostility toward the agency after it revoked Bob Jones University's tax-exempt status in the 1970s (a decision upheld in 1983 by another villain, the U.S. Supreme Court, in *Bob Jones University v. United States*). As the IRS paid closer attention to organizations seeking tax-exempt status — in part because conservative Christians themselves had recently become more politically active, increasing the potential for tax-code abuse — it necessarily had to wrestle with the question of what imbued an organization, or its activities, with a "religious" character. Though the very notion of tax exemption for religious endeavors necessarily involves the government in the business of determining what qualifies as "religious" — how else could such a determination be made? — religious conservatives such as Whitehead complained about the very notion of government officials making such distinctions. In parceling out tax exemptions, Whitehead contended, the IRS was "moving perilously close to defining what is and is not permitted in terms of religion," adding that this activity was "much like that of the Roman Empire" (*The Stealing of America,* 98). In fact, he continued, under today's IRS the early church might not have even been considered a religion. Granting tax exemption, in other words, was a way of "placing the church under the dominance of the state" (100). This criticism, though true, merely begged the question of what alternative Whitehead would have preferred. His critique undoubtedly resonated with Christian conservatives frustrated by a government they perceived to be increasingly hostile to their worldview, but few citizens of any religious stripe would have responded positively to a call for rejecting tax exemption. By the mid-1990s, however, Whitehead had become so averse to state meddling in religious affairs that he suggested just that; see John Whitehead, *Church vs. State,* Faith and Freedom series (Chicago: Moody Press, 1996), 43 (discussed further below).

14. For example, in previous writings the following line would likely have stood alone, without concrete support: "Infanticide, once unthinkable, burst into the open and became thinkable." This time, however, Whitehead offered evidence for his claim, citing a 1982 decision by an Indiana court that allowed a six-day-old infant to be "starved to death" because of congenital birth defects; *The Stealing of America,* 43. Later he referred to the 1927 Supreme Court case *Buck v. Bell,* which allowed the forced sterilization of a retarded woman. The opinion was written by one of the author's favorite targets, Justice Holmes, who was quoted in the same section as opining elsewhere, "I see no reason for attributing to man a significance different in kind from that which belongs to a baboon or a grain of sand" (on 48).

media" joined the enemies list as well; the author cited it as "an indispensable ally" in the current campaign of infanticide by replacing the term "baby" with the dehumanizing "fetus." These "gatekeepers of information" publicly show the slaughtering of baby seals while refusing to show abortions, Whitehead claimed, proving themselves "as much a tool for antilife propaganda as was the media of Nazi Germany" (50).

As in previous writings, Whitehead sought to convince his audience that things had not always been so awful — and then added the rarely latent corollary that things need not stay this way. Before 1900, "society operated from a set of presuppositions largely derived from the Christian ethic." Distancing himself a shade from his earlier, more extravagant claims about the devout faith of early Americans, he nevertheless clung to the notion that the new nation had been a Christian one: "This is not to say that the majority of Americans were ever Christians," he wrote, "but that the majority were *influenced* by Christian principles" (31). This Christian foundation included a sense of man's createdness, which "afforded man great worth and dignity"; a sense of individual rights that were absolute because they were derived from the Creator; and an understanding that the state's primary purpose for existing was to protect the God-given rights of men (32). "This was the base for political freedom in America," Whitehead summarized — the base that was now repressed, ignored, or generally forgotten.

Indeed, the author suggested to his readers, if one only contrasted that original Christian foundation with the contemporary circumstance, the depth of the current crisis would become clear. As memory of the country's Christian base — which underwrote and guaranteed freedom — has faded, "the tendency has been toward centralized, authoritarian government" (31). Secularists such as Francis Crick and B. F. Skinner profess a philosophy that is "a complete repudiation of what the framers of the Declaration and the drafters of the Constitution believed. It means there is no Creator and that man has only relative rights" (32). Theism has been replaced by humanism, "the predominant thought form undergirding the basic institutions of our society, especially since the 1930s" (33). The consequences could not have been more disastrous. "Cosmic secularism" was now the empty faith of today's society, in which, Whitehead wrote, "Anything goes" (34).[15]

One rueful aspect of the current environment, according to White-

15. Whitehead quoted G. K. Chesterton to the same end: "When a man ceases to believe in God, he does not believe in nothing. He believes in anything" (40).

head, was the disappearance of "a family-oriented society." He provided a long list of reasons why the American family had long been declining. The birthrate had decreased (not least because of increasing abortions), divorces had increased, "untraditional" and "new" family units had been formed, women had joined the workforce in unprecedented numbers, the legitimacy of male headship had been questioned, cohabitation and unwed pregnancies skyrocketed, children began to turn toward peers and the media for moral formation.[16] All these factors, and more, contributed to society's disintegration.

The state had played a critical role in the family's decline. Whitehead suggested both that the state had contributed mightily to the family's decline, and that the state itself had grown as a consequence of that decline. "Traditionally," the author wrote, "the family has served as a buffer zone between the individual and the state. With the decline of the family the logical consequence has been the governmental bureaucracies and the massive state school systems — in effect, a 'brave new world' type of all-encompassing 'health and human services' welfare state" (65). As families disappeared, the state moved in and took control. Indeed, the state had in effect nationalized the family, making it "a mere extension of the state," one more arm of the "octogovernment." The author frequently reiterated the transformation to drive home the point: "the decline of the traditional family unit has been accompanied by the transference of functions once administered by the family (such as education, health, and welfare services) to other institutions, primarily the state" (60).[17] Given this analysis, it can be no accident that the author's biography rarely failed to mention that Whitehead was married with several children, holding himself up to readers as a "traditional" model to emulate in the midst of moral and social chaos.

His personal example, however, would not be enough to reverse this complicated situation, so Whitehead tried to awaken the country's Chris-

16. Whitehead cited Neil Postman, *The Disappearance of Childhood* (New York: Delacorte Press, 1982), claiming that American society was returning to the Middle Ages, a time when "it was common for children to be present at even ribald events, and fondling the genitals of children was not an uncommon form of entertainment" (68-69). Even for the nostalgic Whitehead, appeals to history had their limits.

17. Echoing themes from the earlier *Schools on Fire*, Whitehead also spent a chapter detailing how the family's decline was matched only by that of the Christian model of public education. Here, as elsewhere, the author pined for a restoration of earlier golden days.

tians to the stealing of America and spur them to action. Christians must first acknowledge that they share some of the blame for contemporary conditions, the author contended. Wasting no opportunity to scare his audience with Nazi references, the author returned to this well again at the end of his book. The current silence of the American churches, he admonished, seemed eerily parallel to that of the German church in the Nazi era. Lest Christians in the United States make the same mistake, they must forgo political quietism and engage the culture before it is too late: "The tendency of many Christians to limit their religious loyalties to the narrow goal of personal redemption has undoubtedly led to sincere and devout lives. However, the failure to carry their Christian principles into political and social life has opened the way for control of the state by the proponents of secularism and humanism, who have no such limitation on living their 'faith'" (*Stealing*, 40-41). Hope still existed, Whitehead assured his readers; time had not yet run out. "There is still enough of the older ethical base — what has been called the Christian memory — that the American people will rebel if they consciously realize what is happening" (6). The fate of the Christian nation, however, hung in the balance. "Recent Christian activism is a good sign," indicated Whitehead; whether or not this has any staying power remained to be seen (107).

1.2. An American Dream

In 1987, four years after *The Stealing of America*, Whitehead repackaged most of its themes into a book-length rumination entitled *An American Dream*.[18] The book's richer bibliography signaled a better acquaintance with history and theology, but Whitehead cited these new sources only in service of previous, familiar positions. *An American Dream* deviated little from the usual rhetorical patterns for the author's books. Whitehead first sounded the alarm: "Realistically speaking, we live in perilous times" (xi). After describing the signs of trouble, the author assigned responsibility to the usual suspects. Finally, he concluded by urging his readers to resist current trends as a means of restoring harmony to the national culture and preserving the "American dream" of individual freedom.

Echoing an attack first launched in *The Separation Illusion*, White-

18. John W. Whitehead, *An American Dream* (Westchester, Ill.: Crossway, 1987). Parenthetical page numbers in the text are to *An American Dream*.

head in his foreword accused modern historians of "prejudice" and a "lack of intellectual integrity" (xi). This time he appeared especially peeved at the version of history presented in the nation's public schools: children, he claimed, "are not given an accurate picture of American historical beginnings." Without such a picture — a picture that assuredly had a Christian hue — children could learn neither what it really meant to be an American nor the content of the "American dream."

According to Whitehead, the "American dream" included three fundamental concepts: "rights, resistance, and a future optimism as they are undergirded by the traditional religion" (18). The Declaration of Independence, the nation's "only true creedal document," best expressed the American dream. Now that the dream had disappeared, Whitehead suggested, the Declaration offered the best blueprint for restoring it: "If there is to be any semblance of political freedom and optimism for the future, it is this author's opinion that we must recapture the ideals that are set forth in this document" (19). In part, the Declaration served as the best clue to the American dream because it "articulated what people of the day were thinking" (22). For Whitehead, this historical location at the country's germination imbued the document with guiding importance. The author willingly granted that the founders had not been perfect men, but their fallibility should not render their truths invalid. "Too often modern historians, many of them Christian, denigrate America's beginnings because of such problems. Such meanderings elude reality. What must be recognized is that without the religious undergirding that allowed for the promulgation of these self-evident truths, Americans could today be living in a much different society where the very concept of self-evident truths would be only a shadow in the corridors of authoritarianism" (31). For Whitehead the Declaration represented a national consensus rooted in religious truths, and this fact should not be — as it so often had been — ignored.

Whitehead's hallowing of the Declaration represented not only his customary reverence for the priority of origins; it also denoted a more sophisticated reflection on what holds the American people together — what constitutes the "American dream" of the title. For the author, the Declaration embodied something of a national consensus, a shared agreement on identity and purpose that derived from divinely established absolutes. The contrast between the republic's early days and contemporary times could not be more stark. Unlike today, Whitehead wrote, when citizens were "steeped in relativism," early Americans agreed on some unbendable truths. The author explained that "The colonists . . . because of the influence of Christianity, were confident that the reason of man could penetrate to ultimate truth, and that truth, once discovered (or apprehended), . . . was both permanent and universal" (27). More than once Whitehead contrasted colonial society with "modern, relativistic society" (see 28ff.). Today, he claimed, the country teetered on the edge of all kinds of anarchy, and the missing ingredient — the foundation that once made possible the shared moral consensus that prevents such anarchy — was Christianity.

This line of thinking naturally set up readers to expect yet another nostalgic call for the restoration of original — meaning Christian — American ideals. And much in *An American Dream* met this expectation. Whitehead complained constantly that religion had been excluded from tales of the nation's founding. He attributed America's current plight to the country having lost its collective soul, and he identified that soul with his own religious tradition. "The soul of the American people," he wrote, "has been the Christian religion. It provided the people with a common morality which allowed individual freedom within moral constraints — a common morality altogether absent in the present American society" (18). Similarly, he later asserted that "the predominance of the Christian religion in colonial America cannot be denied" (31).[19]

Whitehead extended this argument to the nation's founders, so critically important for making his case in both the cultural and legal realms. The "American mind," so intelligently expressed by the founders, was religious in nature. Christianity had always "been the main religious stream flowing through the American consciousness" (18).[20] The framers in particular shared this Christian sensibility: the nation's "early leaders were ei-

---

19. For a dissent from this viewpoint, see Jon Butler, "Why Revolutionary America Wasn't a 'Christian Nation,'" in *Religion and the New Republic: Faith in the Founding of America*, ed. James H. Hutson (Lanham, Md.: Rowman and Littlefield, 2000), 187-202.

20. Whitehead spent a healthy portion of his narrative detailing exactly how early America was Christian, noting the clergy's critical role in shaping colonial sensibilities and the pervasive influence of Puritan ideals upon American life and thought. He also highlighted the compatibility of George Whitefield's evangelism with revolutionary ideals. In this discussion he relied greedily on the then-new work of Mark Noll and Harry Stout, another sign of his increasingly nuanced sense of American history. Whitehead also provided an extended account of John Locke's political philosophy in this book. While perhaps too simply privileging those accounts that underscore the Englishman's Christianity, he nevertheless admitted to his audience that this formative thinker was something less than an orthodox Christian. Though he quickly insisted that the latter fact should be beside the point, this nevertheless indicated a more ready willingness to wrestle with the complexities of history and to share them with his readers.

ther religious or held a religious view on life." Whitehead granted that the
founders had not all been Christians, but he insisted that they could properly be considered "churchmen." There was no question that the Christian
sensibilities of the founders, "combined with the influence of the clergy, . . .
generally created a transcendent view of life and government in early
America" (126). Whether lay, clerical, or political, Whitehead contended,
early Americans acted and thought within an unavoidably Christian framework. Readers who finished *An American Dream* would not have escaped
without sensing that, at least in Whitehead's estimation, the founding era
indeed constituted the good old days.

In spite of this undisguised wistfulness, Whitehead expressed a peculiar ambivalence about the relevance of the nation's past. Indeed, this more
complicated, nuanced sense of the past's relevance most distinguished this
otherwise rehashed narrative from its predecessors. Though he hastened to
add that Christianity should still have a "tremendous influence" on the culture, the author admitted — somewhat grudgingly — that "there can be, in
all likelihood, no such thing as a 'Christian nation' in our time. Moreover,
there were problems with the idea that a nation could be Christian in the
sense of what the Bible terms 'Christian'" (32). This was perhaps a frank,
practical acknowledgment of reality, for in contemporary America only
"shadowy vestiges of Christianity remain." But Whitehead also indicated a
pessimism about the current state of American Christianity. "Its lack of
spiritual depth," he complained, "renders modern Christianity nearly powerless to shape and influence contemporary American culture" (18). Early
on he told readers that "We cannot relive the past" (xi). Later he emphasized that "there are no golden ages" (170). Even to an audience presumably friendly to — if not hungry for — a restored Christian America,
Whitehead could not unequivocally recommend this as a realistic political
goal.

The author did unhesitatingly recommend one restorationist goal: returning to the original American ideal of limited government. This particular aim justified the otherwise inordinate amount of attention Whitehead
paid to the complicated vagaries of American political thought in the
founding period. Knowing his audience to be both Christian and American, Whitehead infused both identities with a resistance to tyranny and a
corresponding preference for keeping government out of individual lives.
He drove the point home with an etymological lesson, telling readers that
the word "tyrant" comes from the Greek *tyrannos*, meaning "a secular ruler,
one who rules without the sanction of religious law" (125). The contempo-

rary American government had become tyrannical, thus forsaking the American dream by trampling individual rights in favor of "cradle-to-grave therapeutic state welfare." Individualism is part of "the liturgy of the American dream," and it "has suffered as a result of the growth of the modern state and collective power" (153). He called the expansion of government "the most significant political development of the twentieth century" and predicted that the number of free to unfree people will be roughly equal by the year 2000 (169). No one, even in the United States, can escape the state and "the spreading of its tentacles" (151).

The grim shadow of totalitarianism overwhelmed the few notes of optimism that Whitehead sounded in *An American Dream*. He wrote that even if he and his readers could recover the original American ideals, "contemporary society may be too rancid to restore freedom" (19). Throughout the book, whenever the author offered a glimmer of hope for the future, he seemed unable to shake his despair. America "appears to be a shrinking island of freedom," Whitehead wrote in a typical passage. Even now, "A looming authoritarianism threatens the United States, and Americans are beginning to feel the squeeze of the iron hand" (17). He warned that "the American tune may soon be only a faint whisper in a storm of totalitarianism. Worse yet, it may be an accident in freedom and a dream that has relapsed to a nightmare" (20).

1.3. The End of Man

In 1986 Whitehead published *The End of Man,* a book he later claimed was "one of the better books I've written."[21] With over six hundred footnotes and a twenty-five-page bibliography, this dense work completed a philosophical triad of sorts: the author wrote in the foreword that it "continues the train of ideas" begun with *The Second American Revolution* and fur-

---

21. John Whitehead, *Slaying Dragons,* 211. Whitehead noted in his autobiography that his publisher's nervousness about the book's fate was confirmed: "The book sold few copies and essentially died after it went into print." Even though this demonstrated that "evangelical audiences were not ready — or interested in — the message" of the book, Whitehead still felt gratified when a man approached him after a speech and related that *The End of Man* had converted him to Christianity. "Who knows? Maybe the purpose of that book was just to encourage one man to reconsider his eternal destiny." In sum, however, *The End of Man's* less than enthusiastic reception was a "frustrating experience" (211-12).

thered in *The Stealing of America.* The first dealt with the metaphysical un-
derpinnings of the American experiment, arguing that a theistic foundation
had been replaced by a secularistic one. The second work detailed the impact of secular philosophies upon the shape of state activity and power.
This third work, Whitehead explained, focused more broadly upon "the
philosophical streams that are directly impacting on people and which . . .
are totally denigrating human beings." TRI's founder claimed in *The End of
Man* that, whether in politics, philosophy, or science, the result had been
the same. "Scientific determinism," entirely devoid of theistic assumptions
and values, has given the world "abortion, infanticide, euthanasia, and co-
ercive population control." Whitehead argued that "we have entered into a
new era of forced death for the generations that would, if they could, follow. *Posterity has become passé.*"[22] Human life had been completely devalued under this new scientific regime: "our society has already been making
funeral preparations for the end of man" (xii).

"The end of man" could be traced to two concurrent and intertwined
intellectual developments. First, in philosophy, the Enlightenment undermined the unity of truth and therefore religion itself. Whitehead wrote that
"the central ideas of the Enlightenment," especially the notion of human
perfectibility, "stand in antithesis to Christian truth" (22). Enlightenment
thinkers subjected people in the West to a "monolithic barrage" of science
and secularism, one difficult to resist. Man, rather than the image of God,
became just one more being in the universe — a universe of relative, rather
than eternal, values.

Whitehead argued that the Enlightenment's introduction of moral relativism contributed directly to the intellectual crisis of the twentieth century, when "impersonalism" provided the greatest metaphysical challenge to
humanity's worth. This mode of thinking reduced people "to nothing more
than cogs in the machinery of our technological society" (15). Secularists
were the primary proponents of this philosophy; by denying the Creator,
they reduced man to mere disposable material. Impersonalism, Whitehead
claimed, stood in direct contrast to "traditional theism," for only in the latter system do "absolute standards exist by which all moral judgments of life
are to be measured" (17). God's love stood as the highest absolute, contended Whitehead, making those living under theism morally accountable
in a way that those under a godless, secularist system simply are not.

22. John W. Whitehead, *The End of Man* (Westchester, Ill.: Crossway, 1986), xi,
author's emphasis. Parenthetical page numbers in the text are to *The End of Man.*

The tragedy of this transition from theism to impersonalism resided not just in the West's abandonment of God as civilization's foundation. In America, it also marked the nation's desertion of its fundamental animating ideals. "Traditional theism is clearly expressed in some of the founding American documents," Whitehead argued (18).[23] The Declaration of Independence, the U.S. Constitution, American law more generally — all were "structured upon a theistic base" (18). In society, theism applied to all areas of life and, Whitehead contended, "Christ's Lordship was emphasized" (20). As impersonalism infected the American mind, the very nature of American identity itself began to disappear.

While philosophers catalyzed this disastrous intellectual transformation, the responsibility for the end of man could also be traced to religious adherents. According to Whitehead, Christians did not stand idly by as philosophers relativized morals and enervated the notion of human dignity. But neither did they resist. In fact, far from being passive, helpless victims or active defenders of theistic principles, religious believers actively assisted in shunting theism from the nation's cultural center. The author claimed that the seventeenth-century Pietist movement, with its exclusive stress upon personal salvation, had turned Protestantism inward and away from engagement with the outside world. "Religion became 'privatized,'" Whitehead declared, "and ceased to affect public life" (20). Those who propagated this culturally debilitating theology, in the author's opinion, had betrayed their own tradition; Pietism "created a non-Christian dichotomy between the spiritual and temporal worlds" (21). Permeated by a Pietist mentality, Christians largely failed to respond to the secular infiltration of Western thought and culture and, if anything, accelerated secularism's advance.

In Whitehead's estimation, political quietism still marked contempo-

23. Whitehead began to step away from the cocksure assertions of previous writings by granting the ephemeral, ambiguous connections between the nation's origins and Christianity. "Although one cannot say that such documents are truly Christian writings," he wrote in reference to the Constitution and the Declaration of Independence, "they do reflect principles that are arguably derivative of theistic thought" (18). Contrast this with his direct, unhesitating pronouncements in *The Separation Illusion* that Christianity "was written into the Constitution" and that "the basic foundation of the government was Christian"; John Whitehead, *The Separation Illusion*, 18, 22. He also backed away from contending that the new nation's population was mostly Christian. Whereas here he granted that the majority of early Americans were not Christians, in *The Separation Illusion* he stated matter-of-factly that, at the time of the Constitution's ratification, 2 million of the nation's 3.5 million citizens were Christian.

rary Christianity. His frustration with this quality seemed to have grown; in *The End of Man*, criticism of his fellow religious followers was no mere afterthought, as it sometimes seemed in earlier works.[24] Perhaps indicative of his growing impatience with an audience willfully indifferent to his message, he lashed out at Christians right from the start, in his first chapter entitled "The Christian Vacuum." Thanks to impersonalism, a "spiritual vacuum" existed throughout the twentieth century, and Christians had failed to fill this void. Thus contemporary church members, still trapped in their "Christian ghettoes," were "largely responsible for the black holes of modern culture" (28, 16).

In *The End of Man* Whitehead tried to have Christians own up to that responsibility and shake off their political inactivity. He urged, even pleaded with, those who might join his cause: "We must *now, at present*, stand and, if possible, rebuild our culture." Continuing disinterest or idleness would bring nothing but ruin; those who hoped for divine rescue are almost assuredly doomed to disappointment. Contemporary Christians may have traded in Pietism for apocalypticism to justify their political pacifism, but this theological error reigned in either case. Whitehead warned those who counseled patience and expected outside intervention. Indicating his distance from former mentor Hal Lindsey, he wrote, "We may fashion 'end times' scenarios and hope and pray to be snatched from the terror of this age." But "as it did not happen for those who preceded us, it may not happen for the present generation" (xii).[25] Whitehead insisted time and again, both in this work and others, that "full-dimensional Christianity . . . means affecting culture" (27).[26] Regardless of time period, theol-

---

24. In *The Separation Illusion*, for example, Whitehead's criticism was cursory, arriving almost as an afterthought at the book's conclusion.

25. It should be noted that Whitehead had not entirely lost his taste for millennial imagery. Near the end of *The End of Man* he granted that "it is virtually impossible to predict the future. There are simply too many variables." Nevertheless, he continued darkly, "the world appears headed for a series of disasters. Rivers of blood could flow" (246).

26. In his call for Christians to reengage American culture, Whitehead — no doubt with an eye cast toward his overtly Reconstructionist past — felt obligated to clarify just what the consequences of such activity would mean. He insisted that "I am not advocating that any particular religious faith, including Christian, should subjugate society." Rather, he wanted faith to have a substantial impact on culture. Elsewhere in the same book, however, he claimed that "true Christianity speaks to all of life" (32), and that "freedom cannot exist externally without the internal freedom that true Christianity offers" (247). Such comments provided ample fodder for critics on the lookout for Whitehead's regnant Reconstructionist designs.

ogy, or historical circumstance, Christians had a duty to participate in and shape the politics and society around them.

Whitehead clearly believed that this obligation had become all the more urgent in the present age, an era distinguished most dramatically from other epochs by the disappearance of absolutes. Always assuming a direct relationship between scientific developments and the wider culture, Whitehead pointed in *The End of Man* to the significance of Albert Einstein's work for crafting the contemporary, morally relativist universe. The modern world, Whitehead claimed, began on 29 May 1919, when photos of a solar eclipse confirmed Einstein's theory of relativity. Whitehead quoted historian Paul Johnson approvingly: "It was as though the spinning globe had been taken off its axis and cast adrift in universe which no longer conformed to accustomed standards of measurement" (24). Radically transforming scientific thought, Einstein's theory also tremendously affected the wider culture. "At the beginning of the 1920s," Whitehead professed, "the belief began to circulate, for the first time at a popular level, that *there were no longer any absolutes.* This included not only time and space, but also good and evil, knowledge and other areas traditionally reserved to moral absolutes" (24). Relativity transmogrified into relativism, with disastrous consequences for Christianity. Again borrowing from Johnson, Whitehead agreed that Einstein's theory of relativity "formed a knife, inadvertently wielded by its author, to help cut society adrift from its traditional moorings in the faith and morals of Judeo-Christian culture" (25). Before 1900, "it was still possible to discuss what was right and wrong (or what was true and false) with the man on the street." Even "non-Christians" before the twentieth century "generally acted on Christian presuppositions." But today's reality stood far distant from that world. "In the battle of ideas," the Christian author pithily pronounced, "Christianity lost" (26).

Whitehead attributed that decisive defeat not just to Christian cultural quietism, but also to the misguided assumption that secularism constituted an appropriate public philosophy — even for Christians — because it placed civilization upon a religiously neutral foundation. Not only was this a mistaken perception, Whitehead asserted, but it was also logically impossible. "One of the great myths of the twentieth century," the author claimed, "is that secularism means the replacement of a world view that is religious with one that is not" (35). Humans are inescapably religious, he stated. The only question, then, concerned what the object of religion — God or man — will be. In discussing "secularism," "modern humanism," "materialistic secularism," or "secular humanism" — terms used more or less as synonyms throughout the book — Whitehead made clear that this "antihuman," anything-goes body of thought could not be further from the intellectual world of "true" Christianity. Secularism was not neutral toward Christianity; secularism repudiated it, along with all theistic religion.[27] Humanism — secularism — was marked by "the fundamental idea that people can begin from human reason without reference to any divine revelation or absolute truth and, by reasoning outward, derive the standards to judge all matters. For such people, *there is no absolute or fixed standard of behavior.* They are quite literally *autonomous . . . a law unto themselves*" (37-38, my emphasis).[28] Like Puritan authorities some three centuries earlier, Whitehead feared that antinomianism posed the most potent threat to the health of both religion and republic.

By relativizing everything, modern humanism reduces man to a mere speck in the grand scheme of the universe. This "leads to the destruction of man. It completely debases man and, in the end, leaves him without a shred of dignity or worth" (39). As proof, Whitehead gleefully indicted prominent twentieth-century intellectuals, often with their own words. For example, psychologist B. F. Skinner wrote that modern man's "abolition has long been overdue. To man *qua* man we readily say good riddance" (44).[29] And John Dewey, Whitehead claimed, helped ensure that evolutionist thought permeated American education. With their "very debased view of people," secularists like Skinner and Dewey fostered a "boozed-out and drugged-out contemporary America" (45, 47).

The consequences of secularism were even more dire than moral decline, wrote Whitehead. In fact, where secularism rules, totalitarianism inevitably comes to characterize the political order. The state becomes the enemy of its people — a situation developing even now, for those with eyes to see. Whitehead noted that presently the "massive bureaucracies — now

---

27. In most of his writings after founding TRI, Whitehead commonly invoked "the Judeo-Christian tradition" and, occasionally, "Judeo-Christianity." Upon the release of *Religious Apartheid* (both the book and the movie) in 1992, Sheila McThenia wrote in TRI's in-house magazine that Whitehead "was careful not to alienate Jews and other religious persons. In fact, he would like to see *Religious Apartheid* used in public school classrooms and civic group meetings." See McThenia, "Religious Apartheid," *Rutherford* 3, no. 6 (June 1994): 5.

28. The notion of an unchristian civilization as inherently morally anarchic appeared often in his legal writings; see chapter 2.

29. Pioneering geneticist Francis Crick came in for similar criticism.

computerized — that administer governmental policy" have become "a *permanent* form of government" (author's emphasis). They lack accountability, remaining free to act as they please (216). Americans now lived under a "giant federal machine" (218).[30] *"People intuitively sense,"* Whitehead knowingly averred, *"that we of the present era are in danger of being consumed by the authoritarian state"* (205, author's emphasis). Whether an employee of the Internal Revenue Service, the National Security Agency (NSA), or some other faceless agency, government bureaucrats seemed little concerned with anything other than spying on other citizens and ensuring the government's perpetual growth.[31]

The fate of religion under such an oppressive regime, Whitehead continued, should not be hard to imagine: "Wherever secularism has predominated within governmental bureaucracies it has been oppressive. It is a closed system. It closes out the spiritual and often actively persecutes the believers" (47). The government's animating secular philosophy, with modern science at its heart, aimed to crowd out religion. In a section describing secularism as "a slow-acting poison," Whitehead wrote: "By conveying the idea of the certainty of scientific knowledge to the general public, man has virtually delegitimized all other ways of understanding. All knees must bow before the god of science" (102). And under this intellectual umbrella, humanity's worth radically diminishes. "With the disappearance of an infinite

30. Though not his primary focus in *The End of Man*, Whitehead did briefly point out that a large, unaccountable federal bureaucracy was not only burdensome, it was practically illegal. The current expansive government, he wrote, represented "the *total* distortion of the Constitution." The current governmental system "is 'too big' and . . . has expanded beyond the borders of its governing document." Whitehead echoed themes treated elsewhere at greater length: "Because of the expansion of power by way of court interpretation of the Constitution, we operate under a document that was never intended to be used the way it is today. As a result, *we no longer operate under a written constitution* but, instead, under the edicts of the courts and the technicians who attempt to impose a national bureaucracy from a centralized (and regionalized) state" (218, author's emphasis). The appearance of this constitutional argument here illustrated not just Whitehead's irrepressible interest in the law, but also the way he integrated his legal activities into a complex cultural matrix of many interrelated elements. This partially explains why Whitehead's writings were often repetitive, digressive, and circular — "However, to return to a point . . ." is a typical transition (112). For the author, a discussion of one particular problem seemed somehow incomplete without noting its connections with others.

31. In discussing the secretive NSA, Whitehead warned that its minions can put chips in wristwatches to keep track of citizens. This transformed America into an "electronic concentration camp" (226).

basis for value-judgment," he argued, "man, too, disappears" (94). Science and technology, increasing in stature and reach, had so radically devalued humanity that "Man and ant are equated" (127).[32] Under secularism, the author submitted, "man is no longer whole. He is a one-dimensional character integrating into the void of the machinations of the universe" (100).[33]

The End of Man sounded a desperate, mournful tone about the fate of humanity and, in particular, citizens of the United States of America. More philosophical dirge than practical manual, the book served to flesh out the intellectual analysis of Western culture that undergirded and motivated John Whitehead's career in legal activism. Though he always injected plenty of philosophical and theological material into his subsequent writings, Whitehead would never again venture so far out onto this theoretical limb. Instead, he devoted his literary energies more fully to motivating his fellow Christians to resisting the secularist trends he identified. If only his religious compatriots could come to view the world with his unique spectacles, Whitehead signaled, those trends could be reversed. If the steadily provocative, plaintive tone of subsequent writings served as any indication, recruiting soldiers for the cultural fight proved to be frustrating, arduous work.

1.4. Religious Apartheid

Ratcheting up the rhetorical volume, Whitehead in 1994 alerted Americans that they were living in a state of "religious apartheid." Both a book and a

---

32. An entire subsection called upon readers to "consider the ant" (100-102).

33. The rise of technology — especially the computer and other intelligent machines — clearly captured Whitehead's imaginative fancy. In a section entitled "The Meat Machine," he claimed that in the hands of secularist scientists, man had become "simply hardware — meat on a metal frame" (156). Humanity is currently engaged in a "sustained drive to mold humanity in the image of the machine," he wrote, and there is trouble ahead: "When we create autonomous machines, we run the risk that before long we will find ourselves in their metallic jaws. It seems to be a perilous path to walk, but a path nevertheless that modern society is traveling" (132). Whitehead continued with the story of "Eliza," a computer that mimicked human interaction in the laboratory. Artificial intelligence signifies that "the scientific elite" has "a great dissatisfaction with man as he exists. It borders on hatred" (147). "If all goes according to plan for the AI people," he wrote, "one can imagine and expect a 'metallic' future. It might go something like this: In some lonely outpost in the distant future, where all the computers in the universe are linked together, some foreboding human servant asks, 'Is there a God?' Striking the questioner down for his impudence, the computers reply, 'Now there is'" (157).

movie shared the same title: *Religious Apartheid: The Separation of Religion from American Public Life.*[34] In these works TRI's founder essentially repackaged *The Separation Illusion* for a newer crowd, one now presumably more familiar with him and his endeavors after a decade of religious advocacy. The half-hour movie from Gospel Films, made with the collaboration of occasional partner Franky Schaeffer, indicated Whitehead's continuing interest in using various media to spread his ideas and further his organization's mission.[35] Available with a study guide, the movie distilled the book's themes and self-consciously targeted church groups around the nation.[36] Both book and movie indicated Whitehead's ongoing outrage over the perceived exclusion of religion from the public sphere, and his desire to have others join the struggle.

In *Religious Apartheid* Whitehead argued that the nation had yet to relinquish the "separation illusion" detailed in his earlier book. If anything, church and state were more at war with each other than before. Contemporary society is characterized by "religious apartheid," defined as "the increasing hostility of secular concerns toward religious interests."[37] *Everson v. Board of Education* in 1947 marked the "official government sanctioning of this apartness," a stance only solidified since then. As well, collections of nongovernmental secularists had sought to reinforce this apartheid regime: "Now various liberal private interest groups, such as the American Civil Liberties Union, often in conjunction with public schools and local governments, search the public arena for any reference to God or Christianity and seek its removal."[38] "On every side and in every phase of life," Whitehead began his first chapter, "Judeo-Christian beliefs and practices are berated and denounced."[39] The time for action against this unjust separation had arrived.

Deliberately chosen, the word "apartheid" undoubtedly sought to in-

---

34. John W. Whitehead, *Religious Apartheid: The Separation of Religion from American Public Life,* directed by Franky Schaeffer (Gospel Films, 1994), videocassette.

35. This goal was quite explicit: an explanation of TRI's mission and a direct plea for funds concluded the movie.

36. An interviewer in TRI's magazine, *Rutherford,* noted that the movie's "primary target audience consists of Bible study groups, Christian schools, pastors, and laymen"; McThenia, "Religious Apartheid."

37. John W. Whitehead, *Religious Apartheid: The Separation of Religion from American Public Life* (Chicago: Moody Press, 1994), 9.

38. John Whitehead, *Religious Apartheid,* 11.

39. John Whitehead, *Religious Apartheid,* 17.

flame, but it did more than that. The term itself made an argument, immediately and viscerally allying his cause with one of the epic injustices of the twentieth century. For Whitehead, America's religious apartheid, like South Africa's racial segregation, represented an illegitimate regime that deserved to be overthrown. In an interview in TRI's magazine, *Rutherford,* Whitehead explained that the image of apartheid seemed most appropriate because both the South African and American systems were marked by unfair distributions of power. In the United States, a secularist minority used the state's power to persecute the Christian majority. Just as black South Africans overthrew their white oppressors, so too should the numerically superior American faithful arise and boot the secularists from power.[40]

Whitehead directly linked a proper church-state arrangement (as he conceived it) with the health of the republic as a whole. In the movie the legally trained narrator spoke directly to the audience, explaining that there were movements afoot that "may very well destroy the basis of religious freedom in America." In fact, Whitehead intoned, "the elimination of traditional religion from public life has occurred throughout the country." Vivid images accompanied this claim, making clear the wider consequences: the movie confronted viewers with scenes of urban decay and destruction, the sounds of sirens and ominous music in the background. Quick jumps from scene to scene, coupled with off-kilter camera angles, helped to artificially heighten the viewers' sense of distress. "America is in trouble," he warned. "Our social fabric is disintegrating." As before in books like *Schools on Fire,* Whitehead argued that the nation's sociological ills could be traced to a distorted church-state arrangement. If the United States persisted in keeping church and state separate from each other, social chaos would only continue to accelerate.

The video format allowed Whitehead to paint broadly, with bright colors, in naming directly those responsible for America's disintegration. For example, while complaining of "political correctness" and those who put forth an "absolutist definition" of the establishment clause, he stood at the edge of Harvard Square. Whitehead explained that the New Left, once the champions of free speech, now constituted the campus and political establishment. But sadly, the narrator carped, they have traded in their ideals in favor of restricting their ideological opponents — especially their religious ones. Academics and cultural elites, the Ivy League image more than suggested, were the ones primarily responsible for creating a general cli-

40. McThenia, "Religious Apartheid."

mate of censorship, preventing people — presumably those most likely to be gathered around the television watching this movie — from speaking out on spiritual issues.

Much less subtle methods helped to clarify to whom blame belonged. Bright-red words in all capital letters, superimposed on the screen, assigned responsibility for "religious apartheid." The ignominious list accumulated throughout the video: SECULARIST, STATE INTERVENTION, BUREAUCRACY, REGULATION, TAXES, SOCIAL ENGINEERING, RADICAL FEMINISM, FAMILY DISINTEGRATION, ENTERTAINMENT CULTURE, TYRANNY. Even those viewers who tuned out the movie's audio would have learned the plot's villains.

A calculated visual parable illustrated the consequences of these trends for the American family. Viewers looked in upon a "traditional family" of father, mother, and children at home, all going about their normal evening routine. All gathered about the dinner table in a Hallmark-hued rendering of life as it ought to be. As dissonant music begins, dark-suited bureaucrats of both genders slowly but purposefully invade the family's home. These government functionaries, faceless and nameless, arrive with briefcases, legal pads, cameras, tape recorders, inquisitive eyes, and intrusive questions. The female bureaucrat approaches the mother, forcibly removes her apron (the not-so-subtle symbol of the mother's proper place in the family hierarchy), outfits her in a dark blue business suit, pulls her maternally long hair back in a professional ponytail, and marches her off into the workforce.

This ominous violation of family privacy might have seemed unsettling enough, but the filmmakers wasted little time in demonstrating the consequences. Now that mom is off at work, television replaces her as the dominant influence in the children's lives. The kids sit stupefied in front of the glowing electronic hearth, transfixed by violence, sex, and video games. Thanks to this corrupting influence, the kids develop a taste for weapons, rock music, and Satanism. The preteen children, disturbingly, begin to act like out-of-control adults: the young-looking daughter sports candy-apple-red lipstick and dances suggestively as she and her equally young brother smoke and drink alcohol. Soon the police arrive and take the children away from the parents; even the baby, wrested from the father's once-protective arms, belongs to the government now.

In many ways the fulcrum of the film, this dark portrait of contemporary America obviously sought to send shudders through the audience. Whitehead and Schaeffer embedded several lessons in this tale, both covert and overt. The government — run by "radical secularizers" — not only had created the conditions that corrupted this "traditional" family, it also then enforced a solution that only hastened the family's nightmarish disintegration. The narrative technique helped to restrict the audience's interpretation. "So-called new forms of family," Whitehead intoned with unmistakable pique, had gained more acceptance, and the traditional family was beset by "special interest groups."[41] The state had transferred traditional family functions away from fathers and mothers and put them into the hands of faceless bureaucrats in charge of the state's "aggressively secularized social agencies." The family had been intentionally weakened by those who want the state to provide nontraditional, nonreligious solutions to today's problems.

Government bureaucrats had accomplished this coup by gaining control of individual minds. "Our modern secular state has replaced the family as educator," Whitehead complained. Mass compulsory school attendance had resulted in making "child-state" the primary relationship. Not only had this usurped the divinely established order of society, but it had caused all manner of troubles: society is a mess, the kids are dumber. Even if one believed that the bureaucratic enforcers of religious apartheid had benevolent intentions, Whitehead suggested, the consequences would still be terrible. As he wrote in the book, "What we are witnessing is the end of religion and morality in the public sphere. As Christianity is driven further from the marketplace, American public life is increasingly vulnerable to radical lifestyles and options that make up the 'closed loop' of a purely secular consensus."[42]

Often willing to use a bazooka when a pistol would do, Whitehead imported into the *Religious Apartheid* movie some of his most provocative, seditious images. Amid complaints about the "antifamily, antitraditional lobby," viewers see swastikas, an SS guard (always shot so as to remain faceless), scenes of medical experimentation, and euthanasia. Schaeffer and Whitehead borrowed a scene from Stanley Kubrick's film *A Clockwork Orange*, depicting a defenseless citizen strapped to a chair, his eyes forcibly held open while he is bombarded with words such as "LOVE," "TOLERANCE," and "DIVERSITY." Minor-key music accompanies the brainwashing session, interspersed

41. The Rutherford Institute was obviously a special interest group itself, one created to counter the actions of others. For more on the ironic consequences of interest-group proliferation, see chapter 5.

42. John Whitehead, *Religious Apartheid,* 12.

with scenes of the SS guard saluting the Nazi flag. A state functionary pins a yellow star on a religious person. As the audience learns that the state of Virginia rejected a memorial to Civil War casualties, a Nazi soldier stomps on a grave marker in the shape of a white cross.[43] An anecdote about a worker prevented from keeping a Bible at her desk is accompanied by another uniformed Nazi ripping pages from the Good Book. Over and over the audience sees an American flag covered over by a Nazi flag. Adolf Hitler himself often appears, as the audience is told that "enforced privatization of religion in America . . . amounts to systematic persecution of religious persons. Dogmatic secularism is becoming intolerant, tyrannical, and totalitarian." Only those who stepped out for popcorn would have come away from *Religious Apartheid* without equating the current American governmental regime not just with the despotic, but with the demonic.

Though the general outline remained virtually identical in both movie and book, the book version allowed Whitehead to expand on his themes. He sounded a familiar note in articulating the book's thesis: "if the Judeo-Christian principles that served as the source of all law governing this republic are not recovered in the near future, the conflict that will naturally emerge over the changes sweeping across the cultural landscape like a fire storm will destroy the structure of our country and its institutions."[44] Why Christianity? Whitehead contended that it alone "provides the basis for both self-correction and value systems by which to limit the actions of government."[45] Indeed, Christian values represented the key to overturning current trends and restoring the nation's health: "Without Judeo-Christian foundations, individual conscience is invalidated as a social norm. There was no longer a basis for challenging institutional tyrannies and the 'compulsory society.'"[46] Echoing the arguments of Washington and Adams, Whitehead argued that the nation's survival depended upon a virtuous citizenry, one dependent upon faith for its moral health. "Rejecting the transcendental truth given to us by Judeo-Christianity is tantamount to committing national suicide," Whitehead stated. "A secular state cannot — as we see in our present cultural crisis — cultivate virtue."[47] Though the tone, not surprisingly, remained dire in both movie and book, Whitehead

43. Recall that in an earlier work, Whitehead interpreted the Civil War as the triumph of federal meddling over states' rights.
44. John Whitehead, *Religious Apartheid*, 12.
45. John Whitehead, *Religious Apartheid*, 40.
46. John Whitehead, *Religious Apartheid*, 41.
47. John Whitehead, *Religious Apartheid*, 42.

offered a sliver of hope for the future. He wrote that "There is still enough of the older ethical base in some countries — what has been called 'Christian memory' — so that people will resist if they understand that their values are being seriously threatened."[48] For Whitehead, knowledge equaled power: if readers would only awaken to their true condition, they would assuredly join him in the struggle.

Perhaps recognizing that elevating Christianity in this way opened him to charges of seeking to replace one unjust legal regime (secularism) with another (Christian particularism), Whitehead also took the time in *Religious Apartheid* to answer his critics' imagined objections. Having attempted to distance himself from Reconstructionist theology before, the author tried again. First of all, the influence of this theological school of thought had been greatly exaggerated, Whitehead wrote reassuringly. The influence of Reconstructionism was like that of the Christian Left: "its influence is often out of proportion to its numbers."[49] He directly dismissed dominion theology as impractical utopianism; even if Christians did seek to re-form the American republic upon the foundations of Old Testament law, this simply could not happen. "In the context of religious liberty," Whitehead explained, "the massive growth and the power of the modern American state makes it highly improbable that any church or religious organization could ever gain control of the whole state government." He continued: "Modern America is too culturally and religiously diverse, and the nonreligious state is too strong and pervasive for any type of religious takeover. The norm of the present is pluralism."[50]

The author also took space in *Religious Apartheid* to address not just those suspicious of his potentially Reconstructionist leanings, but also those in his audience who might have shared the impulse toward Christian domination of American society.

> Christians have every right to be involved in the political process, but they must rid themselves of the notion that they are destined to assume control of other people and governments and rule the world. The believer's claim must not be for absolute power but for equality of access to society's marketplace of ideas where true Christianity, and the worldview that springs from it, can more than hold its own. Claims of

48. John Whitehead, *Religious Apartheid*, 38.
49. John Whitehead, *Religious Apartheid*, 169.
50. John Whitehead, *Religious Apartheid*, 153.

special holiness and a divine right to rule will not help Christians gain this equal access. Indeed, it may well . . . create a reactionary back-lash.[51]

Dominion-minded believers were not only utopian, they hampered the achievement of realizable goals by unnecessarily frightening their fellow citizens.[52] Even if Christians could agree to follow a particular set of moral principles, Whitehead argued, they should not seek to force them upon other citizens. "From the acknowledgment that Judeo-Christian ab-solutes are a source of objective norms," the author wrote, "it does not automatically follow (as some may assume) that such norms should be enforced through any state mechanisms (such as governmental edict, leg-islation, and so on). To the contrary, if such absolutes are practiced con-sistently by those people who advocate them, then, by the principle of cultural absorption, they will serve society well."[53] Christians best serve the religious code they profess by exemplifying it themselves, Whitehead suggested in *Religious Apartheid*, not by legally coercing others to behave similarly.

1.5. Grasping for the Wind

John Whitehead maintained a keen interest in using visual media to reach a wide audience. Several years after the movie version of *Religious Apartheid*, he sought to create a more in-depth, sweeping cultural analysis that might

51. John Whitehead, *Religious Apartheid*, 170.

52. Whitehead offered a further word of understanding to those who feared the designs of Christian activists, admitting that the popular rise of televangelism had made it seem more likely that Christians were seeking, and actually could accomplish, the re-Christianization of America. He dismissed this possibility, however, claiming that these operations have "an aura of influence and substance out of proportion to reality." Tele-vangelism had actually fostered religious apartheid by creating "an illusion of power and importance that fosters fears of Christian reconstruction, a theocracy, or at minimum the imposition of religious views upon a people accustomed to significant freedom in the matter of religious beliefs." Moreover, because of its medium, televangelism must enter-tain, and therefore often it presented the faith in a more exaggerated, more emotional manner than is accurate; *Religious Apartheid*, 151-52. The contrast between the movie and the book provided evidence in support of this latter point, though the irony seemed to have escaped the author.

53. John Whitehead, *Religious Apartheid*, 44.

appeal to people both within and beyond the Christian community. In 1998 he crafted *Grasping for the Wind: Humanity's Search for Meaning,* a seven-episode film series.[54] In this magnum opus Whitehead walked viewers through the last four hundred years of Western history, allowing them to see cultural transformation through his peculiar eyes.[55] Clad in a sober blue suit, Whitehead introduced the guiding questions behind the series: "Who are we? What is our destiny? What gives us as human beings worth and dignity?"[56] The narrator recounted the story of how the answers had changed; it quickly became clear that the transformation described had been for the worse. Humanity once located the meaning and purpose of existence in the divine, Whitehead intoned, but this no longer was the case: with the Enlightenment, humanity began to believe that our capacity to reason — not our status as children of God — imbued people with worth. "Breaking with the past" (also the title to the first episode), Western civilization cast itself adrift. "The history of ideas from this point on," he said, "is a journal of humanity's attempt to redefine itself in the absence of the traditional notion of God."

According to Whitehead, history teaches us that this attempt has failed, and the nature of this quixotic quest provides the series title: "In modern humanity's search for meaning we have, in a sense, been grasping for the wind." For the rest of the series Whitehead marshaled a remarkably wide-ranging case for this assertion. Referring by name to politicians, philosophers, scientists, poets, musicians, painters, theologians, and film directors (to name only a few), the narrator exhaustively documented the West's complicated cultural decline.

For Whitehead three pieces of art summarily captured the nature of the West's transformation. Rembrandt's painting *Adoration of the Shepherds* (1646), Whitehead argued, represented the proper order of things in the Reformation era, with everyone and everything on earth properly oriented toward the heavens. Life has meaning, the painting acknowledged, because

---

54. *Grasping for the Wind: Humanity's Search for Meaning,* directed by Franky Schaeffer, hosted by John W. Whitehead, 7 episodes (MPI Home Video, 1998). The creative collaboration of Whitehead and Schaeffer proved much less harmonious than it had several years earlier on *Religious Apartheid,* and Whitehead removed Schaeffer from the project before it was finished. For more on their "creative differences," see John Whitehead, *Slaying Dragons,* 256-59.

55. Indeed, Whitehead often *literally* walked viewers through historical topics, wandering in and out of oversized panels displaying works of art and photographs.

56. *Episode 1: Breaking with the Past,* from *Grasping for the Wind.*

humans are created with a divine purpose. A second artwork from the early twentieth century, *God,* by Morton Schaumburg (1917), revealed just how far the West had since traveled. In the sculpture of a disconnected plumber's pipe, the God of *God* is disconnected, cold, impersonal, only faintly resembling the personal, caring God of the "Judeo-Christian" tradition. Finally, the painting *Three Studies for Figures at the Base of a Crucifixion* by Francis Bacon (1944) ratified humanity's radical rejection of God by depicting man in primitive isolation from any meaning. (Spooky music helped reinforce the emotional message Whitehead sought to convey.) How the West journeyed from the halcyon days of Rembrandt to the horrifying world of Bacon served as another form of the questions Whitehead's video series sought to answer.

In documenting the West's decline, Whitehead attempted to inculcate a particular moral lesson. As he put it in the first episode, "When a culture abandons its religious traditions as a matter of survival, it should find something strong enough to replace these traditions, to give people a sense of meaning and purpose." So far, nothing had proven adequate to replace Judeo-Christian theism as a viable cultural adhesive. Without the certainties ensured by religion, we inhabited "a world of hard edges, a world of no absolutes."[57] "The results," Whitehead intoned while shrouded in shadows and surrounded by images of Adolf Hitler, Nazi flags, and gas ovens, "have been catastrophic."[58] Images and rhetoric once again converged to make an already unsubtle point inescapable.

One of the critical themes in *Grasping for the Wind,* as in every literary and visual effort created by TRI's founder, was that *ideas matter.* In Whitehead's historical scheme, intellectual changes preceded and caused historical events. Had it not abandoned the divine as the center of meaning, in other words, the West would not have declined so precipitously — if at

---

57. *Episode 2: Where Are We Going?* from *Grasping for the Wind.* Whitehead used the Impressionists to make this point. Their blurring of the edges, their equating of individual perception with reality, signified the disappearance of absolute truth. He took the title of this episode from a painting by Gauguin entitled *Where Do We Come From? What Are We? Where Are We Going?* The Frenchman was trying to recapture the humanity muted by the Impressionists, Whitehead argued, but the questions still remain unanswered.

58. *Breaking with the Past.* Nazism loomed as perhaps Whitehead's favorite trope when he wanted to suggest the consequences of quietism in the face of godlessness and tyranny. His message to Americans was a simple one: resist secularism, or what happened in Germany just might happen here.

all. The ideological vacuum created by the Enlightenment had been filled by a roster of evils: communism, fascism, evolutionary thinking, racism, all of which proved disastrous for humanity. Only after "the denial of absolute truth" became "the defining characteristic of Western civilization" did Hitler take the stage, abortion become frequent and legal, Timothy McVeigh murder hundreds in Oklahoma City, and physicians indiscriminately euthanize the elderly. With "the loss of basic truths to live our lives by," Whitehead argued, anything goes.[59]

In *Grasping for the Wind* Whitehead expended considerable energy explaining how "the central questions of the nineteenth and twentieth centuries still have no answers."[60] The third episode documented how Westerners had become "children of the machine." In the twentieth century, Whitehead submitted, modern technology attacked man's sense of himself as significant. Human beings became faceless in the machine age. Psychology, cubism, surrealism, jazz, mechanized warfare, abstract expressionism, existentialism, birth control, Bauhaus architecture, Beat poetry, television, rock and roll music, feminism, pop art, sexual liberation,[61] computers, quantum physics, UFO cults — all unsuccessfully tried to grapple with the moral anomie ensuing from a devaluation of humanity's uniqueness, from civilization's divorce from tradition and its guiding absolutes. All have failed to replace the meaningfulness dispatched when the Enlightenment relocated God further from human endeavor; in fact, many of these phenomena had accelerated the West's decline. For instance, according to Whitehead, Einstein's scientific insights seemed to reduce the idea of moral absolutes to irrelevance. Newton's ordered and predictable universe became a world of comprehensive chaos: "Relativity . . . became confused with relativism."[62] Chaos came to reign.

In the last episode of *Grasping for the Wind*, Whitehead summarized the desperate contemporary circumstance and suggested what the future might hold. "By the 1970s," Whitehead claimed, "the Judeo-Christian worldview was no longer accepted in the West." As a result, "Western cul-

59. All quotes in this paragraph come from *Breaking with the Past*.
60. *Where Are We Going?*
61. Included in this category was homosexuality. As proof of the destructive force of this "movement," Whitehead claimed that 30 percent of all suicides are related to gender confusion; *Episode 7: The Narcissistic Culture*, from *Grasping for the Wind*.
62. *Episode 3: The Lost Generation*, from *Grasping for the Wind*. In the second episode, Whitehead singled out T. S. Eliot as one of the few cultural shapers who sought to respond to the machine age with Christian answers.

ture was splintering." Little united the Western world at century's end except a morally bankrupt narcissism.[63] Could society overcome such pandemonium? Typically, Whitehead proved to be less than sanguine about the West's prospects: "Democratic society may be unable to survive the loss of the internal restraints once provided by Judeo-Christian ethics." Since he defined "culture" as "a set of consistent moral beliefs," the narrator clearly believed that people in the West, and in particular the United States, no longer possessed a culture at all.

Viewers who persisted through all seven episodes experienced an extended jeremiad. We are at the end of a long experiment to see if humans can live orderly, meaningful lives without the Judeo-Christian ethic, Whitehead told his audience. Clearly society has failed to do so. "If there is to be a restoration of hope and beauty," he urged, we must return to the sentiments reflected in Rembrandt's worshipful painting. "Can we rediscover the spiritual hope that for so many centuries enlightened Western culture? Can we rediscover the spiritual certainties" that once cemented civilization together?[64] The ominous, despairing tone of the entire series suggested that rediscovery, though desirable, was unlikely.

For Whitehead the rise of the bureaucratic state proved to be another critical theme, one that cropped up time and again not only throughout *Grasping for the Wind*, but also in more specific legal contexts. In this film series he analyzed Nazi and fascist architecture, pointing to the way it symbolized how an all-powerful state sought to subsume the individual. And lest his audience believe this to be a purely European phenomenon, Whitehead quickly noted how the same terrible transformation had been happening in the United States. He juxtaposed images of Nazi buildings with the Empire State Plaza in Albany, New York — the similarities between German totalitarians and modern American bureaucrats, Whitehead more than suggested, were not purely aesthetic. Dwarfed by the imposing buildings, surrounded by them on all sides, Whitehead asked viewers, "Where do human beings fit in all of this?" These buildings could have a swastika on them, he contended; whether Nazi or American, such twentieth-century architecture revealed "the faceless power of the state over the individual."

63. Whitehead began *The Narcissistic Culture* with an epigraph from Tom Wolfe: "We now live in an age in which science is a court from which there is no appeal. And this issue this time around, at the end of the twentieth century, is not the evolution of the species . . . but the nature of our own precious inner selves."

64. *The Narcissistic Culture.*

Whitehead continued on the same theme, this time accompanied by visuals of the headquarters of the FBI and the IRS: "An unstoppable, face-less machine seems to be running things behind closed doors." People have lost touch with their elected representatives; politicians seem beyond the reach of the ballot box. "Many people," according to a Gallup poll, think the government is out to get them. The U.S. Capitol came into focus as dissonant music played. A shot of the Murrah Federal Building in Oklahoma City, just after the murderous bombing in 1995 by an antigovernment loner, concluded the sequence.[65] Whitehead's journey through four hundred years of Western history argued that those who have abandoned God had come to be ruled by the godless. The awful consequences could be found in every cranny of the culture.

2. Ideas in Practice

From the time he founded The Rutherford Institute in 1982 through century's end, John W. Whitehead sought diligently to explain the motivations for his legal advocacy work. Through his books and movies, the lawyer made a strenuous effort to convince others to join him in reversing the current situation, one he described as drastically different from the way things used to — and ought to — be. In *The Stealing of America, An American Dream, The End of Man, Religious Apartheid,* and *Grasping for the Wind,* Whitehead revealed his belief that ideas matter, that history could be altered by the activism of right-thinking and right-acting people, and that people could be motivated to engage in public cultural battles by being shown how to correctly perceive the world around them.

In addition to exploring the theological and philosophical foundations for his public activism, Whitehead, through his newly founded non-

---

65. Whitehead usually took care to urge only lawful activism in many of his writings. For example, in John Whitehead, *The Right to Picket and the Freedom of Public Discourse,* TRI Report 3 (Westchester, Ill.: Crossway, 1984), he entitled a chapter "The Outer Limits of Expression" in which he cautioned dissenters to stay within certain moral boundaries. In *Grasping for the Wind* he seemed to be offering only an explanation for antigovernment sentiment, not an endorsement of murderous antigovernment activities. Nevertheless, having virtually equated America with Nazi totalitarianism, and having subjected viewers to incendiary imagery designed to frighten them about the consequences of such an ideology, Whitehead revealed some ambivalence about the true limits of acceptable resistance.

profit organization, also strove to provide practical information and advice to citizens ignorant of their legal rights as religious individuals. In a variety of books, pamphlets, newsletters, magazines, and booklets issued under the auspices of TRI, the Christian lawyer and his organization positioned themselves as knowledge brokers and reliable advocates for those civically dispossessed because of religion. Simultaneously serving to drum up support and publicity for TRI's advocacy efforts, these materials — as in his other works — dispensed a sticky confection of theology, history, argumentation, and information. Perhaps even more than Whitehead's more serious books, these vehicles presented The Rutherford Institute to the American public and communicated most clearly TRI's sense of its own identity and mission in late twentieth-century America.

2.1. The Rutherford Institute Reports

Early in TRI's history Whitehead and his colleagues began to treat the particularities of several freedoms in a series of books called The Rutherford Institute Reports (also called TRI Reports). The books' self-explanatory titles reflected the less abstract, more practical nature of the content. The series included five books in all. *The Freedom of Religious Expression in Public High Schools* (1983) explained what rights students had under current law.[66] (This analysis was expanded to all of public education in a subsequent book, *The Freedom of Religious Expression in Public Universities and High Schools,* three years later.)[67] The second TRI Report, *Home Education and Constitutional Liberties: The Historical and Constitutional Arguments in Support of Home Instruction* (1984), marshaled a case in support of a growing movement among evangelical and especially fundamentalist Christians disenchanted with public education.[68] TRI then issued *The Right to Picket and the Freedom of Public Discourse* (1984) and, a year later, *Arresting Abortion: Practical Ways to Save Unborn Children* (1985), both seeking to contribute intellectual support and practical advice to would-be activist con-

66. John W. Whitehead, *The Freedom of Religious Expression in Public High Schools,* 1st ed., TRI Report 1 (Westchester, Ill.: Crossway, 1983).

67. John W. Whitehead, *The Freedom of Religious Expression in Public Universities and High Schools,* 2nd ed., TRI Report 1 (Westchester, Ill.: Crossway, 1986).

68. John W. Whitehead and Wendell R. Bird, *Home Education and Constitutional Liberties: The Historical and Constitutional Arguments in Support of Home Instruction,* TRI Report 2 (Westchester, Ill.: Crossway, 1984).

servatives.[69] The final volume of TRI Reports proved to be the most theoretical and sophisticated of the set. In 1987 legal scholar Daniel Dreisbach contributed *Real Threat and Mere Shadow: Religious Liberty and the First Amendment,* an in-depth and technical examination of original intent and subsequent jurisprudence.[70]

The revised version of the first TRI Report, *The Freedom of Religious Expression in Public Universities and High Schools,* combined brief historical argumentation and practical information in a manner characteristic of the entire series. In his first chapter Whitehead sought to locate religious expression in public schools firmly within the American tradition. "Our forefathers," he wrote in the preface, "would have permitted much more latitude toward religious expression than is commonly found in our modern secular society."[71] In support he summarized the evidence for accommodationism he first detailed in *The Separation Illusion,* highlighting especially those facts related to education. For example, he noted that the language in the Northwest Ordinance of 1787 lifted up both religion and education as vital to the republic's health. He further explained that in the nineteenth century, "textbooks referred to God without embarrassment, and public schools considered one of their major tasks to be the development of character through the teaching of religion." The religion-rich McGuffey's Reader predominated in classrooms, selling more than 120 million copies between 1836 and 1920; Whitehead contended that this reflected the sentiments of the founders. "The great men who built this country from the ground up," he wrote, "sat under McGuffey-type teaching."[72]

69. John Whitehead, *The Right to Picket and the Freedom of Public Discourse;* John W. Whitehead, ed., *Arresting Abortion: Practical Ways to Save Unborn Children,* TRI Report 4 (Westchester, Ill.: Crossway, 1985).

70. Daniel L. Dreisbach, *Real Threat and Mere Shadow: Religious Liberty and the First Amendment,* TRI Report 5 (Westchester, Ill.: Crossway, 1987). Written solely by Dreisbach, an Oxford graduate, this volume differed from the other four TRI Reports in that it was written by someone with impressive academic credentials and it conformed most closely to scholarly conventions. Indeed, subsequent studies of the First Amendment would rarely fail to take into account Dreisbach's work, and it became a credible touchstone for conservative lawyers (like John Whitehead) and like-minded activists who sought to make a public, credible case for accommodationism as the most historically accurate interpretation of the religion clauses.

71. John Whitehead, *The Freedom of Religious Expression in Public Universities and High Schools,* 11.

72. John Whitehead, *The Freedom of Religious Expression in Public Universities and High Schools,* 14.

This kind of teaching "produced a spirit of accommodation toward the exercise of religion in early America."[73] Even Thomas Jefferson — who in the author's opinion was too often misperceived as a separationist — signed a treaty with the Kaskaskian Indians in 1803 that provided federal money for a Catholic mission. And as the first president of the Washington, D.C., school board, he raised no objection to including the Bible and the Watts hymnal in the curriculum. Whitehead concluded his historical survey in an authoritative tone: "As one can readily see, history clearly teaches that from our country's inception the prevailing mood toward religion has been one of accommodation. The founding fathers and those who administered and taught in the public schools throughout the nineteenth century defended and perpetuated this accommodation."[74]

TRI's founder devoted the rest of the work to explaining what was and was not appropriate under current law. He wrote the book in part, he said, because so many school districts had overreacted when dealing with religious issues. Whitehead explained that the United States Supreme Court's attitude toward religion in the public schools was best understood as one of "accommodating neutrality." The Court, he noted unhappily, had granted secularism the same status as religion under the First Amendment, which meant that the state must remain neutral among all competing belief systems. Under that regime of neutrality, many religious expressions were appropriate and must be allowed. Whitehead devoted separate chapters to the rights of students, the rights of faculty, the rights of nonstudents, and a thorough exegesis of the Equal Access Act (passed in 1984). Religious adherents in need of information and advice about appropriate actions and behavior, it was clearly hoped, would find this book indispensable.

Whitehead wrote the first TRI Report by himself, but he turned to theologically like-minded authors in *Arresting Abortion: Practical Ways to Save Unborn Children*. With essays by Franky Schaeffer, D. James Kennedy, and Joseph M. Scheidler, this book variously offered advice on how to picket, how to perform effective "sidewalk counseling" to women arriving at abortion clinics, and how to support "rescue" adoption agencies. Editor

73. John Whitehead, *The Freedom of Religious Expression in Public Universities and High Schools*, 15.

74. John Whitehead, *The Freedom of Religious Expression in Public Universities and High Schools*, 16. Whitehead relied on two more recent resources to support his case: Robert L. Cord, *The Separation of Church and State: Historical Fact and Current Fiction* (New York: Lambeth Press, 1982), and Justice William Rehnquist's dissent in *Wallace v. Jaffree* (1985).

Whitehead provided clues in his introduction that the battle against abortion and the battle against what he often called "religious apartheid" formed parts of the same struggle against humanism and relativism. "The most important single issue facing this generation," he wrote, "is the devaluation of human life." For him the responsibility for this societal transformation could be easily assigned to a degenerate philosophy: "As traditional values have waned, we have seen our entire culture shift to a relativistic view of all things, even life."[75] Once humans become the center of the universe, once they replace God as the proper focus of existence, then those who do not match up to society's definition of "acceptable" humanity can be dispatched with little notice.

2.2. Faith and Freedom

Whether written solely by Whitehead or with many others, The Rutherford Institute Reports provided legal information in what the organization clearly hoped was an easily digestible form. This trend continued into the next decade, as Whitehead and The Rutherford Institute continued to publish works that combined philosophical argumentation and practical legal advice.[76] In the mid-1990s TRI joined with Moody Press to issue six pamphlet-sized books on a variety of topics. These booklets served as more portable, pithy, updated versions of TRI Reports, coupling succinct philosophical and legal analyses with practical legal and activist advice for sympathetic constituencies. Promoted on TRI's Web site, these brief but densely packed booklets provided another useful snapshot of what issues continued to animate Whitehead and his organization's legal work. The resources not only indicated an interest in keeping updated legal information before the public, but they also tacitly proved that Whitehead's cultural arguments had yet to gain sufficient traction. Catalyzed by the misunderstanding and misapplication of the First Amendment, the

75. John Whitehead, *Arresting Abortion*, ix-x.

76. One example not discussed here is John W. Whitehead and Alexis Irene Crowe, *Home Education: Rights and Reasons* (Wheaton, Ill.: Crossway, 1993). In this book Whitehead and Crowe, TRI's longtime legal director, followed the earlier model of TRI Reports, providing homeschoolers and curious others with a vigorous defense of the practice and a guide to understanding their legal rights. This essentially updated and expanded Whitehead's earlier volume, John Whitehead and Bird, *Home Education and Constitutional Liberties*.

crisis TRI's founder had first pointed to in the late 1970s still existed; in fact, it had grown more complicated. Readers of the Faith and Freedom series learned that Christians still had a duty to respond to this crisis, and if they would only awaken to their duty to be the salt of the earth, Whitehead and The Rutherford Institute would help them channel their energies effectively.

Three volumes in this series came out in 1994. The first booklet, *Christians Involved in the Political Process*, made a vigorous case for Christians to shake off political pacifism and labor diligently to shape the culture in their own moral image.[77] *Censored on the Job: Your Religious Rights* provided a reference for religious people unsure of what passed for religiously and legally appropriate behavior in the workplace.[78] Whitehead and TRI issued a third booklet that year entitled *State vs. Parents: Threats to Raising Your Children*.[79] In this work Whitehead echoed themes from earlier works, raising the alarm over the increase in state intervention in once-sacrosanct spheres of family life and individual rights.

Whitehead followed the next year with three more booklets in the series. In *Politically Correct: Censorship in American Culture*, TRI's leader recapitulated themes from his book and movie combination of 1994, *Religious Apartheid*. Although a short booklet, *Politically Correct* offered Whitehead's most nuanced argument against the concept of neutrality, or fairness. With telling quotation marks, he entitled his first section "'Neutral' Terminology." Although those behind political correctness purported to seek the elimination of prejudice, the author argued that in reality this movement's hallowing of fairness was merely a ruse to purge public life of opinions deemed out of bounds by the cultural elite. "One of the hallmarks of political correctness," Whitehead explained, "is inconsistency in the treatment of ideas that are deemed 'correct' and 'incorrect.'"[80] And too often those ideas ruled "incorrect" were religious ones. In the name of seemingly incontrovertible American values — free speech, fairness, equality, diversity,

77. John W. Whitehead, *Christians Involved in the Political Process*, Faith and Freedom series (Chicago: Moody Press, 1994).

78. John W. Whitehead, *Censored on the Job: Your Religious Rights*, Faith and Freedom series (Chicago: Moody Press, 1994).

79. John W. Whitehead, *State vs. Parents: Threats to Raising Your Children*, Faith and Freedom series (Chicago: Moody Press, 1994).

80. John W. Whitehead, *Politically Correct: Censorship in American Culture*, Faith and Freedom series (Chicago: Moody Press, 1995), 6-7. Parenthetical page numbers in the next few paragraphs refer to *Politically Correct*.

justice, tolerance — political correctness actually restricted the ability of religious people to proclaim their values in the public sphere. "Both formally and informally," he wrote, "notions of political correctness inhibit the freedom to dissent from a lengthening litany of 'approved' positions on matters of family, gender, and sexual orientation" (7).

With the author's corrective lenses, the losers in this charged political battle came quickly and clearly into focus. Whitehead elucidated: "some people — most often religious people and others with a traditional moral view — are unable to speak and act according to their convictions. This too often results in religious apartheid, or the separation of those who express or hold religiously based views from those who espouse views that are deemed politically correct" (8). This situation of forced separation steadily worsened. He wrote that the "rejection of religion, and Christianity in particular, continues to grow" (38). In large part the "zealously secular" media bear responsibility for "the stigmatization of religion as evil." Given the media's power, "it is no surprise that religion is being derided and removed from American public life." In fact, the religious were the most persecuted group under "the regime" of political correctness. These days, Whitehead complained, "Christians largely remain the only group that may be publicly defamed with impunity" (39). Political correctness was an ideological wolf in sheep's clothing, and religious viewpoints had become the preferred prey.

Whitehead also fretted over the wider implications of restricting religious expression.[81] Early on he rued the disappearance of free speech in higher education, which he thought would cut off tomorrow's leaders from important sources of innovation and social change. Thanks to political correctness, the next generation of citizens "will not be educated as to the religious and philosophical heritage inherent in this country's foundation and development as a great nation." He worried that "many of the important values and precepts of our forebears will not be included in the education of the nation's future leaders" (16). If the politically correct exclude religion from campus, students' education would not be complete and our nation will suffer for it.

Whitehead pushed beyond just religion, however, portraying himself in *Politically Correct* to be a First Amendment absolutist on the subject of

---

81. Those outside the PC boundaries had even fewer friends. Whitehead complained that "persons with politically incorrect views are no longer included in many social events" (43).

free speech. He contended that even hate speech should be allowed, for exposing it often served as the best way to stamp it out. "Free speech is often the best way to uncover truth," Whitehead explained. "By allowing a free marketplace of ideas, open to even the most offensive ideas and expressions, truth will generally ultimately triumph" (25). In defense of this position, the author even displayed some uncharacteristic humility about the fragility of certainty: "In light of history's record of human fallibility in recognizing truth, freedom of expression must include freedom for all expression and not just the promulgation of one view as the only and correct one" (28). Whitehead again pointed to a recent case taken by TRI as evidence that he practiced what he preached: the organization assisted a Virginian in suing the state of Virginia for disallowing his request for a license plate that read "ATHEIST." After all, "if you can't put ATHEIST on a license plate, you can't put THEIST," Whitehead elsewhere told a reporter. "Sometimes, for the protection of liberties, personal repugnancies must be subverted."[82] Boldly drawing on intellectual support from Justice William Brennan of the Supreme Court and Nadine Strossen, head of the American Civil Liberties Union, Whitehead also communicated to his readers that defending free speech often results in unfamiliar alliances (*Politically Correct*, 30-31). Ideological wheat and tares must be allowed to grow together to ensure the free speech rights of everyone.

Whitehead concluded *Politically Correct* by advising readers "what you can do." For the author, knowledge equaled power, and he called upon Christians to become better informed. The nation's guiding philosophy had become secularist, and people must realize that "secularism is not compatible with Judeo-Christian beliefs and values" (43). Once sufficiently outraged, Whitehead continued, religious people must direct their energies appropriately. Do not retreat, for "withdrawal is not Christianity" (46). Instead, get busy, and have the courage of one's "politically incorrect" positions, for "involvement in *all* areas of the culture is a necessary part of true Christianity." Do not fight censorship with censorship, Whitehead advised: "Christians must vigorously support the right of others to express opposing views" in order to ensure the right to express their own. "After all," he maintained in an undoubtedly self-conscious Jeffersonian key, "the Christian message *is* truth, and the free marketplace of ideas is where truth will flourish" (47).

In 1996 Whitehead and Moody Press published the final two book-

82. Karen Augustine, "Interview," *Rutherford* 3, no. 1 (Jan. 1994): 12-13.

lets in the Faith and Freedom series.[83] The final one, *Church vs. State,* served primarily as a repository of practical advice and legal information for church leaders, but, as its title suggested, a familiar defense of accommodationism — first articulated by Whitehead almost twenty years earlier in *The Separation Illusion* — underpinned the narrative. We must shed the "so-called doctrine" of the separation of church and state, Whitehead urged, for it does not accurately reflect the nation's founding principles.[84] "The United States was," Whitehead claimed, "at one time in its history, a nation greatly influenced by Christianity."[85] Here Whitehead also recapitulated his contention that the state constituted a — if not *the* — formidable enemy of Christianity and individual freedom. Churches should strive to avoid contact with government bureaucrats at all costs, the author counseled. Stretching the boundaries of "practical" advice, Whitehead even suggested a radical antigovernment step: due to "the pro-IRS sentiment demonstrated by the courts and the anti-church stance taken by much of modern government," perhaps it was time for the churches to forgo exemption from federal taxes.[86]

3. A Breed Apart

The themes carefully argued in The Rutherford Institute Reports and the Faith and Freedom series appeared in more succinct form throughout TRI's other written materials. Audiotapes and pamphlets on a variety of topics, from church-state separation to homeschooling, could be purchased from the institute. Additionally, in the early 1990s Whitehead created a syndicated radio show, *Freedom under Fire,* that spotlighted particular cases or issues. Virtually from the beginning, TRI published a newsletter, journal, or magazine to inform, to alert, and to maintain connections with its financial and theological supporters.[87] TRI's *Rutherford,* a glossy, handsomely pro-

83. Foreshadowing his assistance to the most famous female litigant of the 1990s, Paula Jones, Whitehead issued the penultimate volume in the Faith and Freedom series: John W. Whitehead, *Women's Rights and the Law,* Faith and Freedom series (Chicago: Moody Press, 1996).

84. John Whitehead, *Church vs. State,* 15.

85. John Whitehead, *Church vs. State,* 14.

86. John Whitehead, *Church vs. State,* 43.

87. Keeping careful track of TRI's publications likely has challenged more than a few library cataloguers. The *Rutherford Institute Journal,* the *Rutherford Journal,* the

duced monthly, provided the most direct and effective means for the institute to explain its endeavors and troll for supporters. Rarely did an issue pass without some article promoting the institute's efforts, and often entire issues were devoted to detailing TRI's identity and activities. The magazine's articles, just like the other materials from Whitehead and TRI, told a familiar story of America's decline into moral chaos and hostility toward religion. Presenting this story over and over allowed TRI to position itself, in the eyes of sympathetic fellow Christians, as the most obvious and effective defense against alarming cultural trends.

All these materials distilled themes from Whitehead's lengthier works and sought to build support for his organization's mission to offer legal assistance to those embroiled in religious issues. That mission became more complicated in the early 1990s, as a host of similar legal organizations gained higher profiles and threatened TRI's niche. Given this increasingly crowded terrain, Whitehead and his organization naturally grew uneasy about the potential competition for money, cases, media attention, and perhaps most importantly, the moral high ground. Fully aware of this wider range of options its conservative Christian constituency had in directing their charitable dollars, The Rutherford Institute devoted considerable energy to distinguishing itself from its apparent clones. In doing so, especially in *Rutherford*, the organization indicated a collective frustration with the crowded landscape, lamenting the difficulties it presented for TRI to perform its urgent work. As well, TRI put forward an argument for its own uniqueness, strenuously making a case for why supporters should send TRI — rather than its many competitors — their donations.

For example, in January 1994 The Rutherford Institute devoted an entire issue of *Rutherford* to itself, promising readers a look "Inside The Rutherford Institute." Staff members interviewed each other, a TRI employee reviewed the founder's latest movie, and John Whitehead's wife, Carol, reflected nostalgically on the organization's early days. Despite the

---

Rutherford Institute Magazine, Rutherford — all were at one time or another published by TRI. The organization experimented with both a quarterly magazine and a newsletter in the mid to late 1980s and into the early 1990s. *Rutherford,* a glossy and culturally wide-ranging monthly, was issued from April 1992 to February 1997, during which time various newsletters also appeared. In March 1997 *Rutherford* disappeared. Whitehead then began publishing the bimonthly *Gadfly,* a much more general journal of culture that was barely connected — so far as its readers could have noticed — with The Rutherford Institute. In the late 1990s TRI's affairs continued to be detailed in the much more mundane *Religious Liberty Bulletin.*

issue's incestuous vibe — an interview of John Whitehead *by* John White-head would not have seemed out of place — subscribers would have learned a great deal about the origins and motivating philosophy of TRI. As well, "Inside The Rutherford Institute" signaled the organization's evolving understanding of itself and its unique place in both conservative Christianity and the wider American culture.

In a column entitled "Why Is The Rutherford Institute Different?" legal coordinator Alexis Crowe responded to a growing sense — shared both by the institute's staff and by its potential supporters — that theirs no longer was the only game in the conservative religious town. By 1994 several similar organizations dotted the landscape, many with the funds and star power to attract considerable attention. The Christian Law Association, the oldest conservative legal advocacy organization, had been around since 1969, though relatively speaking it operated with few funds and below the public radar. The Center for Law and Religious Freedom, an arm of the Christian Legal Society, also predated TRI (it was founded in 1976), but it had a similarly indistinct public profile. After TRI emerged in 1982, the legal advocacy scene soon become more crowded. The National Legal Foundation formed in 1985. The high-wattage preacher Jerry Falwell created his own legal organization, the Liberty Counsel, in 1989. The American Center for Law and Justice (ACLJ) was founded in 1990 by media-savvy lawyer Jay A. Sekulow and televangelist and erstwhile presidential candidate Pat Robertson. In 1994 the Becket Fund for Religious Liberty came on the scene, and the same year a collection of conservative religious leaders founded the Alliance Defense Fund as a fund-raising clearinghouse for litigation efforts. All these organizations threatened to glean from the same fund-raising fields, and TRI's resentment began to grow.

In *Rutherford* the organization directly addressed this issue. Undoubtedly deluged with fund-raising pleas from all comers, how were potential supporters to distinguish among the many religiously conservative players in the legal arena? Clearly sensitive to this concern and its implications for her own organization's financial health, Crowe began her column by reporting that "Almost daily people ask me how The Rutherford Institute is different from other legal organizations that defend religious freedom." People also want to know why all these groups have not combined their efforts. Crowe's response: we're older, we're bigger, and we're better.

As befitted an organization whose founder revered history as the surest guide to solving contemporary constitutional questions, Crowe claimed the moral high ground from similar groups by insisting that TRI was the first to undertake this kind of legal advocacy. "We have been defending religious freedom longer than any other group in this country," she asserted.[88] Moreover, this mission had remained unchanged since the early days: "We pour all our resources into one single purpose: to defend the rights of religious persons. That was our mission in 1982, and it's our mission today." Crowe suggested that by honoring TRI's "original intent," by remaining consistent in its agenda, the institute had more than demonstrated its moral soundness.

In Crowe's estimation, TRI's single-mindedness contrasted sharply with the scattershot approach of similar organizations. She suggested that their competitors "often have a myriad of objectives," some of which strayed far from defending the rights of religious people. She pointed out that when the ACLJ was created, founder Pat Robertson's first hire was not a lawyer but a fund-raiser — a clear sign of impure motives, the essay transparently implied. Though TRI must have been similarly concerned with raising funds, Crowe suggested that TRI — unlike others — had remained blissfully free from the taint of moneygrubbing. The author later reinforced this lesson by proclaiming proudly that TRI had always been financially accountable; fully audited every year by outsiders, TRI was the only legal advocacy group fully compliant with the Better Business Bureau's standards for philanthropic organizations. Financial watchdogs had never questioned TRI's financial integrity, Crowe bragged. "The same is not true of several similar organizations."

This tone of moral superiority permeated Crowe's column. TRI "handles the majority of the religious liberty cases in this country," readers learned, because the institute "doesn't turn the tough cases away." What "makes us very different" from similar legal organizations, Crowe emphasized, was that, unlike them, "We take all the cases — including the ones that will never make the headlines and the ones that you can't win hands down." Baldly naming names, she cited another magazine's claim that the ACLJ took on only those cases with ideal, precedent-setting, headline-generating legal potential. In further contrast to the ACLJ, The Rutherford Institute "has no 'star' litigators." TRI's cases were pursued by "a vast network of volunteer lawyers coached and trained by Institute attorneys." And TRI staff did not hog the publicity if cases made it to the Supreme Court,

88. This would obviously have come as news to staffers at the Christian Law Association and the Christian Legal Society's Center for Law and Religious Freedom, organizations both older than TRI.

readers learned; unlike the ACLJ, whose "star," Jay Sekulow, dedicated himself solely to high-profile arguments before the nation's highest court, TRI allowed its volunteers to see cases all the way to the end. Through Crowe's disdainful eyes, the ACLJ was distastefully desperate for publicity; The Rutherford Institute, meanwhile, remained motivated only by noble principles.

Elsewhere in the same issue, both John Whitehead and his wife, Carol, reinforced this institutional mythology of humility and authenticity. TRI's founder told an interviewer that "We're not an elitist organization, and we try to meet people's needs at the grassroots level."[89] Carol Whitehead, in "Looking Back at the Early Days," made sure to follow the standard narrative arc. She noted that the difference between TRI and similar groups "is that most of them are tied to big Christian ministries and thus have a large financial network to draw from." TRI, by contrast, sprang forth from their home basement and had never lost touch with its humble roots. TRI "has been built one step at a time through the generosity and sacrificial giving of supporters." Though "its finances have always been on a tight shoestring," she wrote, and life had always been a struggle, "John and his dedicated staff . . . will never give up." The "growing pains" the Whitehead family and The Rutherford Institute had "always" experienced were well worth it, Carol concluded.[90]

Other issues of *Rutherford* reinforced this romanticization of its own grassroots sensibilities. Perhaps the most overt example came in the form of a child's letter to TRI's founder, reproduced on the inside cover of an issue in 1994. "Dear Mr. Whitehead," the young boy began, "I am sending $40 to you because I raised pigs, and this is my tithe money. And I thought I would give it to you instead of anywhere else. I am nine years old. From Caleb Ehlers."[91] Here, as in virtually every account of the institute's founding and its subsequent activities, an instance of humble sacrifice provided the truest seal of TRI's organizational righteousness.[92]

89. Augustine, "Interview."
90. Carol Whitehead, "Looking Back at the Early Days," *Rutherford* 3, no. 1 (Jan. 1994): 14.
91. Caleb Ehlers, "Letter to the Editor," *Rutherford* 3, no. 2 (Feb. 1994): 2.
92. This theme was further solidified by a brief section asking staff members, "What sacrifices have you made to work for TRI?" Kelly Shackelford noted the "danger" of working at a place that wouldn't advance his legal career in traditional fashion, but concluded that nevertheless "I want to argue on behalf of righteousness." David Melton related that he could be making more money elsewhere, and Melanie Davis Stockwell

The next year, in 1995, Whitehead and TRI continued to try to distinguish themselves from their imitators by echoing many of the same themes. As Crowe had done before, Whitehead disdained the "big case" mentality of other advocacy groups. "We can't fight just the legal battles that might set a so-called 'important precedent' or only take on the cases that might make it to the Supreme Court," he sniped in his monthly column. "There aren't many of these cases, and they take a long time to come to fruition."[93] The real work took place out of the spotlight and on behalf of ordinary people. Crowe picked up this subject again. "Our client-centered emphasis," she argued, "is what makes The Rutherford Institute unique." She claimed that other legal advocacy organizations often referred people to TRI, who "takes most cases from the beginning."[94] Throughout, Crowe suggested unsubtly that even their imitators knew, deep in their institutional souls, that TRI stood as first among equals.[95]

Crowe and her colleagues became more direct in professing TRI's superiority vis-à-vis other organizations. Crowe complained of "the low level of ethics of many leaders in the evangelical field," and asked readers of *Rutherford* to contrast those unnamed others with TRI's own impeccable model. With an eye toward financial troubles in the evangelical community, Whitehead reminded readers that "To date, The Rutherford Institute is one of the only nonprofit Christian legal defense organizations with a membership with the Better Business Bureau."[96] Did others, unlike TRI, have something to hide?

In the 1990s The Rutherford Institute sought in other ways to distin-

---

similarly admitted that "I've definitely given up . . . prestige and . . . financial security." Anne-Marie Amiel rued that in working for TRI, "you don't have a life." Brad Dacus offered the most direct answer: "I'm 29 and still single, need I say more?" My point is not to minimize the possible sacrifices made by most employees of nonprofits, including The Rutherford Institute, but instead to note how the organization's mythology of virtue was replicated at many different levels, including the personal.

93. John W. Whitehead, "Why We Do What We Do," *Rutherford* 4, no. 2 (Feb. 1995): 11.

94. In fact, she explained to inquisitive subscribers, this was why TRI refused to join the Alliance Defense Fund (ADF). Despite the apparent overlap in mission, Crowe claimed that the ADF remained too bureaucratically cumbersome to react to individual emergencies.

95. T. Stanciu and Nisha N. Mohammed, "Committed to the 'Little Guy' (Interview with Alexis Crowe)," *Rutherford* 4, no. 2 (Feb. 1995): 13-15.

96. John W. Whitehead, "The Rutherford Institute Story: Responding to a Need," *Rutherford* 4, no. 2 (Feb. 1995): 16-17, 23.

guish itself from its competitors. For example, TRI began to claim that its principles transcended a narrow evangelical constituency, and to act accordingly. In an organizational profile in *Rutherford,* author Jim Travisano admitted that almost all TRI staffers would happily self-identify as evangelical Christians. But that did not mean that TRI advocated only on behalf of this religious community, for TRI "is not easily pigeonholed." The institute, Travisano noted, "has also defended Jews, American Indians, and, once, even a vehement atheist." This made TRI practically ecumenical. Though "at first glance, it might appear that the organization defines 'religious people' as evangelical Christians," Travisano argued, "in fact, The Rutherford Institute is nonsectarian, defending people's rights to religious expression regardless of religious faith."[97] The diversity of viewpoints printed in *Rutherford,* wrote the author, further proves the institute's open-mindedness.[98] As the organization grew older, TRI's founder diligently cultivated this image.[99]

As another means of carving out a particular identity apart from a narrow-minded religious conservatism, Whitehead sought on several occasions to distance himself from Reconstructionism.[100] In 1995 he wrote of the *mistaken* assumption by some evangelicals "that Christians should rule the world." Believing this, he argued, committed the sin of investing the state with redemptive power. He recognized that many — probably including himself, early in his literary career — turned to history in support of a biblical American republic: "Many Evangelicals refer to America's Christian

97. Jim Travisano, "Fighting for Religious Freedom," *Rutherford* 3, no. 1 (Jan. 1994): 3-11.

98. Travisano made his case: "Look at its *Rutherford* publication, and you may see an article by commentator Phyllis Schlafly. Yet if you turn to another issue you just might find the column 'A Different View' written by a homosexual or an avowed feminist. You could even find song lyrics by Bob Dylan. It's safe to say that The Rutherford Institute not only vigorously battles its adversaries — but is also willing to challenge its own members from time to time." Though the diversity of perspectives might have been exaggerated, this magazine's increasingly eclectic nature eventually disenchanted many subscribers. This led Whitehead to cease publication of *Rutherford* and divide its content between the *Religious Liberty Bulletin* and *Gadfly.* The latter magazine allowed TRI's founder an outlet for his cultural interests that did not risk alienating potential donors. As mentioned above, Whitehead divorced *Gadfly* completely from TRI; readers of the magazine would find no hint of a connection with that organization.

99. A common example, frequently cited as proof of extra-Christian activities, was TRI's defense of the Virginian who wanted "ATHEIST" on his license plate; see above.

100. See the discussion of Whitehead and Reconstructionism in chapter 2.

heritage to justify a restoration of her Christian roots." But, he emphasized, this should not translate into a Christian will to power. Even history proves to be less than reliable for making such claims, for "despite the Framers' biblical ethos and world view, their finest piece of political advocacy, the Federalist Papers, contains scant references to God or Scripture."[101] So interested in "rescuing" the Christian influence upon America's origins in *The Separation Illusion,* Whitehead two decades later turned to history to persuade his fellow evangelicals that the United States was in fact more than a Christian nation.

A more vigorous repudiation of Reconstructionism came in *Church vs. State,* where Whitehead directly declared his complete independence from that theology's more undemocratic aspects. The author argued that equal access, not totalitarian governance, should be the goal of Christian activism.

> Too many Christians busy themselves with activities designed to take over and rule the world, or at least America. They want to take "dominion" over the political process until the "righteous," namely themselves, hold the reins of power and reinstitute Old Testament law. God could then rule through them, his chosen intermediaries. Utopianism, reconstructionism, or whatever other name the notion uses, is incorrect biblically. . . . The believer's claim must not be for political domination, but for equal access to the world's marketplace of ideas, where true Christianity, and the worldview that springs from it, can more than hold its own.[102]

Critics would dismiss such passages as little more than a smoke screen for Christian exclusivism, but Whitehead presented no clearer repudiation of his previous theological leanings.[103]

101. John W. Whitehead, "Political Stones or Spiritual Bread?" *Rutherford* 4, no. 4 (Apr. 1995): 11.

102. John Whitehead, *Church vs. State,* 10-11.

103. In *Church vs. State* Whitehead also demonstrated his distance from apocalyptic prophets such as Hal Lindsey — whose book served as the catalyst for his conversion to Christianity — by citing belief in prophecy as one important factor in causing Christians to abdicate their political responsibilities (10).

4. Conclusion

Even as Whitehead apparently rejected the idea of remaking American institutions in Christian form, he nonetheless pushed himself and his organization into the culture with undiminished vigor. In a variety of media he relentlessly expounded his worldview, laying a complicated theological and
historical foundation for his more practical endeavors. At the same time,
The Rutherford Institute positioned itself as a broker of legal information
regarding religious rights in an age of growing litigation. By surveying carefully the church-state terrain, Whitehead and TRI sought to empower people to resist the government's attempt to eradicate religion from the nation's
public culture.

TRI's founder viewed his legal work as his Christian obligation. As
Christians, he wrote, "we are duty-bound to assist the oppressed." For him,
a convert to Christianity in the last decades of the twentieth century, the law
proved to be an appropriate and necessary arena in which to offer that assistance. "Attorneys have special skills," he explained, "which can be especially effective in assisting the oppressed. So attorneys have a special obligation to act as Good Samaritans."[104] Viewed in this way, The Rutherford
Institute represented a new kind of rescue mission, particularly suited to the
late twentieth century, one that sought to serve up not food and clothing to
the down-and-out, but legal expertise to the religiously downtrodden.

104. John Whitehead, "Why We Do What We Do."

4

Cleaning Up "the Dungheap of Constitutional Jurisprudence": The Rutherford Institute as Friend of the Court

We are under a Constitution, but the Constitution is what the judges say it is.

Justice Charles Evans Hughes, 1907[1]

When the Constitution is utilized by interpretation to accomplish the wishes of the presiding justices it then renders the Constitution worthless. No longer is it law; it is relativism. There is no morality because morality deals with absolute right and wrong. If there is no morality then an institution like the Supreme Court can adulterate the basic document of its country without thinking twice.

John W. Whitehead, 1977[2]

As Christian legal advocacy groups multiplied at century's end, The Rutherford Institute became more and more self-conscious, and it sought to distinguish itself from competing organizations by emphasizing its populist character. Whitehead himself claimed that "We're not an elitist organization, and we try to meet people's needs at the grassroots level."[3] House publications insisted that, unlike other groups that could tap huge donors to finance their operations, TRI relied upon people such as Caleb Ehlers,

1. *The Autobiography of Charles Evans Hughes*, ed. Daniel J. Danelski and Joseph S. Tulchin (Cambridge: Harvard University Press, 1973), 143.
2. John W. Whitehead, *The Separation Illusion: A Lawyer Examines the First Amendment* (Milford, Mich.: Mott Media, 1977), 59-60.
3. Karen Augustine, "Interview," *Rutherford* 3, no. 1 (Jan. 1994): 12-13.

the nine-year-old pig farmer who selflessly tithed forty dollars to the cause. As well, according to TRI's self-understanding, the organization eschewed publicity-mongering and precedent-setting cases in order to support common citizens in their fights for religious freedom. While other Christian legal advocacy groups maintained a "big case" mentality, the institute adamantly maintained that it stood out because of its "client-centered emphasis." "We can't fight just the legal battles that might set a so-called 'important precedent' or only take on the cases that might make it to the Supreme Court," Whitehead explained. The headline to an interview with TRI's legal director, Alexis Crowe, said it all: "The Rutherford Institute: Committed to the 'Little Guy.'"[4]

TRI sought to befriend not just the little guy but also the nation's highest courts. Whitehead's organization filed dozens of amicus curiae briefs in state and federal courts from 1982 to 2000, indicating that despite TRI's passion for populism, its lawyers remained intensely concerned with the cultural impact of ideas. In virtually all his writings Whitehead revealed himself to be someone for whom ideas matter; they have always created and continue to create the world around us. As the location for considering and establishing important principles and as a key, powerful agent for enforcing — and, Whitehead and other critics argued, *making* — national laws, the higher courts seemed a natural arena for TRI to enter. Indeed, since the courts shaped the context in which even local fights for religious freedom took place, filing amicus briefs could be viewed as one important aspect of a two-pronged strategy. However, in pushing a particular understanding of the First Amendment in amicus briefs, The Rutherford Institute unwittingly risked dearly held theological commitments and raised difficult questions about the wisdom of its original legal mission.

1. Amici Curiae in Twentieth-Century American Courts

Amici curiae have existed since long before there even was an American legal system. In English law they originally served as impartial assistants to the magistrate; only more recently, in the twentieth-century American setting, have they directly and independently advocated for particular parties

4. T. Stanciu and Nisha N. Mohammed, "Committed to the 'Little Guy' (Interview with Alexis Crowe)," *Rutherford* 4, no. 2 (Feb. 1995): 13-15.

and positions.[5] In late twentieth-century practice, amici briefs took various forms: some presented actual legal arguments, directly referring to the case at hand; others argued for particular public policies or suggested fresh interpretations and principles.[6] In 1992 a scholar commented on the amici's multiplicity of roles: "No longer a mere friend of the court, the amicus has become a lobbyist, an advocate, and, most recently, the vindicator of the politically powerless."[7]

Not only did amici serve many more functions in the last half of the twentieth century, they also filed many more briefs.[8] Writing in 1984 (just two years after TRI was founded), Bruce J. Ennis showed that at the Supreme Court level, "their use is steadily and dramatically increasing," both in sheer number and in number of briefs per case. Briefs from amici had grown so plentiful, Ennis suggested, that "it is quite possible that the Supreme Court now reviews more briefs from amici than from parties."[9] Though in the early twentieth century amici filed briefs in only about 10 percent of cases, by century's end the briefs had multiplied exponentially. From 1946 through 1995, though the caseload remained stable, the number of amicus briefs filed before the Court increased by more than 800 percent. Two scholars noted that "At the close of the twentieth century, cases without amicus briefs have become nearly as rare as cases *with* amicus briefs were at the beginning of the century." This development was nothing less than "a major transformation in Supreme Court practice."[10]

A few factors help explain this phenomenon. In part, according to

5. On the history of amici curiae briefs, see especially Samuel Krislov, "The Amicus Curiae Brief: From Friendship to Advocacy," *Yale Law Journal* 72 (1963), and Frank M. Covey, Jr., "Amicus Curiae: Friend of the Court," *DePaul Law Review* 9 (1959-60). For a helpful summary, see Andrew P. Moriss, "Symposium: Private Amici Curiae and the Supreme Court's 1997-1998 Term; Employment Law Jurisprudence," *William and Mary Bill of Rights Journal* 7 (1999): 830-34.

6. Moriss, "Symposium," 826.

7. Michael K. Lowman, "Comment: The Litigating Amicus Curiae; When Does the Party Begin after the Friends Leave?" *American University Law Review* 41 (1992): 1245.

8. Susan J. Becker, "Amicus Filings on the Rise," *Litigation News* 23, no. 1 (1998), provides a useful summary.

9. Bruce J. Ennis, "Symposium on Supreme Court Advocacy: Effective Amicus Briefs," *Catholic University Law Review* 33 (1984): 603, 604.

10. Joseph D. Kearney and Thomas W. Merrill, "The Influence of Amicus Curiae Briefs on the Supreme Court," *University of Pennsylvania Law Review* 148 (2000): 744, 749.

Andrew Moriss, this rise in amicus filings could be attributed to "the Supreme Court's increased willingness, since the 1950s, to tackle public policy issues that it previously avoided." Moreover, "not only has the Court taken a more expansive view of its role than in earlier decades, but it also has done so in the context of interpreting an increasing number of federal statutes aimed at contentious social issues."[11] It was little wonder, then, that Christian conservatives noticed this, identifying the courts as a critical agent of American cultural change — change they invariably characterized as negative. In entering the courts, then, advocates such as John Whitehead had decided to meet the enemy directly in order to halt the nation's moral decline.

Part of the proliferation of amici in late twentieth-century America, The Rutherford Institute also contributed enthusiastically during its first eighteen years to the corresponding increase in amicus curiae briefs. Entering the courts on behalf of religious freedom, TRI's lawyers consistently pushed the same key points.[12] The courts should reach church-state decisions, TRI believed, only after consulting history, specifically the First Amendment's original intent. TRI argued that accommodation of religion should be the guiding principle derived from that history. If judicial precedents fell into line with American history, they should be followed, but if not, they should be jettisoned as recent misapplications of the law. As well, when considering issues related to the free exercise of religion, TRI wanted the courts to consider religion as a subset of free speech, a kind of speech no less deserving of protection because of its religious content. If "neutrality" meant the eradication of religion from public life, then it should be abandoned as a hermeneutical principle; but if "neutrality" meant the equal — or even special — treatment of religious beliefs and practices in a benevolent, accommodating manner, then the courts should feel confident that they were reaching decisions in harmony with American tradition.[13]

11. Moriss, "Symposium," 832.

12. A whole host of factors lead advocates to employ different strategies in amicus briefs filed at different judicial levels, of course — the particular facts of the specific case, previous rulings on the issue, and the potential for setting precedent, to name only a few. These distinctions are important, but in this chapter I will treat TRI's briefs as one coherent body of evidence because I believe that such factors minimally impacted the substance of the arguments Whitehead and his colleagues put forward.

13. Defining "neutrality" has been a difficult task for both the Supreme Court and legal scholars. Steven K. Green has noted the Court's "often discordant" uses of the term; "Of (Un)Equal Jurisprudential Pedigree: Rectifying the Imbalance between Neutrality

2. First Principles

The Rutherford Institute filed its first significant amicus curiae brief in the case of *Lynch v. Donnelly,* a brief noteworthy not just because it was the organization's first foray as friend of the court, but also because in this brief TRI and Whitehead introduced characteristic lines of argumentation that persisted in subsequent years.[14] The First Circuit Court of Appeals had ruled that the city of Pawtucket, Rhode Island, had violated the First Amendment's establishment clause by financially supporting a holiday display that included a crèche. Separationists argued that any government provision for religion, such as the cost borne by the city to erect the display, ran afoul of constitutional law. Accommodationists pointed to America's long history of general support for religion, and noted that because the crèche appeared on private property amid a host of secular holiday symbols, it formed part of a general holiday celebration rather than an endorsement of a particular faith.[15]

In *Lynch* The Rutherford Institute filed an amicus brief on behalf of two organizations, the Coalition for Religious Liberty and the Freedom Council.[16] With the encouragement — and presumably the financial back-

---

and Separationism," *Boston College Law Review* 43 (Sept. 2002): 1113. In detailing several alternative meanings, Douglas Laycock has shown that we can "agree on the principle of neutrality without having agreed upon anything at all"; Laycock, "Formal, Substantive, and Disaggregated Neutrality toward Religion," *DePaul Law Review* 39 (1990): 994. As Whitehead himself had argued elsewhere, "The Supreme Court's theory of neutrality by the state is merely a hopeful illusion"; John W. Whitehead and John Conlan, "The Establishment of the Religion of Secular Humanism and Its First Amendment Implications," *Texas Tech Law Review* 10, no. 1 (1978): 22. Here, as before, Whitehead and his colleagues were using the language of "neutrality" to urge an accommodationist paradigm. This subject is discussed further below.

14. Brief Amici Curiae of the Coalition for Religious Liberty and the Freedom Council on Writ of Certiorari to the U.S. Court of Appeals for the First Circuit in Support of Petitioners, Lynch, et al., No. 82-1256 (1982); hereafter Lynch Brief.

15. TRI made sure to point out the crèche's context in its brief: "It was placed on private property, with the crèche situated amidst lighted Christmas trees, reindeer, snowmen, stars, a wishing well, a large lighted sign proclaiming 'Seasons Greetings,' a Santa's house inhabited by a live Santa and 21 figurines including a clown, dancing elephant, robot and teddy bear." For more on the details of this case and the Supreme Court opinions it generated, see Winnifred Fallers Sullivan, *Paying the Words Extra: Religious Discourse in the Supreme Court of the United States* (Cambridge: Harvard University Press, 1994).

16. The Freedom Council, based in Virginia and affiliated with Pat Robertson's Christian Broadcasting Network, identified itself in this brief as "a non-profit corpora-

ing — of these institutional allies, Whitehead and co-counsel James Knicely sought to persuade the court that publicly financed crèches, far from violating the Constitution, properly honored America's heritage and identity. TRI's first brief addressed two specific concerns: the historical record with respect to civic support of religious observances, with an eye toward the "correct" understanding of the establishment clause; and whether or not the city of Pawtucket had in fact violated that clause in this particular instance.

From the beginning, the brief's authors made it clear that history was a weapon in *their* arsenal. "The Court's disposition of this case," they wrote, "will affect many centuries-old American customs and traditions observed as part of the Christmas holiday in thousands of communities in every state of the Union" (1-2).[17] Indeed, the tradition in question predated the Constitution itself, the lawyers argued, for "Christmas has been observed in America continuously . . . from the early days of the first settlement at Jamestown, Virginia" (1). To restrict the celebration of Christmas would be to repudiate something so fundamental to the American character that it literally arrived on the ship with the very first colonists.

That religion-friendly atmosphere persisted right into the Revolutionary period, Whitehead and Knicely continued. They cited several authorities, including Supreme Court Justice Joseph Story (who served from 1811 to 1845), who attested to America's accommodationist climate. Whitehead had noted Story's opinions elsewhere, and happily imported his words into the Lynch Brief:

> Probably at the time of the adoption of the Constitution, and of the first amendment to it . . . the general if not the universal sentiment in America was, that Christianity ought to receive encouragement by the state

tion organized to defend, restore, and preserve religious liberties guaranteed by the Constitution." The Coalition for Religious Liberty, headed by conservative preacher D. James Kennedy of Ft. Lauderdale's Coral Ridge Presbyterian Church, identified itself as "a coalition of Jewish, Roman Catholic and Protestant lawyers and lay persons" that "was founded to educate the public on important issues affecting religious liberties, to support efforts to promote religious liberty and toleration in American life and to oppose the use of law and the court system as a vehicle for imposing secular religion on American society." This alliance signaled an initial interest in collaborative efforts that in later years would prove much less likely and, for Whitehead, much less desirable.

17. In-text parenthetical citations in this chapter will refer to the page numbers of the original briefs. Hence this reference is to the Lynch Brief, pp. 1-2. For a complete list of briefs, see "Amicus Curiae Briefs" in the bibliography.

so far as was not incompatible with the private rights of conscience and the freedom of religious worship. Any attempt to level all religions, and to make it a matter of state policy to hold all in utter indifference, would have created universal disapprobation, if not universal indignation. . . . The real object of the amendment was . . . to prevent any national ecclesiastical establishment which should give to a hierarchy the exclusive patronage of the national government (4).[18]

According to these advocates, the historical record demonstrated and Justice Story confirmed that the new nation's citizens welcomed, and perhaps expected, civic acknowledgments of the Christmas season.

Perhaps more importantly, they continued, the framers themselves would have been comfortable with Pawtucket's holiday spirit. "There is substantial historical evidence," TRI argued, "that the Framers actively sanctioned in their official capacities religious observances and activities having a far greater religious impact than the mere display of a crèche in the midst of a secular holiday exhibit" (3). From holding chapel services in the House of Representatives to funding a congressional chaplain, from Washington's endorsement of religion in his Farewell Address to Congress's invocation of religion in the Northwest Ordinance of 1787, the record was not just suggestive, it was convincing. "There is a wealth of historical data illuminating the meaning of the First Amendment and the intent of the Framers in this regard," they claimed. The Constitution's authors directly "participated in and authorized" official religious observances. "Thus, it is the previous Court of Appeals decision, not the display in issue, that conflicts with long-standing First Amendment values" (4). In short, Whitehead summarized for the court, "the Framers would have been appalled that the First Amendment could be utilized to prohibit the practice in question here" (6). The Court had often relied upon the framers to reach constitutional decisions, Knicely and Whitehead continued, and now was no time to discard their guidance.

As they returned from the eighteenth to the twentieth century, TRI's lawyers also contended that the appeals court had relied on the wrong standard of review in deciding the case. Since the 1940s the U.S. Supreme Court had wrestled with exactly how to judge when the government had transgressed the boundaries of the establishment clause, a struggle that

18. The original quotation came from Joseph Story, *Two Commentaries on the Constitution of the United States,* 2nd ed. (1851), 593-95.

continued through the end of the twentieth century. In 1971 the Court devised a tripartite standard, called the *Lemon* test, for considering establishment-clause violations. Justice Warren Burger looked back upon the Court's previous rulings in outlining the test's components: "Every analysis in this area must begin with consideration of the cumulative criteria developed by the Court over many years. Three such tests may be gleaned from our cases. First, the statute must have a secular legislative purpose; second, its principal or primary effect must be one that neither advances nor inhibits religion . . . ; finally, the state must not foster 'an excessive entanglement with religion.'"[19] Justices subsequently disputed its utility and it failed to become a universal standard, but the *Lemon* test formed a critical part of the Court's church-state jurisprudence in the last three decades of the twentieth century.[20]

In *Lynch* the appeals court had ignored the *Lemon* test and used a "strict scrutiny" standard; TRI argued for a return to the previous standard as more appropriate for correctly deciding this case. Though not surprising, this appeal to recent judicial precedent nevertheless had presumably unintended consequences. In the process of arguing for using the *Lemon* test in deciding the case, TRI's lawyers, though clearly interested in showing that general government support for religion fell within the bounds of constitutionally acceptable practice, also tried to explain away the religious nature of the crèche. Pawtucket's display does not celebrate a central Christian event, they contended; rather, it "serves an overriding secular goal of depicting and announcing observance of the Christmas holiday. The religious component of the display represents at most a governmental accommodation, in de minimus fashion, of the historical-cultural elements of Christmas as a national holiday" (7). The anniversary of the birth of the Christian savior, Whitehead and Knicely were suggesting, was publicly important for secular rather than religious reasons.

19. *Lemon v. Kurtzman*, 403 U.S. 602, 613 (1971).

20. At least four standards have been variously deployed for deciding disestablishment clause cases: a neutrality test (government must not favor one religion over another or religion over nonreligion), the *Lemon* test, the endorsement test (government actions must not appear to endorse one religion over another or prefer religion to nonreligion), and the coercion test (government may not orchestrate religious rituals or ceremonies in such a way that coerces participation from those who do not wish to participate). See Elizabeth A. Harvey, "Casenote: *Freiler v. Tangipahoa Board of Education;* Squeeze the *Lemon* Test out of Establishment Clause Jurisprudence," *George Mason Law Review* 10 (2001): 299-320.

As well, they continued, the crèche's cluttered context should be considered when determining constitutionality. Whitehead and Knicely argued that "its appearance in the midst of a myriad of other Christmas symbols, some with pagan and some with religious origins, does not constitute state approval or advocacy of religious belief or non-belief. It merely acknowledges the advent of the Christmas holiday as one of many traditional symbols that are part of the heritage of the American people" (7). Because the crèche "is positioned in the midst of and as part of a comprehensive display acknowledging in symbolic form the celebration of the American Christmas holiday and not as an object of veneration, worship or private devotion," they wrote, "its display serves a secular purpose and does not transgress the line separating church and state" (8). Again, in this line of thinking, announcing the arrival of a central Christian holiday served a legitimate secular, not religious, purpose: "The overall effect of the Christmas display is a secular message that the Christmas holiday is at hand" (8). As such, the crèche cannot be considered unconstitutional.

Whitehead and Knicely emphasized repeatedly that the crèche is really no different from other, decidedly unchristian symbols of the season. "The crèche, as with secular Christmas symbols such as Santa Claus and reindeer, has been absorbed into the American culture" (8). Hence the crèche should no longer be considered threatening, having been gutted of all particularist connotations. Reassuring any skeptical justices, the lawyers urged that "the religious impact is greatly diluted, if not emasculated, by the secular elements." Indeed, given the context, "the religious impact of the nativity scene is remote and incidental" (9). Even separationists, the lawyers communicated, need not be nervous about the Pawtucket display having violated the First Amendment, for there was no "church" in the display from which the city should have kept itself separate.

Though the appeals court had sought to bar Pawtucket's display in the interest of religious neutrality, Whitehead and company argued, this reasoning constituted "extreme logic" in service of "an unrelenting dogma that would eradicate from public life every vestige, root and branch, of America's Judeo-Christian religious tradition" (2). To agree with that earlier decision, the advocates clearly meant the court to understand, would be to cleanse American culture of one of its most time-honored, constitutive elements. Allowing the appellate court decision to stand would have far-reaching, undesirable consequences. Barring civic religious displays would not just affect one practice, they insisted; rather, this would undermine "the display of religious symbols in all aspects of public life" (2).

In this brief, then, two contradictory arguments seemed to be at work. On the one hand, TRI contended that religion represented an important, constitutionally acceptable part of American culture and should be allowed a public, symbolic presence. The nation's founders and overall history supported — and perhaps even necessitated — this sort of accommodation. In their conclusion, TRI's attorneys wrote that "There was no intention on the part of the Framers to censor or eradicate religion from public life. And such has never occurred" (10). On the other hand, they argued that the appearance of religious symbols in public contexts can be supported by government precisely because the symbols no longer carry any religious valence. Surrounded by Santa Claus, reindeer, and a menorah, the crèche had been sufficiently neutered of any religious import, its baby Jesus retaining no more spiritual significance than the robot placed next to him. In the end, to muster the most effective legal argument, John Whitehead and The Rutherford Institute proclaimed both the time-tested salience and the present public powerlessness of the symbols they sought to reinclude in American public life.

TRI's amicus brief in *Lynch* revealed how pursuing a desired legal outcome might require uncomfortable ideological compromises. Whitehead and Knicely believed that marshaling their most persuasive argument in this case required putting forward positions that were philosophically incompatible. Was the crèche religious? Yes, and American history demands that such public symbols retain civic importance. Was the crèche religious? No, and therefore the *Lemon* test had not been violated. Such a strategy, though unsurprising and quite common in legal argumentation, nevertheless confirmed that in amicus briefs Whitehead and TRI seemed to value a preferred outcome over ideological consistency.

A divided Supreme Court ruled five to four in favor of Pawtucket and its holiday display. William Brennan, joined by three others in dissent, shared TRI's argument that the crèche was in fact religious, but he reached the opposite conclusion: it therefore was unconstitutional. In his majority opinion, Warren Burger shared TRI's contradictory reasoning that the crèche, because symbolically inert, was constitutional. "To forbid the use of this one passive symbol," Burger wrote, "would be a stilted overreaction contrary to our history and our holdings."[21] In putting forth this rationale — the crèche as one among many legitimate forms of symbolic speech — TRI's amicus brief hinted at the idea of placing religion on a truly neutral

21. *Lynch v. Donnelly,* 465 U.S. 668, 686 (1984).

footing with other ideologies. Though the appellate court thought it neutral to ban the crèche, thus keeping church and state separate, in fact it had thwarted the legitimate secular purpose of announcing the Christmas holiday. To ignore such an important occasion would have been to discriminate against an occasion just because it was religious. This line of thought gently foreshadowed TRI's later push for "true neutrality" and the rejection of "invidious content-based discrimination."

In July 1984 Whitehead and Knicely again filed an amicus curiae brief on behalf of the Freedom Council, this time in *Wallace v. Jaffree*.[22] Given the context of the case, it was no surprise that the newly formed Rutherford Institute wanted to join the conversation. In 1962 the U.S. Supreme Court had ruled unconstitutional the practice of officially led prayer in public schools.[23] Many outraged citizens, especially Southerners, sought to circumvent this decision by enabling school districts to provide a "moment of silence" wherein students could voluntarily pray. The state of Alabama had passed such a law, and the district court upheld it, contending that the First Amendment did not apply to the states. The appeals court disagreed, applying the establishment clause to Alabama's law in finding it unconstitutional. To resolve the dispute the Supreme Court consented to hear the case.[24]

In its basic presuppositions The Rutherford Institute's brief in this case matched its earlier one in *Lynch*. Whitehead and Knicely argued that the Alabama statute "does not advance religion. It merely provides for a period of silence that recognizes in neutral fashion the freedom of conscience of each teacher and student" (1). Observing a period of silence, the brief's authors continued, "merely advances the spirit of pluralism and toleration intended by the First Amendment and does not constitute an unlawful establishment of religion" (1). Since no one is required to pray, let alone pray a particular, particularist prayer, the law should be upheld.

As they had in *Lynch*, the advocates turned to the framers to help advance their position. The relevance of Revolutionary-era ideas could hardly be more important: "concrete, specific historical evidence of the Framers' views on religion and religious practices in public life," they wrote, "must be placed at a premium to understand the reach and meaning of the First

22. Brief Amicus Curiae of the Freedom Council on Appeal from the U.S. Court of Appeals for the Eleventh Circuit in Support of the Appellants, Wallace et al., No. 83-812, No. 83-929 (1983); hereafter Freedom Council Brief, Wallace.

23. *Engel v. Vitale*, 370 U.S. 421 (1962).

24. *Wallace v. Jaffree*, 105 S. Ct. 2479 (1985).

Amendment Religion Clauses" (3). The marshaled evidence remained identical to that offered in the Lynch Brief; if anything, they adopted a tone even more confident about how effectively history served their position.

> History provides *varied and ample evidence* that among the founders of this Republic and its early presidents and congresses, the *universal* sentiment towards religion was one of accommodation, not merely toleration. It is *unequivocably* clear from the language, intent, and history surrounding the adoption of the First Amendment that the separation of church and state intended by the Bill of Rights was of limited defect and that *amicability,* not hostility to the free exercise of religion, *was the shibboleth* of that era. (3, my emphasis)

No one, it seemed, dare deploy history in the service of anything other than an accommodationist interpretation of the First Amendment.

Whitehead and his co-counsel took on at length those who turned to James Madison and Thomas Jefferson to refute their claims about original intent. They devoted an entire section of the brief to these framers, expending considerable energy to diminish the two Virginians' relevance for determining the original meaning of the First Amendment. Though Madison and Jefferson had demonstrated a "fervor for disestablishment," they argued, many others had held more moderate views on church and state. "In many ways," they insisted in the brief with some scholarly support, "the views of Madison and Jefferson were not representative of those of the Framers of the Constitution" (4).[25] Look at the mainstream, TRI's lawyers seemed to insist, not at these extremists.

For those justices who remained unpersuaded by this portrait of the two founders, Whitehead and Knicely made sure to provide an accommodationist gloss. A close examination of Jefferson's writings and actions, they claimed, showed that his version of disestablishment "did not require the eradication of religion from public schools" (5). As for Madison, "although often cited as antagonistic toward religion," he nevertheless "par-

25. They quoted extensively from C. Antieau, A. Downey, and E. Roberts, *Freedom from Federal Establishment* (Milwaukee: Bruce, 1964), esp. 207-9. Those authors argued that "the First Amendment was hardly the exclusive product of any one person. Subsequent interpretations . . . should not be controlled by the singular statements of Madison [or] Jefferson." TRI's advocates also made considerable use of a then-new accommodationist book, Robert L. Cord, *The Separation of Church and State: Historical Fact and Current Fiction* (New York: Lambeth Press, 1982).

ticipated in the creation of several government sponsored religious practices" (5-6). In sum, "the evidence is clear that both Virginians advocated, participated in and authorized federal government funding and sponsorship of patently religious activities which generally exceeded that degree of accommodation fostered by the Alabama law involved in the present case" (6). Whether or not they were decisively influential, TRI's lawyers argued, Madison and Jefferson could nevertheless not be used as hermeneutical talismans to ward off an accommodationist understanding of the First Amendment.

As in *Lynch,* TRI's lawyers believed that history certainly favored those who considered a moment of silence to be constitutional. "Our national history is replete with examples of government, in a spirit of toleration and accommodation, recognizing, as the State of Alabama has in this case, America's religious tradition and culture," TRI's lawyers wrote, "but without infringing on the rights of conscience of those who do not subscribe to particular tenets of that tradition or culture" (2). Each individual under this "permissive" Alabama law "may meditate or voluntarily pray" according to one's conscience. Hence the law "merely advances in neutral fashion the freedom to believe (or not to believe) and constitutes the type of affirmative, yet neutral, accommodation mandated by the First Amendment" (2).[26] After having expended great energy detailing the historical evidence in favor of accommodation, TRI's lawyers sounded frustrated by the need to explain it at all. They wrote that "It is blinking at reality to say that the practices and actions [of all three governmental branches] described above do not provide concrete, specific historical evidence upon which to evaluate the constitutional validity of the Alabama statute. In light of this rich heritage of governmental benevolence towards religion, the result is inevitable" (9).

Echoing themes consistent with Whitehead's other writings, TRI's lawyers argued in this brief that to disallow a moment of silence because religious reflections might occur was in fact to discriminate against religion. It was to protect speech and thought only as long as it was secular in nature — a notion clearly contrary to the Constitution. "It would be inapropos

26. Although Whitehead had criticized Justice Holmes repeatedly in his popular works, he apparently had no qualms about invoking him before the bar. "In Religion Clause adjudication, no less than any other area of law," Whitehead wrote in support of his argument, "Justice Holmes' statement is most fitting: 'A page of history is worth a volume of logic.'" Holmes's original quotation is from *New York Trust Co. v. Eisner,* 256 U.S. 345, 349 (1921).

[*sic*] to so fervently protect the liberties of speech, press, assembly, and petition in the school forum, while curtailing that freedom of conscience which is their root and origin" (11). Prohibiting a moment of silence because of the possibility of religious thinking amounted to "content-based censorship of thoughts." They claimed that far from maintaining a constitutionally appropriate, neutral sphere in public schools, banning the moment of silence "would prefer those who believe in no religion over those who believe" (11). Neutrality was a mere cloak for a decidedly unneutral secularist agenda, the last refuge of the religious bigot. "It is constitutionally impermissible for government fanatically to seal religion from the classroom," they stated. "Such a secularization would prefer nonbelief over belief" (12).[27]

As in *Lynch,* Whitehead and his co-counsel again sought to reassure the Court that the practice in question did not violate the *Lemon* test of constitutionality. The law was in fact a secular one, for many reasons, they argued. First, because the content of a moment of silence "may be wholly secular, or wholly religious, depending on the individual's exercise of conscience," it can be considered a practice devoid of religious pressure (14). Second, the law recognizes religious liberty, something that actually constitutes "an important secular interest" because it honors a critical part of our national heritage. "Recognition of our religious-cultural heritage," they stated, "is clearly a legitimate educational goal" (14). As well, the moment of silence quiets and focuses schoolchildren, and perhaps even teaches students self-discipline and greater respect for the teacher's authority. "Surely, it is consistent with the public schools [*sic*] secular educational goals," they wrote, "to encourage students to turn silently towards serious thoughts and values" (14). If those thoughts and values happened to be religious in character, that result would be merely incidental.

In the end, the U.S. Supreme Court did not so much disagree with TRI's substantive reasons as it decided the case on other grounds. Justice John Paul Stevens, writing for the majority, found that the Alabama law had violated the first part of the *Lemon* test. In fact, not only did the law not

27. Whitehead's fondness for images of state totalitarianism, so evident in his movies, crept into the Wallace brief as he sought to make the point that a religion-free school is not a neutral one. "Just as religious indoctrination may convey — indeed inculcate — doctrines contrary to the views of the children's parents, here the placing of the governmental hand upon the shoulder of a young religious adherent for holding and expressing those views would be equally inappropriate"; Freedom Council Brief, Wallace, 12.

have a secular purpose, it had in fact been motivated directly by the legislature's decidedly nonsecular desire to return prayer to public schools. (In the majority's opinion, the Alabama legislature's debates on the measure provided ample proof for this charge.)[28] Though dissenting justices seemed in harmony with TRI's perspective in *Wallace v. Jaffree*,[29] in the end they stopped short of considering the institute's line of argument.

3. History Matters Most . . .

The arguments that appeared in TRI's first two briefs would be repeated — occasionally verbatim — in subsequent amicus curiae filings. Indeed, over the next several years Whitehead and company constructed their briefs upon the same two bedrock assumptions. First, history should matter the most when deciding church-state issues, and history clearly comes down on the side of accommodation. Second, religion should be considered a form of free speech, and free speech should not be restricted merely because it happens to be religious. True neutrality required the accommodation of religion in the public sphere; if religion were excluded, the result would not be neutrality but a clear preference for secularism.

28. Justice Stevens cited this evidence in his majority opinion. State Senator Donald G. Holmes, the Alabama law's primary sponsor, had said before the district court that he intended "to return voluntary prayer to our public schools"; indeed, he had "no other purpose in mind." However, according to Burger's dissent, Stevens's comments came *after* the legislature had passed the statute in question. And regardless of the timing of Holmes's justification for the bill, he was only one of many legislators who voted for the bill, and "No case in the 195-year history of this Court supports the disconcerting idea that postenactment statements by individual legislators are relevant in determining the constitutionality of legislation."

29. Burger began his dissent by noting the irony of juxtaposing the majority's opinion with the fact that that day's Supreme Court session had "opened with an invocation for Divine protection." William Rehnquist, also in dissent, provided a comprehensive and stinging critique of the Court's rationale and, indeed, of the Court's entire line of thinking since *Everson:* "It is impossible to build sound constitutional doctrine upon a mistaken understanding of constitutional history, but unfortunately the Establishment Clause has been expressly freighted with Jefferson's misleading metaphor for nearly forty years." Jefferson's "wall of separation between church and state" had appeared only in "a short note of courtesy" written over a decade after Congress passed the Bill of Rights. Rehnquist concluded that the history of the First Amendment, "properly understood," reveals no barrier to any generalized "endorsement" of prayer. See *Wallace v. Jaffree,* 2479.

In *Bender v. Williamsport Area School District* (1986), the courts considered the legality of students who voluntarily engaged in religious endeavors during an unstructured activity time during the school day.[30] Students who formed the group Petros, devoted to promoting "spiritual
growth and positive attitudes in the lives of its members," sought to meet
on campus to pray, read the Bible, and discuss religious subjects. School officials denied Petros permission to convene; the U.S. district court reversed
that decision, ruling that the district had violated the First Amendment. A
school board member appealed. TRI took notice and filed an amicus brief
on behalf of the students.[31]

In that brief TRI counsel deployed the by-now-ritually-cited argument from history that urged the government to accommodate religious
belief and practice.[32] Whitehead seemed frustrated with the conflict between the court's and his own understanding of American history (sig-

30. *Bender et al. v. Williamsport Area School District et al.,* 475 U.S. 534 (1986).

31. The case's fate was complicated: the appellate court reversed the district
court's decision, ruling that had the school district approved Petros's request to meet
during school hours, it would have impermissibly advanced religion. The U.S. Supreme
Court granted certiorari once the students appealed that decision and, in a five to four
vote, asserted that the board member did not have standing to appeal. This vacated the
appellate court's decision, allowing the district court's original ruling to stand and con-
fining that decision's impact to the immediate local context. For more on the details of
this case and possible reasons for rejecting the board member's standing, see Robert T.
Miller and Ronald B. Flowers, *Toward Benevolent Neutrality: Church, State, and the Supreme Court,* 3rd ed. (Waco, Tex.: Markham Press Fund, 1987), 248-49. The district
court, in affirming Petros's right to meet during noncurricular time, matched the sentiments of the Congress, which in 1984 passed the Equal Access Act, guaranteeing religious groups the same rights as others within public school districts.

32. Brief Amicus Curiae of The Rutherford Institute on Writ of Certiorari to the
U.S. Court of Appeals for the Third Circuit in Support of the Petitioners, Bender et al.,
No. 84-773 (1984); hereafter TRI Brief, Bender. Another "ritual" invocation in TRI's
briefs was its increasingly lengthy list of affiliates. Not content to file as merely The
Rutherford Institute, TRI's lawyers listed each associate office directly underneath. In addition to its headquarters in Virginia, in TRI Brief, Bender, The Rutherford Institute proclaimed the existence of chapters in Alabama, Georgia, Minnesota, Montana, Tennessee,
and Texas. By 1987 the list included Arkansas, California, Colorado, Connecticut, Dela-
ware, Florida, Kentucky, Michigan, Ohio, Pennsylvania, and West Virginia. In 1989 TRI
had affiliates in Hawaii, Illinois, Louisiana, Maryland, Nebraska, New York, North
Carolina, South Carolina, and Washington. Kansas, Oklahoma, Oregon, and Wisconsin
joined the roster in 1991. Common to amici briefs, this list nonetheless served to signal
the courts that even as their arguments were dismissed, the organization devoted to
pressing those arguments continued to grow.

naled by the Court's decision against TRI and other accommodationists in *Wallace v. Jaffree* a year earlier).[33] "If this Court is to maintain at least some semblance of allegiance to history and the intentions of the Framers," TRI's lawyers wrote, "it will vigorously protect the Petitioners' freedom to associate voluntarily in public secondary schools for self-directed religious activity. To rule otherwise would distort the law and run contrary to the wishes of the very men who drafted the document upon which we base our freedoms" (7).

For TRI's advocates, this was especially exasperating because, thanks to the Supreme Court, historical misunderstanding had spread like a virus throughout America. People continued to mischaracterize the proper relationship between church and state, TRI's brief complained: "For decades and even to this day . . . American educators and students have labored under the dark shadow of the layman's belief that the United States Supreme Court has ruled that nothing of a religious nature can take place on the campus of a publicly supported educational institution even if there is no connection between the activity and the school" (15).

Whitehead hoped the Court could help dispel this misunderstanding with a correct decision in this case. "It is urged," the brief read, "that this Court put to rest in the strongest possible terms the insidious and simplistic idea that any religious expression in the public schools is automatically suspect" (15). The perceived influence of the Supreme Court helps to explain why TRI bothered filing amicus briefs: ideas mattered to TRI's founder and his attorneys, never more so when expressed by the highest court in the land. The consequences of misunderstanding — both intellectual and practical — could ripple far and wide throughout the culture.

That same year Whitehead criticized the Washington Supreme Court for the same sins. On the basis of the establishment clause, and specifically the U.S. Supreme Court's insistence in *Lemon* that a law cannot have the "primary" effect of advancing religion, the Washington Supreme Court de-

33. It is important to note that, thanks in large part to Justice (soon Chief Justice) William Rehnquist, the Supreme Court's previous understanding of American history in regard to the First Amendment began to change. His dissent in *Wallace v. Jaffree* provided a comprehensive critique of post-*Everson* understandings of church and state, providing an alternative narrative that paralleled that pushed by Whitehead and The Rutherford Institute. Warren Burger shared much of this perspective as well. Indeed, the presence of justices sympathetic to an accommodationist history of the First Amendment may have encouraged TRI and similarly minded advocates to continue pushing this understanding.

nied state-provided financial assistance for the blind to Larry Witters because he wanted to use those state funds for pursuing a religious vocation.
(On appeal, the U.S. Supreme Court rejected this reasoning and remanded
the case back to Washington for consideration on the basis of the Washington State Constitution.)[34] "The Washington Supreme Court decision,"
TRI's brief argued, "runs contrary to this central historical and political
truth. It could lead to the exclusion of religious persons from many, if not
most, areas of public life. It is tantamount to a de facto establishment of
what this Court has previously identified as a 'religion of secularism'"
(12).[35] Bitterness about this persisted, as another brief a year later revealed.
"The First Amendment . . . was not a fortuitous memoralization [sic] of a
passing political philosophy," Whitehead argued, "but a representation of a
considered moral view — a moral view whose dimensions have deepened
and broadened with the enriching experiences and thought of the past 200
years" (5).[36] How could judges willfully ignore the historical evidence in
deciding church-state cases?

The frustration eased briefly in a brief later that year, when Whitehead flattered the Court for having previously "indicated its obedience to

34. *Witters v. Washington Department of Services for the Blind,* 474 U.S. 481 (1986).
The Court's majority ruled that because the recipient of state aid to the blind, and not the
state itself, decided where the financial aid would be applied, the state would not be
guilty of violating the establishment clause by supporting religion.

35. Brief Amicus Curiae of The Rutherford Institute on Writ of Certiorari to the
Supreme Court of Washington in Support of the Petitioner, Witters, No. 84-1070
(1984); hereafter TRI Brief, Witters.

36. Brief Amicus Curiae of The Rutherford Institute on Writ of Certiorari to the
U.S. Court of Appeals for the District of Columbia in Support of the Petitioner,
Goldman, No. 84-1097 (1984). In this case TRI demonstrated relatively early in its institutional life that its advocacy would not be confined to conservative Christian litigants.
In *Goldman v. Weinberger,* airman and observant Jew Simcha Goldman had been told he
could not wear his yarmulke on duty; he sued (and eventually lost). TRI's brief favored
Goldman's position, and provided an explanation of the skullcap's significance that, although unoriginal, was nevertheless eloquent: "The wearing of the yarmulke is, for Petitioner, no less a matter of conscience than stating his belief in God would be if required
as a test for public office. Both are absolutely required by his religion and one is not, as a
matter of conscience, any 'less required' than the other. To put it conversely, to coerce Petitioner into wearing Air Force headgear in lieu of his yarmulke would work, it is fair to
say, as much torture on his conscience as would coercing him to deny some religious belief. For him, wearing the yarmulke is a matter of obedience to his religion, one that he
has faithfully and fastidiously executed throughout his adult life. To coerce him into forsaking it now would cause him to violate his conscience on a fundamental level."

history in the development of the right of privacy" (5).[37] But he took no chances, using a great deal of space to explain just what constituted the "correct" version of history. In arguing in favor of Georgia's antisodomy laws, Whitehead and his fellow advocates reached far back beyond America — where sodomy has always been forbidden, he claimed — to the roots of Western civilization itself. "American laws against such practices can be traced back to the Judeo-Christian Scriptures, Roman law, the teachings of the Christian Church, and early English common and statutory law" (8). Those traditions were maintained in the American situation; colonies proscribed sodomy, and up until 1961 "all American states had criminal statutes forbidding the practice of sodomy, even of a private and consensual nature" (10). An accurate understanding of history leads to some "obvious" conclusions: "American and Western society in general have historically and traditionally forbidden through criminal law the practice of sodomy. From the very outset of our society, criminal law has regulated even private consensual sodomy. Prior to the recent decriminalization movement, there has never been a time when the practice of private consensual sodomy has been considered beyond the proper scope of government regulation. . . . [T]he history and traditions of this Nation do not support a right to the private consensual practice of sodomy" (10). Hence the conclusion that sodomy can be banned by the state "is irresistable" (12).

According to The Rutherford Institute, the Supreme Court also failed to take into account America's history when deciding abortion cases. In a brief in a 1988 abortion case, TRI's counsel looked back to *Roe v. Wade*.[38] This decision was miserable for all kinds of reasons, according to Whitehead, but the first was that "its premises were not rooted in the tradition of the Nation. Its reading of history was flawed" (3). That, combined with a misapplication of precedent and its usurpation of the legislature, resulted

37. Brief Amicus Curiae of The Rutherford Institute on Writ of Certiorari to the Eleventh Circuit Court of Appeals in Support of Petitioner, Bowers, No. 85-140 (1985); hereafter TRI Brief, Bowers. Ten years later another TRI brief noted approvingly "the demonstrated interests by the Justices of the Court in First Amendment history" and the Court's "alertness to how purported 'neutrality' can mask hostility"; see Brief Amicus Curiae of The Rutherford Institute on Writ of Certiorari to the U.S. Court of Appeals for the Eleventh Circuit in Support of Petitioners, Church of the Lukumi Babalu Aye, Inc., and Ernest Picardo, 1991 U.S. Briefs 948, 2.

38. Brief Amicus Curiae of The Rutherford Institute on Appeal from the U.S. Court of Appeals for the Eighth Circuit in Support of Appellants, Webster et al., 1988 U.S. Briefs 605.

in a "failure of jurisprudence" that "rivals this Court's decision in the Dred Scott Case" (3).[39]

In arguing for the constitutionality of graduation prayers, TRI's lawyers also appealed to history. "The tradition of including invocations and benedictions in a graduation ceremony began in America at Harvard in 1642," they wrote. And "the practice has become so ingrained in American commencement exercises that a typical commencement" has included both an invocation and a benediction.[40] If graduation prayers were prohibited, then other public religious practices and symbols equally as embedded in American history and supported by the founders would have to be abolished. Is the Court prepared to prohibit the Pledge of Allegiance, patriotic anthems, all writings that refer to a deity, America's Thanksgiving holiday, the National Day of Prayer, the national Christmas tree, and presidential invocations of God's blessings on the nation (14)? If one practice is restricted, TRI's brief contended, then all could be restricted. To decide against prayers at graduation would be to reject long-standing American tradition.[41]

In a later brief, in the case of *Boerne v. Flores,* TRI indicated its continuing affinity for history as the best and final arbiter of how to apply the First Amendment.[42] TRI's founder insisted that "The Court must examine

39. Though granting that the Court's "deficiencies" in historical interpretation had been detailed elsewhere, TRI felt it necessary to at least summarize the Court's myriad errors: "The historical exegesis undertaken in Roe is distinctly problematical." There now existed a "well-documented view that the Court had misread history. . . . The historical difficulties in Roe arise from the Court's cursory and incomplete treatment of the ancient history of abortion, its skewed view of the ancient Greek Hippocratic Oath (which forbade abortion), its blinking at over 1000 years of Judeo-Christian ethics and law (where opposition to abortion was predominantly constant) and, perhaps most importantly, its distortion of the common law and statutory tradition" (8). This line of criticism appeared each time TRI filed a brief in an abortion-related case. See, for example, Brief Amicus Curiae of The Rutherford Institute on Appeal from the U.S. Court of Appeals for the Seventh Circuit in Support of Appellants, Turnock et al., No. 88-790 (1988).

40. Brief Amicus Curiae of The Rutherford Institute on Writ of Certiorari to the U.S. Court of Appeals for the First Circuit in Support of Petitioners, Lee et al., 1990 U.S. Briefs 1014, 6; hereafter TRI Brief, Lee.

41. In 1992 the Court narrowly sided with the litigants against the school district that had sponsored a graduation prayer by a local religious leader; see *Lee v. Weisman,* 505 U.S. 577 (1992). This decision ruled out only prayers directly sponsored by public school officials; the constitutionality of voluntary student prayers at graduation continued to be litigated through century's end.

42. Brief Amicus Curiae of The Rutherford Institute on Writ of Certiorari to the

the historical roots of the free exercise of religion in this country in order to understand the original meaning of the Free Exercise Clause" (4). In arguing for the constitutionality of the Religious Freedom Restoration Act (RFRA), TRI's brief relies heavily on the historical scholarship of Michael McConnell to prove that the act was consonant with original intent.[43] TRI's brief recommended the constitutionality of the RFRA precisely and primarily because history demonstrated that exempting religious practices from generally applicable laws (the RFRA's purpose) was a "long-standing method," one "consistent with the Framers' intent" (4). Such exceptions were constitutionally appropriate because they "embodied the understanding of the Framers of the Free Exercise Clause" (9). If the nation's founders would have approved of the RFRA, Whitehead argued, then so should the Court.[44]

Why was using history as the primary interpretive lens in church-state cases so important to Whitehead and TRI? When the Court did inter-

---

U.S. Court of Appeals for the Fifth Circuit in Support of Respondents, Flores and U.S.A., 1995 U.S. Briefs 2074.

43. So heavily did this brief borrow from McConnell's article (Michael W. McConnell, "The Origins and Historical Understanding of the Free Exercise of Religion," *Harvard Law Review* 109 [May 1990]: 1409ff.) that TRI might simply have submitted it instead. Few wrote so extensively on the First Amendment's religion clauses during the last two decades of the twentieth century, but relying upon his conclusions was not without problems. Some questioned McConnell's reliability as a historian. For example, in *Boerne v. Flores,* Justice Scalia mocked those in dissent (O'Connor in particular) who relied upon McConnell's historical conclusions. McConnell had criticized the Court's *Smith* decision (which Scalia authored), and the justice now chastised McConnell for his timidity in applying history in critiquing *Smith.* Scalia wrote that McConnell, "the most prominent scholarly critic of *Smith,* after examining the historical record, was willing to venture no more than" that the framers might have thought appropriate religious exemptions from neutrally applicable laws. McConnell responded directly to Scalia's dismissal; see McConnell, "Freedom from Persecution or Protection of the Rights of Conscience? A Critique of Justice Scalia's Historical Arguments in *City of Boerne v. Flores," William and Mary Law Review* 39 (1998): 819-47. Mark Tushnet offered a more thorough critique of McConnell's historical scholarship, summarizing that "As a historian, McConnell is a fine lawyer"; see Mark Tushnet, "The Rhetoric of Free Exercise Discourse," *Brigham Young University Law Review,* 1993, 127.

44. Tangential here, the history of the RFRA is not irrelevant to the context in which TRI is operating. On *Smith* (the U.S. Supreme Court decision that sparked the RFRA) and its consequences, see especially Carolyn N. Long, *Religious Freedom and Indian Rights: The Case of Oregon v. Smith* (Lawrence: University Press of Kansas, 2001), and Garrett Epps, *To an Unknown God: Religious Freedom on Trial* (New York: St. Martin's Press, 2001).

pret history as TRI wished, it did not go unnoticed. In a 1988 brief, for example, Whitehead and co-counsel praised the Supreme Court's "obedience to history" in deciding previous euthanasia cases.[45] But even assuming that all parties could agree on what the founders intended in crafting the First Amendment, why should judges obey this master instead of others?

Whitehead rarely justified his historicism, preferring instead to assume tradition's relevance and move on to explain the details of that history. But revealing glimpses did appear here and there in TRI's amicus briefs that offered clues to why history should be privileged. In a brief in *Bowers v. Hardwick,* Whitehead suggested that history can act as an important check against arbitrary preference. "Without the constraint and guidance of history in discerning the fundamental rights protected against the states," TRI's counsel contended, "judges would be free to legislate their own preferences at the expense of those of the American people as expressed through their elected representatives" (6).[46] History prevents the Court from becoming the "Legis-Court," as he had described the Supreme Court in *The Second American Revolution.* History retrains judicial prejudice, especially the antireligious kind. To leave judges to their own capricious whims invited secularization and, eventually, anarchy. "A rejection of the tether of history," he wrote, "would also constitute a renunciation of any restrictions on judicial decisions." To avoid chaos, judges should embrace the "restraints of the historical approach" (15).

He returned to the same argument several times in this brief. The very soundness of the U.S. Constitution, Whitehead argued, depends upon how tied it is to its history. If the Court chose to ignore history, nothing less than "the integrity of constitutional construction will suffer" (13). Similarly, he insisted that "it would also seriously undermine the integrity of constitutional construction" by redefining the constitutional function of the Court (13). If the Court acted as other than a mere interpreter of the Constitution's original meaning, it undermined that very document by becoming something else entirely. Sounding a theme familiar to readers of his popular works, Whitehead identified for the justices their proper role: "the Court is not a 'super-legislature' . . . empowered to adjudicate according to the personal preferences or political agendas of its members or any other

45. Brief Amicus Curiae of The Rutherford Institute on Writ of Certiorari to the Missouri Supreme Court in Support of Respondents, Harmon et al., 1988 U.S. Briefs (1503), 6.

46. TRI Brief, Bowers.

persons or institutions. Instead, the Court's job is to expound the Constitution" (16). To reject history and reconfigure the First Amendment's meaning, Whitehead wrote colorfully in another case, "would relegate the Free Exercise Clause to the dungheap of constitutional jurisprudence."[47]

What happens when history's restraints are lifted? Whitehead's most vivid answers came in his multiform "sky is falling" literary critiques of Western and American cultures, in his unsubtle use of Nazi imagery in books and films. He refrained from importing Hitler into TRI's amicus briefs, but occasionally the sense of panic found in his nonlegal writings seeped into his professional legal documents. In the *Bowers* brief Whitehead not only insisted upon historical understanding as the proper restraint on judicial whim, he also suggested what would happen if the justices ignored the past: "A rejection of historical analysis in favor of any of the tests proposed above, including that of the Eleventh Circuit, would appear to legalize polygamy, homosexual marriage, incest, necrophilia, private use and possession of many controlled substances, bestiality, fornication, adultery, and perhaps prostitution" (16). Without history, Whitehead claimed, moral anarchy will rush into the vacuum. Ignoring history means that anything goes.

As well, TRI's advocates asserted, if the courts ignore American history, they will eradicate many of the necessary cultural checks and balances on governmental power. In arguing for Dayton Christian Schools to be exempt from Ohio civil rights laws, TRI posited a rather technical argument about democratic theory and the role of associations.[48] Civic associations have a critical counterbalancing role to play in democratic society, Rutherford's attorneys held. "In democratic theory . . . associations perform a critical checking function by locating a portion of the power to define society in numerous, diverse, autocephalous power centers, which together offset the state's power of definition. . . . The dispersion of power creates a variegated and uneven political landscape resistant to the strong levelling tendencies of the state" (5). Associations act so as to "enable them to offset government power" (5). American history reveals the value of independent associations, TRI's lawyers wrote, and we should continue

47. Brief Amicus Curiae of The Rutherford Institute on Appeal from the District Court of Appeal of the State of Florida, Fifth District, in Support of Appellant, Hobbie, No. 85-993 (1985), 10; hereafter TRI Brief, Hobbie.

48. Brief Amicus Curiae of The Rutherford Institute on Appeal from the Sixth Circuit Court of Appeals in Support of the Appellees, Dayton Christian Schools, No. 85-488 (1985); hereafter TRI Brief, Dayton.

to preserve that independence in a day when the government has grown more power hungry.

Again, TRI's lawyers insisted, the consequences of ignoring history in the Dayton case should not be underestimated. If the government remains unchecked, it may re-create civic organizations in the image of the state. Though buried in a footnote, the brief's authors left little doubt about what such a development would mean. They quoted at length from a scholar writing in *Democracy and Natural Law* (1960), who claimed:

> One of the earmarks of the totalitarian understanding of society is that it seeks to make all subcommittees — family, school, business, press, church — completely subject to control by the State. The State then is not one vital institution among others: a policeman, a referee, and a source of initiative for the common good. Instead, it seeks to be coextensive with family and school, press, business community, and Church, so that all of these component interest groups are, in principle, reduced to organs and agencies of the state. In a democratic political order, this megatherian concept is expressly rejected as out of accord with the democratic understanding of social good, and with the actual make-up of the human community.[49]

For the state to regulate private associations, then, would be for the state to violate the very principles that provide its legitimacy.

Without the tether of history, TRI's lawyers argued, government will also become more overtly hostile toward religion. In his books and movies, Whitehead had claimed that this already had begun to happen, and TRI's founder discovered evidence for the same trend in the courts. For example, in the early 1980s Paula A. Hobbie was denied unemployment benefits after being fired for refusing to work on the Sabbath.[50] She had recently converted, and the state took this as evidence of convenience rather than religious sincerity. Whitehead was outraged. In TRI's brief, he wrote that in this case "the state policy demonstrates an animus against anyone who would change his or her belief structure. This official hostility to religious liberties, in general, and religious conversion, in particular, cannot be permitted to stand" (3). Antireligious sentiment had come out of hiding and

---

49. TRI Brief, Dayton, 6 n. 2. The original quotation came from Calhoun, "Democracy and Natural Law," *Natural Law Forum* 5 (1960): 31, 36.

50. TRI Brief, Hobbie.

become encoded in the laws of Florida. Hobbie had to confront "a state animus against a change in her belief structure." She had unwillingly received "the stigma of a state-imposed badge of 'misconduct' for her actions" and must have felt "pressure not to change her beliefs or modify her behavior, as well as the pressure to violate her beliefs" (7). Once government has freed itself from the tether of America's accommodationist history, TRI's brief claimed, the nation's faithful were clearly in trouble.

4. . . . But Contemporary Context Matters Too: Government Growth and Religion as Speech

The Rutherford Institute's hallowing of America's early history and its exclusive privileging of original intent imbued its amicus curiae briefs with a firm, even rigid character. History should serve as the one mold into which judges were to pour any church-state case so that the outcome would match the sentiments of the republic's framers and the sensibilities of the new nation's citizens. However, TRI frequently coupled this apparent interpretive inflexibility with an emphasis upon recent historical trends as an important factor in applying that original intent. Separation might have made sense in 1800, they argued in many briefs, but "separation" in its original nineteenth-century context still allowed the founders to accommodate religion. However, in an age when the once-limited government has become all-encompassing, it is no longer possible to keep church and state separate while still preserving the original goal of having a religion-friendly republic.

While the bedrock principle of accommodation should remain the same, TRI's lawyers insisted, the context in which that principle now must be applied required a reconfiguring of both language and, in the end, reality. To remain faithful to history, in other words, required adaptation. To their opponents — and perhaps even to themselves — they seemed to be textual fundamentalists: judges who learn what the First Amendment says and understand what it originally meant have all they need to make correct decisions. However, in actuality they often called for the courts to adhere to the spirit, not the letter, of original intent and the rest of the historical record.

In the mid-1980s Whitehead's familiar complaints about big government began to appear in TRI's amicus curiae briefs. "We live in an age when Government assumes it has an all-pervasive authority to intervene in virtually all phases of life" was not an unfamiliar incantation.[51] But occasionally these complaints transcended rote bleating and became substantive, in that TRI's lawyers sought to show the courts how bureaucratic expansion had affected religious freedom in America, and thus how it should alter the way they think about deciding church-state cases. Contemporary circumstances — which were characterized by what one TRI brief called "the collision of pervasive government welfare programs with religious activity and practice"[52] — demanded an appropriate response.

Although The Rutherford Institute, in its amicus briefs, continued to try to chip away at any separationist understanding of original intent, it also sought to reach those judges for whom an exclusively historical argument would never be convincing. In a brief in a 1986 case, TRI granted that while a "Separation Paradigm" might have worked as an understanding of the First Amendment in its original context, the twentieth century demanded a different mode of applying the law. TRI's counsel wrote:

> In particular, early establishment clause doctrine drew on an image of separation that pictured government and religion in discrete terms, as if there were discernible boundaries that marked off the separate spheres of religion and government; the critical characteristic of this conception was its commitment to the notion that government and religion occupied mutually exclusive, independent territories, that each could carry on its business without trenching upon the affairs of the other. The problem was that even as this Separation Paradigm was being articulated at the middle of this century, the extremely limited government model it presupposed was, with the death of laissez-faire capitalism, passing away. (3)[53]

A new era called for a new paradigm.

51. Brief Amicus Curiae of The Rutherford Institute on Appeal from the U.S. District Court for the Middle District of Pennsylvania in Support of Appellees, Roy et al., No. 84-780 (1984), 13.

52. Brief Amicus Curiae of The Rutherford Institute on Writ of Certiorari to the New York Court of Appeals in Support of Petitioners, Board of Education of the Kiryas Joel Village School District et al., 1993 U.S. Briefs 517, 5.

53. Brief Amicus Curiae of The Rutherford Institute on Writ of Certiorari to the U.S. Court of Appeals for the Third Circuit in Support of Appellants, Karcher et al., No. 85-1551 (1985); hereafter TRI Brief, Karcher. This idea was repeated later: "The problem was that even as this Separation Paradigm was being born, the era to which it might possibly have applied was rapidly dying out" (8).

This historical interpretation implied that, short of shrinking the government's enormous size (a desirable but practically impossible goal), the Court must reject the separationist paradigm in order to correctly apply the First Amendment. Even if justices chose to ignore TRI's "proof" that such an understanding of original intent was historically counterfeit, they should nevertheless realize that it was an interpretive model that ill suited the present era. An unwieldy section title summarized the change: "The Separation Paradigm, Like the Era to Which the Image It Evokes Corresponds, Is Now Anachronistic and No Longer Helps to Explain or to Guide Modern Establishment Clause Doctrine Which Focuses on Overseeing, as Opposed to Renouncing, the Interface between Religion and Government" (8-9). When government occupied much less public space, the separationist paradigm might have been appropriate; church and state could have existed more or less separately and, since government was small, religion had plenty of civic space in which to breathe. But in the contemporary period, when government has invaded every area of culture and threatens to choke off religion's air supply, a rigid separationism in fact violated the spirit of the First Amendment and should no longer apply. "Accommodation of religious beliefs and practices," TRI's attorneys urged, "has a central role in adapting the religion clauses to the breadth of governmental involvement in our modern welfare state" (17).

This understanding was carried forward in another brief that same year.[54] TRI's lawyers recognized that the doctrine of accommodationism they were pushing the courts to adopt had come under substantial, and to some extent effective, attack. So they sought to prove that accommodation in fact had "an affirmative, salutary role in achieving the purposes of the establishment clause in a modern welfare state" (6). This argument preserved the familiar privileging of original intent, while at the same time calling for adapting that intent to changed circumstances. TRI's counsel wrote that the image "of a world in which government and religion exist in discrete, mutually exclusive, spheres with discernible boundaries, itself presupposes an extremely limited government model, or, what amounts to the same thing, a model in which one could say of some things that they were exclusively the business of government, and of other things that they were exclusively

---

54. Brief Amicus Curiae of The Rutherford Institute on Writ of Certiorari to the U.S. Court of Appeals for the Third Circuit in Support of Appellant, Bowen, No. 87-253 (1987). F. Tayton Dencer seems to have been the primary author of both Karcher and Bowen; those TRI briefs to which Dencer contributed were more dense and philosophically abstract than others.

the business of the church. It might be questioned whether life was ever this simple, but if it ever was, it certainly is not now" (6-7). In an era when the state dispenses so many benefits and organizes so much of the social order, the brief contended, religious people and groups should not be rigidly excluded from public culture. Instead, they should be placed on an equal footing with others. Otherwise, if separation continues to be the operative understanding of church-state relationships, religion's sphere will shrink more and more as the state continues to expand. As TRI's lawyers argued in a footnote, "The greater the role of government, the more narrow one's definition of religion has to be in order to continue to see this basic picture of separation as true of our world" (6-7 n. 7). Religion may disappear entirely, TRI's briefs suggested, unless the Separation Paradigm gives way to an accommodationist one. Life under the "octogovernment" — Whitehead's earlier term for the all-encompassing, invasive federal bureaucracy — required the active preservation of religious freedom.

In articulating this new accommodationist paradigm, The Rutherford Institute's attorneys often pushed for "neutrality" as an appropriate goal for justices in deciding church-state cases. In TRI's amicus curiae brief in *Witters,* Whitehead wrote that to allow religious people to participate on equal footing with others in government programs "is merely the most neutral course for government to take, and therefore the course which most fully realizes the values embodied in the Establishment Clause" (4).[55] This neutrality, according to Whitehead's logic, was preferable to the only other possible option, the establishment of secularism. A neutrality that accommodated religious belief and did not exclude it from public life should provide the theoretical skeleton for replacing the Separation Paradigm with something better.

"Neutrality" was a concept to be handled with care, however, so The Rutherford Institute meticulously explained what it meant. Too often separationists had invoked neutrality as a means to suppress religious freedom and establish secularism in its place at the center of American culture. In a case in the early 1980s, when Washington State denied Larry Witters generally available financial aid to the blind because he wanted to use the money for religious education, the state and its supporters claimed they were merely trying to preserve neutrality in church-state relations. Neutrality in this case did not avoid the establishment of religion, TRI's lawyers insisted. Instead, it served merely as a cloak for the establishment of secular-

55. TRI Brief, Witters.

ism. "Amici believe that the decision of the court . . . is consonant with the views of some that the Establishment Clause requires the secularization of American society. A decision by this Court upholding the denial of assistance to Petitioner would be interpreted by many as validating this thesis. Moreover, it could well be interpreted by public administrators and others in public authority as a mandate to remove all religious influence from the public sphere" (9).[56] This was not the kind of neutrality The Rutherford Institute had in mind.

Instead, Whitehead and his lawyers carefully contrasted this sort of neutrality with "true neutrality." In a complicated philosophical argument in 1986, TRI's counsel argued that justices should adopt an interpretive scheme called the "*True* Neutrality Paradigm."[57] Having contended that the old Separation Paradigm, one that sought to keep church and state completely apart, no longer worked in an era of all-pervasive government, TRI's brief urged that a True Neutrality Paradigm should take its place. Under this scheme justices would require "government to take religious interest into account, with a view toward protecting religious voluntarism, in its management of the social order" (14).[58] Such a shift in constitutional understanding would not represent a rejection of the animating principles behind the Separation Paradigm, the brief continued. Instead, the True Neutrality Paradigm would represent an adaptation of the old paradigm for changed circumstances: "it is, in a word, the Separation Paradigm come of age" (14).[59]

56. TRI Brief, Witters.

57. TRI Brief, Karcher, 9ff., my emphasis.

58. This argument is not unlike that later advanced by Michael W. McConnell, "The Problem of Singling Out Religion," *DePaul Law Review* 50, no. 1 (2000): 1-47. He argued that "'singling out religion' for special constitutional consideration is fully consistent with our constitutional tradition" (3). As the founders indicated in the First Amendment, McConnell wrote, "religion has a special and unique place in our constitutional order" and should be treated as such (15). TRI's advocates seemed to argue that because what McConnell reports is true, "true neutrality" would not mean equality between all competing worldviews, both secular and religious; instead, "true neutrality" would mean "special treatment for religion according to the First Amendment's original design." According to McConnell, such special treatment is not an unfair privilege, "but rather, a comprehensive attempt to minimize government power over religious decisions" (38). In an era when that power is so omnipresent, Whitehead would say, it is this attempt — in McConnell's language, this "singling out" — that would most closely approximate "true neutrality" according to the Constitution.

59. TRI's collective heart did not seem to be in granting the historical legitimacy

Closely related to this understanding of "true" neutrality, in TRI's amicus briefs, was the notion of "true" open-mindedness. In a nationally significant case, *Edwards v. Aguillard* (1987), TRI joined many others in filing an amicus curiae brief.[60] Louisiana had passed a law requiring equal time for creation science in the public school classroom, a law ruled unconstitutional by the Fifth Circuit Court of Appeals. TRI assisted a diverse gathering of interested parties in crafting an argument against that decision.[61] Just as before, when TRI had argued that those pushing "neutrality" really were seeking to replace religious accommodation with antireligious secularism, TRI in this case accused those who characterized creation-science advocates as narrow-minded and intolerant of the very same sins. By seeking to prevent equal time for creation science in the classroom, evolutionists were restricting knowledge and freedom of inquiry — the very ideals they professed to espouse.

In spite of criticism to the contrary, the brief argued, the law requiring "balanced treatment" for creation science served the very secular purpose of enhancing academic freedom and diversifying the "marketplace of ideas" (2). Indeed, this purpose reflected the very heart of the First Amendment. The political theory underlying the First Amendment was one that "assigns government a role outside of ideological controversy. It denied government the authority to interfere in the competition among ideas. It denied, in short, the right of government to impose upon society its view of truth and falsity in ideological matters" (5).[62]

---

of the Separation Paradigm. TRI Brief, Karcher, recommended Cord, *The Separation of Church and State,* as evidence that "The notion that the establishment clause requires neutrality between religion and irreligion, while appropriate given the vastly different cultures of the twentieth and eighteenth centuries, is a distinctly modern notion" (8 n. 6). A paradigm with shallow historical roots, TRI implied, should be intellectually easier to uproot and replace.

60. *Edwards v. Aguillard,* 482 U.S. 578 (1987).

61. Brief Amici Curiae of the Rabbinical Alliance of America, the Catholic Center, the Free Methodist Church of North America, the Honorable Robert K. Dornan [U.S. representative from California], the Honorable William E. Dannemeyer [U.S. representative from California], the Honorable Patrick L. Swindall [U.S. representative from Georgia], and the Committee on Openness in Science, in Support of the Appellants, Aguillard, et al., No. 85-1513 (1985); hereafter TRI Brief, Aguillard. Three TRI staffers, including Whitehead, served as "participating attorneys."

62. This statement formed part of a highly technical, philosophically dense discussion about modern epistemology and its relationship to American democracy. One not atypical subsection of the brief was entitled "The Dominant Post-Kantian View of In-

The entire controversy had become one pitting evolutionary "facts" against the supposedly untenable claims of creation science, TRI's attorneys complained. This was mistaken, a misunderstanding of both the tenuous nature of evolutionist claims and the kind of truth creation science presents. They bemoaned the "hubris" of scientists, and those who obeyed them unquestioningly, who have "blurred the distinction between empirical data and hypotheses" so that scientific propositions have unjustifiably acquired an aura of unassailability (10). The dispute over origins, despite appearances, was really "non-empirical"; both theories, in fact, shared a similar nonfactual basis (11).[63] Both were hypotheses, competing interpretations of the same data, and hence deserved "balanced treatment" in the free marketplace of ideas that should characterize the public schools. To deny schoolchildren exposure to creation science, on this reasoning, "would involve the imposition of ideological limitations on meaning and would, therefore, violate the First Amendment" (12).

As the brief in *Edwards v. Aguillard* drew to a conclusion, TRI's argument had transferred the charge of close-mindedness and illiberality from creation science proponents — its side — to their persecutors: "There is, of course, a strong psychological tendency to seek closure in relation to questions of meaning. The urge to exclude a competing account of our origins is thus understandable. However, the First Amendment requires us to conquer this yearning for closure; it is the teaching of all of liberal political and philosophical thought, as well as the requirement of our form of government, that we master the fear of interpretations that pose a threat to our world view and overcome the visceral (one is tempted to say prehensile) urge to intolerance" (12). Liberal advocates of evolution were nothing short of illiberal; devotees of scientific inquiry were denying the free rein of intellectual curiosity; champions of toleration who thought resisting creation science fulfilled that goal actually thwarted it.[64] Dogmatic evolution-

---

terpretation Recognizes a Dualistic, Though Heavily Contingent, Separation between 'Reality' and Interpretation That Allows for the Proliferation of Meanings without Denying the Possibility Of Meaning Itself"; TRI Brief, Aguillard, 9.

63. The lawyers delighted in pointing to the tenuous nature of some evolutionists' claims. Punctuated equilibrium — the positing of rapid change to explain the lack of transitional organisms in the fossil record — is, according to the brief, "on a conceptual level . . . virtually a euphemism for special creation" (12).

64. Justice Scalia, dissenting from the Court's eventual decision not to hear the case (thus leaving intact the lower court's ruling that invalidated the Louisiana law), agreed with this logic. Scalia wrote that "today we permit a Court of Appeals to push the

ists must get over their "yearning for closure" and allow truth to find its own way.[65]

In 1989 The Rutherford Institute argued similarly that opponents of religious groups were the illiberal ones in America's supposedly liberal democracy. The Equal Access Act of 1984, which provided the use of public school facilities by religious groups on an equal basis with other civic groups, had been challenged in court. In a brief arguing for the constitutionality of the act, TRI's lawyers placed themselves squarely on the side of religious tolerance. "The schools serve as poor role models for the ideals of freedom and tolerance," the brief suggested, "when they discriminate against and deny equal access to religious student groups."[66]

One strategy TRI employed to push for "equal access" for religion in all public arenas was to reconfigure religious expression as free speech. In a truly liberal democracy, properly organized under a paradigm of "true neutrality," freedom of speech should be guaranteed. If religion is understood as a subset of free speech, TRI's counsel urged, then it too should be guaranteed the same public freedoms that other forms of speech have been granted. If religious speech or action was prohibited solely because of its religious nature, then the First Amendment's guarantee of freedom of speech was hollow. Such prohibitions amounted to "discrimination," no less morally and constitutionally offensive than other forms of the same.

---

much beloved secular legend of the Monkey Trial one step further. We stand by in silence while a deeply divided Fifth Circuit bars a school district from even suggesting to students that other theories besides evolution — including, but not limited to, the Biblical theory of creation — are worthy of their consideration. I dissent." See Dissent, Denial of Petition for Writ of Certiorari to the U.S. Court of Appeals for the Fifth District, Tangipahoa Parish Board of Education et al. v. Herb Freiler et al, No. 99-1625 (2000).

65. In *Edwards v. Aguillard* the U.S. Supreme Court — using the *Lemon* test — ruled the "equal time" law unconstitutional because it had the primary purpose of advancing a particular religion. Justice Scalia, in a dissent joined by Rehnquist, questioned the wisdom of the majority's attempt to discern legislative intent and attacked the coherence of the *Lemon* test itself. As well, Scalia took seriously the notion — as had Justice Black in *Epperson v. Arkansas*, 399 U.S. 97 (1968) — that teaching evolution exclusively may in fact be *antireligious*. From Scalia's perspective, the Louisiana "equal time" law did not threaten to establish a religion; it may in fact have been legitimately designed to *prevent* an establishment — that of secularism. Whitehead and TRI would have agreed; see especially the discussion of Whitehead and Conlan, "Establishment of the Religion of Secular Humanism and Its First Amendment Implications," in chapter 2.

66. Brief Amicus Curiae of The Rutherford Institute on Writ of Certiorari to the U.S. Court of Appeals for the Eighth Circuit in Support of Respondents, Mergens et al., 1988 U.S. Briefs 1597, 8.

In *Bender,* as in *Wallace v. Jaffree,* TRI attorneys made clear that to bar students from independently organizing for religious purposes during an unstructured activity time was to unfairly discriminate against those students "solely on account of the content of their speech" (3). In TRI's estimation, "Once access for voluntary, self-directed free speech activity is accorded to some, it should be accorded to all" (4). Denying students the ability to meet for religious reasons, when all other reasons are valid, "would prefer those who believe in no religion over those who believe" (7).[67]

TRI applied the same argument in *Witters.* TRI's lawyers argued that to deny Witters benefits amounted to religious prejudice: "a state policy which excludes a person from generally available benefits, solely on religious grounds, constitutes invidious discrimination and places an impermissible burden upon that person's free exercise of religion" (2). That Witters used public money for religious education, TRI claimed, was no more inappropriate than public money paying for fire and police protection for houses of worship. To rule against him would be to suggest that Social Security recipients, GI Bill beneficiaries, and federal student-loan recipients should be barred from using their monies for any religious purposes; and doing this would be "converting the clause into a sword against religion" (7). To keep the state's policy in place amounted to "invidious discrimination" against religion (3).[68]

TRI found another case in which speech had been outlawed simply because of its religious content. Jews for Jesus, Inc., had been barred from distributing literature and preaching inside Los Angeles International Airport. They sued the city, and TRI wrote on their behalf. TRI believed all speech must be allowed in a traditional public forum. "The overriding issue in this case is, plainly and simply, how free will speech be in this country," TRI's lawyers wrote.[69] To disallow religious speech would be to discriminate against religion.

The Rutherford Institute's increasingly intense devotion to free speech persisted into the 1990s, appearing most noticeably in an amicus brief filed in *Lee v. Weisman.*[70] Daniel Weisman had sued on behalf of his daughter when prayers were offered as part of her middle school gradua-

67. TRI Brief, Bender.

68. TRI Brief, Witters.

69. Brief Amicus Curiae of The Rutherford Institute on Writ of Certiorari to the U.S. Court of Appeals for the Ninth Circuit in Support of Respondents, Jews for Jesus, Inc., No. 86-104 (1986), 5.

70. TRI Brief, Lee.

tion ceremony. Weisman's lawyers argued that since the school administra-
tion had invited the cleric to speak, this practice violated the First Amendment's establishment clause. No matter how nondenominational or
inoffensive, the prayers, since they had in effect been officially sponsored
by the public school, signaled an unconstitutional endorsement of religion.

The district court agreed with the Weismans, and the school district
appealed. The Rutherford Institute filed an amicus brief in support of the
appeal, which argued that in fact this school prayer case had nothing to do
with the establishment clause. Instead, it was "really about censorship" (3).
To refuse to allow graduation prayers amounted to "the content-based exclusion of religious speech," censorship that violated "one of the core values of the First Amendment" (3-4). Some may think that this particular restriction does not amount to something significant, TRI's lawyers wrote.
However, those people are mistaken, for this case formed part of a larger
plan: "Such a prohibition may appear reasonable to some. . . . However,
such an exclusion is, in reality, yet another step toward large-scale censorship of religion and wholesale eradication of religious messages, references
and symbols from American public life" (4). The brief drew to a climax as
the attorneys invoked America's long tradition of freedom of speech:
"American schoolchildren are taught that they have the constitutional right
to speak. It is ironic that, at the threshold of their educational adulthood,
the government is asked to publicly abridge that right and censor the very
speech that celebrates their graduation. Such censorship is a far cry from
what our forefathers envisioned when they wrote the document that would
govern this nation and protect our most treasured freedoms" (14). To reject
graduation prayers, according to Whitehead and his attorneys, would be to
reject America's most fundamental values.[71]

In 1992 TRI resurrected complaints about discrimination against religious speech in an amicus brief filed on behalf of a New York State church
that sought, and had been denied, the use of public school facilities.[72]
Other civic groups had been granted access, but the school district rejected
the request of Lamb's Chapel for similar access because, school officials believed, this would have violated the establishment clause. Such a policy,

71. In 1992 the U.S. Supreme Court upheld the lower court's ruling that the
prayers at a public school graduation ceremony ran afoul of the establishment clause; see
Lee v. Weisman.

72. Brief Amicus Curiae of The Rutherford Institute on Writ of Certiorari on Appeal from the U.S. Court of Appeals for the Second Circuit in Support of Appellants,
Lamb's Chapel et al., 1991 U.S. Briefs 2024.

TRI contended, constituted "content-based invidious discrimination which, if sustained, will create a religious apartheid not unlike the Jim Crow laws that denied blacks the equal use of public facilities because of race" (1).[73] In fact, according to TRI's brief, the school's rejection of Lamb's Chapel demonstrated that religious groups had it *worse* than African Americans in the Jim Crow South. "The exclusion of blacks from privately-owned lunch counters, or their relegation to the back of the bus is tame compared to this New York policy which contains a wholesale ban and outright exclusion from public facilities based on the content of the message. The Plessy v. Ferguson 'separate but equal' doctrine, though broader in reach, pales in light of a government policy that effects 'total exclusion and total inequality' — disabling the speech of religious citizens and disenfranchising them from an important part of the public arena" (5). The members of Lamb's Chapel had been unconstitutionally disenfranchised in this situation, solely on account of the content of their speech.[74]

A few years later TRI's amicus curiae brief filed in *University of Wisconsin v. Southworth* adopted the same line of reasoning. Three university law students had sued the university for using their mandatory student activity fees to subsidize "objectionable" organizations that did not match their values. The First Amendment, they argued, granted them the right *not* to fund groups that expressed values different from their own. The university argued that the fees helped them establish a free marketplace of ideas, one that enhanced the university's educational mission. TRI, weighing in on the students' side, contended that not only did the mandatory student fee "unlawfully compel students to subsidize speech with which they disagree," it also "significantly burdens the students' First Amendment freedom of speech rights" since they were not allowed to graduate without paying the student fee (2). For these students, expressing their free speech rights resulted in "an academic 'death penalty'" (9).[75]

73. The rhetoric of "religious apartheid" appeared in the courts three years before Whitehead would publish a book of the same name.

74. The U.S. Supreme Court eventually ruled in favor of Lamb's Chapel; see *Lamb's Chapel v. Center Moriches School District,* 508 U.S. 384 (1993).

75. Brief Amicus Curiae of The Rutherford Institute on Writ of Certiorari to the U.S. Court of Appeals for the Seventh Circuit in Support of Respondents, Southworth et al., 1998 U.S. Briefs 1189. *Southworth* appeared before the Seventh Circuit four separate times from 1996 to 2000. After going up to the Supreme Court and back again, the issue remaining was whether the University of Wisconsin's mandatory fee system "unconstitutionally granted the student government unbridled discretion for deciding which stu-

In *Santa Fe v. Doe* The Rutherford Institute made a similar claim about the inviolability of private free speech rights.[76] The Santa Fe School District had been sued for permitting prayers at high school football games, even after district officials had absented themselves from choosing whether or not a prayer would actually be given or, if students voted to have prayer, which student would deliver it. TRI argued that once school officials absented themselves from the process, the prayers became a form of private speech protected by the First Amendment's guarantee of freedom of speech. To restrict the content of student speech after they had voted to have a prayer would be to submit them to "government censorship" (8).[77] Banning these voluntary prayers would be tantamount to requiring government approval for individual expression, something against which the Constitution — especially the First Amendment — so clearly stood.

5. Conclusion

Throughout its first two decades, The Rutherford Institute consistently sought to convince the courts through amicus curiae briefs that religion had

---

dent organizations to fund"; *Southworth v. Wisconsin,* 307 F. 3d 566, 1. If the student government had that discretion, the plaintiffs argued, then the university would be unable to guarantee that those mandatory fees would be distributed, as required, in a viewpoint-neutral fashion. (Previously the plaintiffs had stipulated that these student funds were distributed in a viewpoint-neutral fashion, but they later amended their complaint to remove this stipulation. The Supreme Court, in *Board of Regents v. Southworth,* 529 U.S. 217 [2000], had ruled that students were entitled to the assurance of viewpoint neutrality in the distribution of mandatory student fees.) The Seventh Circuit Court ruled against the plaintiffs, agreeing with the University of Wisconsin that a student-funding organization was not granted "unbridled discretion" in distributing the funds and therefore did not violate the plaintiffs' rights to viewpoint neutrality.

76. Brief Amicus Curiae of The Rutherford Institute on Writ of Certiorari to the U.S. Court of Appeals for the Fifth Circuit in Support of Respondents, Doe and Doe, 1999 U.S. Briefs 62.

77. TRI viewed this restriction of religious speech as part of a larger conspiracy. In a 1995 brief TRI accused those who opposed anti-abortion picketing of advocating "the totalitarian view of society which requires all speech to be in accordance with official government policy"; Brief Amicus Curiae of The Rutherford Institute on Writ of Certiorari to the U.S. Court of Appeals for the Second Circuit in Support of Petitioners, Schenck and Saunders, 1995 U.S. Briefs 1065, 2. In the same case the attorneys complained that "We live in an age of increasing intolerance toward anyone with a different point of view. Rejection of such intolerance was one of the major reasons for the founding of this nation" (8).

become the undeserving target of discrimination and censorship, and therefore merited protection. The so-called separation of church and state might, once upon a time, have been a satisfactory understanding of how the two realms ought to coexist, TRI's briefs occasionally granted. But the founders approved the First Amendment in an era when government was limited and religious individuals and institutions could roam freely about the culture. In the contemporary era, when government had spread like kudzu across the civic landscape, threatening to choke off once-independent spheres of culture, a new paradigm was needed to remain faithful to the founders' accommodationist aspirations. To continue to pursue the rigorous segregation of religion from government was to reinforce a discriminatory system no less morally offensive or constitutionally odious than that in the Jim Crow South. To continue to prohibit religious expression in the public sphere was no less illegal or inconsonant with the Constitution's original purposes than silencing opinions merely because the government disagreed.

The attempted rescue of religious free exercise from "the dungheap of constitutional jurisprudence" meshed comfortably with John Whitehead's cultural analysis and TRI's overall mission. In fact, because TRI's founder held the courts responsible for so much of America's currently sorry state, legal activism did not just make sense, it seemed required. Though it was important to help "the little guy" in his fight against the "octogovernment" and the antidemocratic "legis-courts," a systemic change in church-state relations could be most efficiently accomplished by establishing legal precedents. Filing amicus briefs allowed TRI to engage a readily identifiable enemy on its home turf.

Whether or not this constituted a wise tactical decision, or met with any real success, remained an open question. In his books, pamphlets, and movies, Whitehead had pressed a cultural analysis in which the courts played only one — albeit significant — role. In those works he complained that American life had been hijacked and reshaped by an antidemocratic, secularist court system. So why turn to that same system to gain relief? Were there not costs to bear in playing a high-stakes cultural game on the opponent's own terms? Assuredly, attacking the problem at its source seemed both emotionally and practically attractive: justices provided easily identifiable enemies, and if they had the power to flout the popular will merely by issuing decisions, then legal activism represented perhaps the quickest, most effective means of pushing back against the secularist tide.

But what if The Rutherford Institute succeeded in convincing the courts of its church-state perspective? What if, through its energetic legal advocacy in the court system, it put itself out of business? What if it (re)created cultural conditions that allowed religious believers to think and practice unfettered by governmentally imposed, secularist restraints? Critics charged that TRI and similar organizations sought to create a comprehensively Christian republic, one in which dissenters might or might not be tolerated. Whitehead often responded that he merely sought to place religious believers — of any tradition — on an equal footing with those of other metaphysical perspectives. The gap between TRI and its critics raised an important question: Just what would it mean for Whitehead to win?

5

The Measure of Success:
Religiously Motivated Legal Activism
and Its Consequences

The Christian must act as the preservative of his culture by guiding it. He must stop thinking small and start thinking in terms of the creation mandate to subdue the earth.

John W. Whitehead, 1977[1]

Our agenda is not to have a Christian nation, but to enable religious people to survive.

John W. Whitehead, 1993[2]

John W. Whitehead and his colleagues at The Rutherford Institute spent two decades spreading a particular gospel of First Amendment originalism in both the culture and the courts. As especially revealed in amicus briefs filed before the U.S. Supreme Court, TRI's lawyers believed that the founders had almost uniformly esteemed religion and recognized how crucial its role would be in making the new national experiment succeed. The original authors of the Constitution and the Bill of Rights had constructed a republic that, although eschewing an official union of religion and government, nevertheless carved out a place of primacy for religion in American life. President Thomas Jefferson's claim that the First Amendment had

1. John W. Whitehead, *The Separation Illusion: A Lawyer Examines the First Amendment* (Milford, Mich.: Mott Media, 1977), 38.
2. Quoted in Tim Stafford, "Move Over, ACLU: A Host of New Public-Interest Law Firms Are Helping American Christians Fight for Their Religious Liberties," *Christianity Today,* 25 Oct. 1993.

erected a "wall of separation between church and state" accurately described only the restricted sphere to which the federal government would
be confined.[3] According to Whitehead and TRI, the framers so esteemed religion's cultural and political importance that they drafted a Constitution
that provided enormous latitude for religious expression in public life.

Therefore, for TRI's advocates, a truly originalist hermeneutic would
allow — if not require — the government to support religion generally, and
to prefer religion over nonreligion. Agreeing wholeheartedly with Justice
Douglas that "We are a religious people whose institutions presuppose a
Supreme Being,"[4] Whitehead and his lawyers insisted that this theistic
foundation should forever remain in place. When in the twentieth century
it seemed to be crumbling, as cultural elites replaced it with a stridently
secularist underpinning, Whitehead argued that the very nature of American identity was being comprehensively and illegitimately altered.

This semi-surreptitious scheme to supersede the framers' intentions
had both public and private dimensions, according to TRI's founder. For as
the nine unelected justices on the Supreme Court made (secularist) law for
the nation, they also affected religious individuals in localized situations.
Indeed, though TRI advanced complex hermeneutical arguments at the
highest judicial levels, it is important to remember that Whitehead found
his professional calling when responding to a single schoolteacher cen-
sured for explaining to her students the cross around her neck.[5] For him
and his organization, First Amendment interpretation was never merely an
academic problem. The tentacles of the "octogovernment" extended far
and wide across the land, threatening not just liberty in the abstract but
also individual religious freedom in particular. This was the crisis that The
Rutherford Institute had been created to address.

The national and the local dimensions of this constitutional calamity
were all interlinked in Whitehead's understanding and TRI's endeavors.
What happened in the highest chambers of federal power could directly affect what transpired in the smallest rural schoolroom or the tiniest workplace cubicle. This interrelatedness was a big part of the problem, White-

---

3. For a Library of Congress exhibition in 1998, the FBI analyzed the original
draft of Jefferson's letter to the Danbury Baptists, discovering that he had initially written
of a wall of "eternal separation" between church and state; see James H. Hutson, ed., *Religion and the New Republic: Faith in the Founding of America* (Lanham, Md.: Rowman and
Littlefield, 2000), 85.

4. *Zorach v. Clauson*, 343 U.S. 306 (1952).

5. See chapter 2.

head believed. The federal government, once small in size and restricted in power, had been illegitimately transformed into an invasive, late twentieth-century behemoth — an "octogovernment." Indeed, this expansion of jurisdiction lay behind almost every church-state problem TRI sought to resolve: had the federal government remained as small as originally intended, the elites that administer it would not have been able to insinuate secularism so efficiently throughout the land.

These complicated, intertwining motivations for The Rutherford Institute's legal activism help explain its multifarious approach to confronting America's cultural dilemma. Despite its specialized mission, TRI engaged in different activities with very different constituencies: it filed amicus curiae briefs before the U.S. Supreme Court, assisted local believers with very local legal problems, and disseminated cultural and legal knowledge to whomever expressed interest. For Whitehead and TRI, simultaneously performing these various tasks made perfect sense: each represented a different attempt to win the same battle to preserve America's true religious character from those who would destroy it. The Rutherford Institute's success, then, must be measured in light of how effectively its strategies facilitated achieving this overall goal.

1. The Rutherford Institute and American Law

1.1. Legal Assistance at the Grass Roots

Any assessment of The Rutherford Institute's efficacy must focus, obviously, upon the law. Begun in 1982 to assist believers in defending their individual liberties, TRI steadfastly offered legal services to believers who needed specialized help. This was its primary task. Measuring just how capably TRI performed this function, however, is not easy. Throughout most of the 1990s Whitehead claimed that his organization handled at least 80 percent of all religious liberty litigation.[6] Anecdotal evidence provided by the organization itself certainly contributed to that impression, as TRI's fund-raising letters and publications highlighted myriad local victories

---

6. See, for example, W. John Moore, "The Lord's Litigators," *National Journal,* 2 July 1994. Steven P. Brown has also noted this claim and suggests that at least before the early 1990s, when the ACLJ and then the Alliance Defense Fund were created, this might have been true; see Steven P. Brown, *Trumping Religion: The New Christian Right, the Free Speech Clause, and the Courts* (Tuscaloosa: University of Alabama Press, 2002), 34.

much more than singular national conflicts. Quantifying those local victories, and measuring them against any defeats, would be required to accurately assess TRI's claims. Even having that data would not be enough, however, for what would constitute "success"? Should TRI's advocacy be measured like a baseball batter's production, for whom getting a hit one out of every three times is exceptional? Or, to extend the metaphor, would TRI's endeavors be better judged like those of a sports team, where "success" requires winning considerably more than half its contests? Or, as with many Christian missionaries, does securing even one convert — one "victory" — in the end make all efforts worthwhile?

Even without an exact scorecard of The Rutherford Institute's endeavors, and allowing for some unavoidable difficulty in determining "success," it is true that during its first twenty years TRI did achieve a significant number of victories in the lower courts. However, although useful, a careful examination of only those lower-court activities would not provide the most complete gauge of TRI's grassroots success. Indeed, if the standard of measurement is the preservation of individual religious liberties, those cases that never made it into court — thanks to a well-timed warning to a school administrator or employer that legal trouble loomed if present policies persisted — should be considered just as important as those cases that were actually litigated. How many school administrators, after hearing from TRI's attorneys, quickly rescinded a ban on teachers wearing religious jewelry? How many teachers grudgingly permitted a student to focus an assignment on her hero, Jesus Christ? How many employers relented to a worker's request to hold a Bible study over lunch or to post an invitation to Friday prayers on the workplace bulletin board? In other words, how many victories did TRI achieve outside of the courtroom by inserting itself, the weight of its information, and the threat of its activism into a dispute? Only with an approximate answer to that question could TRI's success in defending individual religious liberties be completely and accurately measured. In 2002 the institute guessed that about 80 percent of its cases were resolved before reaching court; if TRI's insistence that it handled 80 percent of *all* religious liberty cases even approached the truth, then the quantity of cases settled before going to court was quite impressive.[7]

7. For TRI's claim to settle about 80 percent of its cases, see Brown, *Trumping Religion,* 121. In 1999 TRI reported answering 280 requests per week, for a total of over 14,500 responses annually. Obviously not all requests were placed on a litigation track:

1.2. Original Intent

In addition to its grassroots efforts, The Rutherford Institute also joined an ongoing conversation in the higher courts over how best to adjudicate both free exercise and establishment issues. Specifically, as revealed in Whitehead's own writings and the organization's amicus curiae briefs, TRI consistently pushed original intent as the most appropriate hermeneutic to decide church-state cases. As with the consideration of TRI's grassroots achievements, assessing the consequences of TRI's interpretive approach proves rather complicated.

In his earlier books, especially in *The Separation Illusion* (1977) and *The Second American Revolution* (1982), John Whitehead connected the illegitimate nature of incorporation with the broader discussion of original intent. In the twentieth century, using the Fourteenth Amendment as the vehicle, the U.S. Supreme Court applied the Bill of Rights to all the states. Whitehead contended that the First Amendment had originally been designed to affect only the federal government, not the individual states. Therefore, when in the twentieth century the Supreme Court applied the Bill of Rights to the states, it entirely repudiated the framers' intentions. The Court also compounded that mistake by using hermeneutical subterfuge to do so. Not only had the Fourteenth Amendment been ratified illegally, Whitehead claimed, but those who wrote it had not intended for it to incorporate the Bill of Rights. Thus, in the twentieth century the U.S. Supreme Court had used an erroneous understanding of one amendment (the Fourteenth) to mistakenly apply another (the First) in a way that unjustifiably expanded federal power.

Curiously, despite his heartfelt conviction about the jurisdictional aspect of original intent, Whitehead did not include this argument in any of TRI's amicus briefs. He never repudiated his view of incorporation's illegitimacy, but he chose not to press it upon the federal courts. This seems strange, both because Whitehead had so strenuously argued this point elsewhere and because a few important judicial players agreed with him. Writing in 1995, Kurt T. Lash amply documented his claim that "Today, more than fifty years after its application to the states, no one seriously believes

---

during that same year TRI opened eighty-five cases and resolved twenty-five (Rutherford Institute, IRS Form 990, 1999). But if even a small portion of the remaining requests amounted to more than merely providing information, a significant number of conflicts would have been settled without going to court.

that this was the original intent of those who drafted and ratified the Fourteenth Amendment."[8] Pushing an anti-incorporation view in the courts would not necessarily have been a lonely endeavor; allies in the academy, and even some on the bench, might have been easily marshaled.[9]

The Rutherford Institute's reluctance to argue against incorporation in its amicus briefs appeared all the more mysterious because reversing the concomitant jurisdictional expansion — however unlikely a prospect — would have played exactly to the organization's grassroots strength. Among similar groups, TRI had established perhaps the most geographically diffuse network of affiliated attorneys and possessed the most local experience handling religious freedom cases.[10] Ejecting the federal government from most church-state disputes by dismantling incorporation would have moved action from the federal courts to the state and local levels — places where Whitehead believed such matters belonged and where his institute had long devoted most of its efforts.

Perhaps for TRI's lawyers, arguing against incorporation seemed too quixotic. As early as 1963 the Court had pronounced the matter of applying the First Amendment to the states "decisively settled,"[11] and taken as a whole, little in jurisprudential history since then indicated that the Court was ready for a change of heart. Indeed, even when provided a golden opportunity to reexamine incorporation, the Supreme Court declined to do

8. Kurt T. Lash, "The Second Adoption of the Establishment Clause: The Rise of the Nonestablishment Principle," *Arizona State Law Journal* 27 (1995): 1086, esp. nn. 4 and 5.

9. Most recently, Justice Clarence Thomas signaled some sympathy with this view: "Whatever the textual and historical merits of incorporating the Establishment Clause, I can accept that the Fourteenth Amendment protects religious liberty rights. But I cannot accept its use to oppose neutral programs of school choice through the incorporation of the Establishment Clause. There would be a tragic irony in converting the Fourteenth Amendment's guarantee of individual liberty into a prohibition on the exercise of educational choice"; *Zelman v. Simmons-Harris,* 000 U.S. 00-1751 (2002), concurring opinion.

10. Even as its budget decreased in the 1990s, shrinking the number of affiliates, in 2001 it still filed tax returns in thirty-five states and the District of Columbia.

11. *District of Abington Township v. Schempp,* 374 U.S. 203, 216 (1963). See also William Brennan's concurring opinion, in which he discusses — and dismisses — objections to incorporation (254-59). Even if it is true that the Fourteenth Amendment's drafters did not intend to connect its language with the First Amendment religion clauses, Brennan wrote, "it is certainly too late in the day to suggest that their assumed inattention to the question dilutes the force of these constitutional guarantees in the application to the States" (258).

so.[12] In view of this, constitutional scholar Leonard Levy concluded that "the incorporation doctrine has a history so fixed that overthrowing it is as likely as bagging snarks on the roof of the Court's building."[13] Like Levy, Whitehead must have recognized that the First Amendment had consistently been applied to the states for some forty years before TRI appeared. Most justices since the 1940s seemed, at least tacitly, to believe with Justice Clark that objections to incorporation "seem entirely untenable and of value only as academic exercises."[14] In the face of such sentiments, it may have appeared fruitless, even counterproductive, to try to reverse the federal government's expansion of power by arguing against incorporation itself. Although apparently an instance of pragmatism outweighing principle, it certainly made sense for TRI to omit an argument that promised only to distract rather than persuade.

Having accepted the reality of the First Amendment's reach, Whitehead and TRI expended considerable energy pressing for original intent as the most faithful way to understand how to apply the First Amendment's religion clauses. Of course, disputes over the appropriateness of this hermeneutical principle proliferated in the legal community before and during The Rutherford Institute's existence, and even those who agreed that original intent or "the text" should guide constitutional interpretation often differed about just what that might mean in practice.[15] Given the literature's depth, the hardened nature of hermeneutical convictions, and the sheer number of voices offered in any one church-state case,[16] it is implausible that TRI greatly affected judicial decisions by strenuously promoting originalism in its amicus briefs. TRI may have tilted the scales ever so slightly in one direction or another, but given the relatively peripheral status of amici and the cacophony generated by their growing numbers, it

12. As Kurt Lash has observed, District Judge Brevard Hand concluded in *Jaffree v. Board of Commissioners of Mobile County* (554 F. Supp. 1104) that crafters of the Fourteenth Amendment had not intended to incorporate the establishment clause, seeming to force the Supreme Court to consider the issue once they consented to hear the case. However, in *Wallace v. Jaffree,* 472 U.S. 38 (1985), they ignored incorporation altogether. See Lash, "Second Adoption," esp. 1086.

13. Leonard W. Levy, *The Establishment Clause: Religion and the First Amendment,* 2nd rev. ed. (Chapel Hill: University of North Carolina Press, 1994), 227.

14. *District of Abington Township v. Schempp,* 217.

15. See, for example, Mark Tushnet, "Religion and Theories of Constitutional Interpretation," *Loyola Law Review* 33 (1987): 221-40.

16. On the contemporary increase in amicus briefs and its consequences, see chapter 4.

alone would not have been the compass consulted by judges for determining their hermeneutical bearings.

Aside from grounding its own legal positions in a plausible theory of constitutional interpretation, what purpose did originalism serve for The Rutherford Institute? One obvious benefit lay in how this legal approach dovetailed with TRI's cultural complaints. In advocating originalism, Whitehead and his lawyers reinforced the belief that legal decline and cultural decline had proceeded hand in hand during the last half of the twentieth century. TRI provided detailed declension narratives in its legal briefs that closely paralleled those in its nonlegal materials. TRI's story by now seems familiar: the nation, like its law, once existed in near-perfect form. At the beginning the United States properly honored its religious roots by preserving a place of political privilege for faith in general and Protestant Christianity in particular. The law as originally intended reinforced this arrangement by keeping the federal government as far away as possible from individual believers. The fall from cultural paradise corresponded closely with a similar judicial fall from interpretive paradise. In the twentieth century, American society had disintegrated in large part at the hands of secularists who unfairly wielded governmental power in a concerted effort to displace religion from its proper place at the culture's center. So, too, had secularists manipulated church-state jurisprudence in order to hijack American identity, dispensing with a fixed, favorable originalism in favor of capricious judicial relativism. According to Whitehead and TRI, American society's regrettable slide into chaotic amorality could not be separated from developments in constitutional law that abetted — and in some cases directly caused — that decline.

The parallel declension narratives, hardly accidental, must have echoed persuasively with a Christian audience predisposed to stories of exile from Eden. Far more than a legal strategy, originalism oriented The Rutherford Institute and its constituency toward a fixed point in time when all was right with the world. Legal literalism had ready allure. As one scholar suggests, in such a worldview the "originary moments become . . . transhistorical, giving the texts produced in that moment a timeless, authentic, and authoritative meaning."[17] Originalism offers the possibility of arresting both time and history, readily nourishing a worldview where truth is unified, not relative, and where those who possess the truth will ultimately determine the outcome over against those who do not.

17. Vincent Crapanzo, *Serving the Word: Literalism in America from the Pulpit to the Bench* (New York: New Press, 2000), xxv.

The possibility of stopping or even reversing history must have appealed broadly to The Rutherford Institute's supporters, a conservative Christian constituency to whom recent history had not — in this telling of the story — been at all kind. As such, originalism could help rally the troops, facilitate nostalgia, and perhaps boost the spirits of those living amid social upheavals and judicial uncertainty.[18] Originalists put forward "a tale of decadence, or hermeneutic corrosion" that at the same time offered an authoritative source of truth, one that purportedly stood independent of personal prejudices.[19] Originalism helped to identify the enemy for religious conservatives, to explain why their beliefs seemed so publicly devalued, to reassure them that this should not be the case, and to provide a map to guide their return to paradise. In other words, originalism did more than place The Rutherford Institute behind a particular constitutional understanding; it also reinforced rhetorically a particular, familiar way of thinking about texts and history for both the organization and its acolytes.

1.3. Religion as Free Speech

According to Vincent Crapanzo, originalists extend influence "less through direct accomplishment — the overturning of a decision they find obnoxious — than by indirection: by forcing their opponents to frame a problem in their terms."[20] Organizations such as TRI did have some measurable success in reframing church-state issues in the last years of the twentieth century. Having watched the U.S. Supreme Court repeatedly reject an originalist, accommodationist understanding of the First Amendment in favor of strict separation,[21] conservatives adopted a savvy strategy. If the free exercise and establishment clauses offered no relief, perhaps the courts

---

18. Indeed, a declension narrative that engenders outrage against current conditions may primarily function not as a spur to action but as a mechanism for adjustment. Ann Burlein suggests that "Mobilizing people through a politics that protests the loss of a past that is already going, going, gone works less to help people assert power over abstract structures that shape their lives and their children's futures and more to help people live with the structures they protest"; Ann Burlein, *Lift High the Cross: Where White Supremacy and the Christian Right Converge* (Durham, N.C.: Duke University Press, 2001), 29.

19. Crapanzo, *Serving the Word,* 254.

20. Crapanzo, *Serving the Word,* xviii.

21. Whether or not this was an accurate description of the Court's activity, this certainly was the impression of religious conservatives. For details, see chapter 1.

could be persuaded to allow religion more room to breathe if it considered religion to be another form of speech.

Christian legal organizations like The Rutherford Institute were not the first ones to import the religion-as-speech argument into the courts.[22] But after groups like TRI appeared, Steven Brown has argued, they succeeded in the "forging of a new jurisprudential relationship between the free speech clause and religion."[23] Such a move allowed TRI and others not only to rely upon a wider body of case law, but also to appeal to notions of antidiscrimination and fairness — values that had become an important part of twentieth-century American society in general, and its jurisprudence in particular.[24]

This strategy had deliciously ironic consequences for religious conservatives, who had watched in horror as the U.S. Supreme Court, with the prompting of liberal special-interest groups, extended constitutional protections to obscenity, pornography, and flag burning. Now they used the same tactics against their liberal enemies, carving out more space for religious freedom with the very same free-speech rationale. As the leader of the Liberty Counsel explained, "What I am fighting for in the 1990s is what civil rights attorneys were fighting for in the 1960s."[25] Turning the tables on those civil libertarians whose very success in the 1960s and 1970s had motivated Christian conservatives to publicly reassert themselves in the first place, TRI joined others in pushing the courts to consider religion as a form of speech. In fact, in one scholar's judgment, Whitehead and TRI pioneered in using this tactic.[26]

22. One could trace this line of thinking to the 1940s: see *Murdock v. Pennsylvania*, 319 U.S. 105 (1943), in which the Court's majority claimed that distributing religious literature door-to-door not only deserved the same First Amendment protection as preaching from the pulpit, but it "also has the same claim . . . to the guarantees of freedom of speech and freedom of the press" (109).

23. Brown, *Trumping Religion*, 47.

24. For an early discussion of the increasing importance of equality and neutrality in judicial decision making, see Mark DeWolfe Howe, *The Garden and the Wilderness: Religion and Government in American Constitutional History* (Chicago: University of Chicago Press, 1965), esp. chapter 5, "Race, Religion, and Education." For a recent exploration of this development as it has affected religion, see Steven D. Smith, *Getting over Equality: A Critical Diagnosis of Religious Freedom in America* (New York: New York University Press, 2001).

25. Quoted in Moore, "The Lord's Litigators."

26. Brown, *Trumping Religion*, 35. Brown provides as evidence of TRI's trailblazing the Virginia license plate case; see chapter 3, note 99. But TRI explicitly used such an ar-

The religion-as-speech argument succeeded in several late twentieth-century Supreme Court decisions, something that no doubt encouraged TRI and other similarly minded groups to continue pressing this rationale.[27] In fact, those organizations contributed to a "highly successful string of precedent-setting cases in which free speech arguments have successfully warded off traditional establishment clause concerns regarding state-sponsored recognition or acknowledgement of religion."[28] Brown has shown that this strategy afforded Christian legal organizations the bulk of their victories from 1980 to 2000. In the lower federal courts, for example, during that period they prevailed in twenty-nine of the forty-five cases in which they raised the religion-as-speech argument. Although barely better than a 50 percent success rate, those victories accounted for nearly two-thirds of their total victories. Thus, Brown has concluded, Christian legal advocacy achieved "consistent success *only* when it has turned to the free speech clause."[29]

As detailed in chapter 4, The Rutherford Institute represented one vigorous proponent of this line of thinking, insisting on religion-as-speech in several amicus curiae briefs and other institute materials. Given this, even though they were not the attorneys of record in any critical Supreme Court cases,[30] TRI's advocates could be said to have shared in these suc-

---

gument at least as early as 1986 and hinted at it even earlier; see chapter 4. In most of these instances TRI filed as an amicus curiae; in terms of direct and visible success, Jay Sekulow and the ACLJ have used this strategy to greater effect.

27. Examples include *Widmar v. Vincent*, 454 U.S. 263 (1981) (that a University of Missouri student group was religious did not give the school the right to prevent it from using school facilities); *Board of Education of the Westside Community Schools v. Mergens*, 496 U.S. 226 (1990); and *Lamb's Chapel v. Center Moriches School District*, 113 S. Ct. 2141 (1993).

28. Brown, *Trumping Religion*, 84.

29. Brown, *Trumping Religion*, 78, my emphasis. Brown reached his conclusion by examining the federal court activities of five religious advocacy groups: TRI, American Center for Law and Justice (ACLJ), Alliance Defense Fund (ADF), Center for Law and Religious Freedom, and Liberty Counsel. These figures are his; see especially chapter 6, "Pathbreakers and Gatekeepers: The Lower Federal Court Response to the New Christian Right," which includes helpful charts detailing the extent and kind of each organization's participation.

30. TRI rejected an opportunity to participate in what became arguably the biggest victory for the religion-as-speech forces, *Rosenberger v. Virginia*, in 1995. TRI both declined a direct request for assistance from Rosenberger himself and refrained from filing an amicus brief in the case. This may have been purely for financial reasons, as TRI may have been unwilling to risk the cost associated with pursuing such a case.

TRI served as counsel of record in only one case before the Supreme Court: *Frazee*

cesses. From 1980 to 2000, in fact, TRI was the most active religiously motivated advocate in the lower federal courts, participating in twenty-seven cases total, nineteen in which it was the primary sponsor and eight in which it filed amicus curiae briefs.[31] In those twenty-seven cases, its position prevailed eleven times.[32] As the first and most energetic advocate among other religiously conservative legal groups, TRI could claim at least some of the credit for those victories achieved by pushing the religion-as-speech argument.

Throughout its first two decades TRI seemed either oblivious or indifferent to the potentially negative consequences engendered by the religion-as-speech rationale. Even in success, organizations such as TRI "also necessarily stretched that clause to protect other forms of speech that may in fact be anathema to many of their conservative Christian supporters."[33] According to some, treating religion as one form of free speech effectively "reduced" it to the level of other forms of speech protected under the First Amendment — pornography, obscenity, the burning of flags and crosses. Support may have plummeted when TRI took on the Paula Jones case, but imagine the precipitous decline in donations if a fund-raising letter had proclaimed, "The Rutherford Institute: Defending Your Religious Liberty by Equating It with Pornography."[34] Cognizant of its legal potential, religiously conservative legal advocates seemed to deny or ignore the possibility that there may have been both a theological and a constitutional price to pay in making this strategic move.

---

v. *Illinois Department of Employment Security*, 489 U.S. 829 (1989). The religion-as-speech argument was not relevant. In a 9-0 decision, the Court ruled in favor of William Frazee, who claimed his personal religious beliefs (untethered to any particular tradition) prevented him from working on Sunday.

31. Brown, *Trumping Religion*, 87-119. If current trends continue, however, this will soon change. The ACLJ participated in just two fewer cases than TRI, despite TRI having had a ten-year head start, and the even younger ADF sponsored nineteen cases. And in 2000 both the ACLJ and the ADF had budgets twice the size of TRI's.

32. Brown's statistics do not allow for breaking down these decisions by rationale, but as my analysis in chapter 4 shows, at least some of those victories pressed a religion-as-speech rationale.

33. Brown, *Trumping Religion*, 10.

34. In one instance Whitehead actually did equate religious faith with pornography to make the opposite point, that religion did *not* belong on the same level: "Christianity has become the pornography of the 90's — something to indulge in privately, but never to practice publicly and surely not in front of the children." See John W. Whitehead, *Engaging the Culture* (Charlottesville, Va.: The Rutherford Institute, 1993), 1.

Whitehead certainly had been aware that the religion-as-speech argument created some very strange bedfellows, but he explained that this was unavoidable. In his 1995 booklet *Politically Correct: Censorship in American Culture,* he argued — in the words of a section title — that Christians must "Support Freedom of Expression for All." Some of his readers "hold as one-sided a view of the First Amendment as do PC adherents," the author chastised. "They want to suppress the expression of ideas inimical to Christianity." However, he continued, "This tendency to control the speech of others is as wrong for Christians as it is for non-Christians. To ensure their own freedom of speech, Christians must vigorously support the right of others to express opposing views." Whitehead hastened to distinguish between the general support of free speech and an endorsement of that speech in all its forms. Standing up for free speech "does not mean that pornography or fighting words should be defended," he insisted. "But it does mean that Christians should be the first to support a free marketplace of ideas. After all, the Christian message *is* truth and the free marketplace of ideas is where truth will flourish."[35] Only by standing for general principle, then, would his readers preserve their particular Christian beliefs and the right to express them publicly. Sleeping among strange bedfellows was the price to be paid for being allowed to sleep safely at all. And, in the end, Whitehead remained confident that his truth would prevail over all other pretenders if given a fair chance.

TRI's equation of religion with other forms of speech had more critical, potentially negative consequences in the legal realm. On the surface this pragmatic hermeneutical strategy had much to recommend it. Twentieth-century justices who rejected the proper accommodationist understanding of the First Amendment's religion clauses might nevertheless comfortably render the same "correct" decisions if they could rely upon notions of equality or neutrality. Steven D. Smith has asserted that "as a historical matter the language of equality and neutrality *has* provided the dominant vocabulary by which religious pluralism has worked itself out."[36] Whitehead invoked the notion of fairness in 1994, claiming that "Our goal is very simple. Religious people should be treated equally in our society."[37] Religion-as-speech not only provided the opportunity for judges to find in

---

35. John W. Whitehead, *Politically Correct: Censorship in American Culture,* Faith and Freedom series (Chicago: Moody Press, 1995), 47.

36. Smith, *Getting over Equality,* 25, author's emphasis.

37. Quoted in Moore, "The Lord's Litigators."

favor of religious beliefs and practices by relying upon seemingly more "democratic" or "fair" principles, it also had the benefit of keeping the courts from determining the nature or authenticity of those beliefs and practices. Treating religion as free speech could still constitutionally protect religion, "but without the invidious difficulties that arise from approaching it as religion."[38] In terms of gaining the outcomes demanded by TRI's originalist hermeneutic, then, the religion-as-speech argument could be employed effectively.

However, this strategy directly contradicted the overall constitutional originalism TRI frequently pushed forward. Whitehead and his organization's advocates had consistently argued that, in the First Amendment, the nation's founders had deliberately set apart religion in order to acknowledge — and approve — its critical cultural importance. The religion-as-speech argument stripped religion of the very constitutional uniqueness it often urged the courts to recognize. Justice Byron White made this observation in *Widmar v. Vincent,* a case decided in 1981 (a year before Whitehead founded The Rutherford Institute). Although the winning side had argued successfully that "religious worship qua speech is not different from any other variety of protected speech as a matter of constitutional principle," White dissented. "I believe that this proposition is plainly wrong," he wrote. "Were it right, the Religion Clauses would be emptied of any independent meaning in circumstances in which religious practice took the form of speech."[39]

More recently, several scholars echoed White's insistence that treating religion as speech misinterprets the First Amendment, especially when considered in light of the founders' intentions. Derek Davis has concluded that "the Founding Fathers believed that religious speech is different from mere speech," and in authoring the First Amendment, "they could scarcely

---

38. John T. Noonan, Jr., *The Lustre of Our Country: The American Experience of Religious Freedom* (Berkeley: University of California Press, 1998), 207. These words are put in the mouth of "John Henry Newman," an imaginary interlocutor in a dialogue on the current state of religious freedom. Newman quickly rejects this argument, however, as explained below.

39. *Widmar v. Vincent,* 284. White argued that the Court must distinguish religious forms of speech from others; indeed, without making such a distinction, its injunctions against requiring religious oaths for office, official school prayer, or the posting of the Ten Commandments in public school classrooms would have no justification. White wrote that "as a speech act, apart from its content, a prayer is indistinguishable from a biology lesson" (285).

have done more to make the point."[40] In *The Lustre of Our Country,* John T. Noonan, Jr., enabled an imaginary interlocutor, "John Henry, sometimes called 'Newman,'" to make a similar point. He argued that

> Religion is speech sui generis. It is attempted communication with God and the report of what God requires. It has been singled out by the Constitution for special protections. That special status reflects the belief of Madison and other makers of the Constitution that the human obligation to God is different from all other human obligations. To allow that acknowledgment of the claims of conscience to lapse into desuetude would be to abandon a precious portion of the Bill of Rights. I would look the Free Speech gift-horse in the mouth and reject it with mixed feelings of regret and pride.[41]

Winnifred Fallers Sullivan has agreed with "Newman," suggesting that equating religion with other forms of speech prompts the question, "do we need the religion clauses of the First Amendment?" Answering no to this question, Sullivan argues, is at the very least not faithful to the nation's history. "Religion is different," she asserts, "or so most Americans have thought." To privilege free speech and neutrality is to participate in "an ahistorical, post-Christian, postmodern, relativist approach to religion that is strongly at odds with both the stated political goals of religious activists and with American religious history." To equate religion with other forms of speech "accommodates religion by emasculating it and denying its power, both constructive and destructive. On this view, religion no longer makes the difference that Madison and Jefferson thought it made. If religion is understood as just a benign point of view that some people happen to have, then by implication religion is harmless, a meaningless difference. It becomes simply a brand name, or a political party, or a Hallmark card sentiment. To take this approach is dangerously ignorant."[42] If this analysis

40. Derek H. Davis, "Equal Treatment: A Christian Separationist Perspective," in *Equal Treatment of Religion in a Pluralistic Society,* ed. Stephen V. Monsma and J. Christopher Soper (Grand Rapids: Eerdmans, 1998), 141.

41. Noonan, *Lustre of Our Country,* 208. In this imagined conversation, Noonan seems to have the most affection for Newman and his perspective.

42. Winnifred Fallers Sullivan, "The Difference Religion Makes: Reflections on *Rosenberger,*" *Christian Century,* 13 Mar. 1996. See also Brown, *Trumping Religion,* who argues that "in considering religion and religious practices as a mere viewpoint, it is dislodged from its lofty dwelling with the divine and placed squarely within the baser realm

is correct, Whitehead and others who favored the religion-as-speech argument essentially endorsed the judicial departure from original intent that had prompted their legal activism in the first place. Based upon its own understanding of constitutional history, TRI consistently insisted that the founders had treated religion separately for a reason — something that subsuming religion under the free speech clause of the First Amendment would seem to disown. But as the religion-as-speech argument indicated, to preserve religion's historical importance in American culture TRI sometimes denied that very history.[43] In endorsing an originalist understanding of church-state relations, then, TRI directly flouted the founders' desire to preserve religion's singular importance.

Whether aware or not of this intellectual contradiction,[44] TRI's advocates might have argued that the end justified the means. After all, in trying to secure a winning majority of justices, lawyers often offer multiple reasons in the hopes that judges will find one they like. Those reasons may be mutually contradictory, constituting what one scholar has described as "a strange mixture of legal pragmatism and faith."[45] But if the outcome is favorable, where is the harm? Religious conservatives, in other words, might not have blanched at implicitly denying the founders' wishes in the service of achieving results that nevertheless faithfully manifested those intentions. From this perspective, critiques such as those of Noonan and Sullivan, however accurate, might be dismissed as academic parlor games, more aesthetic than useful. Effective lawyers cannot fairly be judged by the overall intellectual coherence of their arguments, these advocates might fairly contend. Results, not reasons, matter most.[46]

A parallel argument could be offered to counter charges of theological inconsistency. Those TRI supporters who might naturally recoil from the strategic equation of religious belief and pornography might be mollified

---

of politics where it is made subject to legislative wrangling, executive caprice, and ultimately adjudication by human judges" (143).

43. As Sullivan summarized, "To efface difference is to forget history."

44. Although Whitehead noted the strange bedfellows created by the religion-as-speech argument, nowhere in his books or articles did he indicate an awareness of how that argument might appear to deny the constitutional uniqueness of religion.

45. Brown, *Trumping Religion,* 139.

46. It is also important to distinguish between an overall coherence of principle and the microcosmic characteristics of a particular case. In responding to specific facts and specific opinions in specific instances, lawyers may be constrained in ways that, although apparently incongruent with a coherent, overall approach, are nevertheless appropriate and effective for a particular case.

by a similar means-ends analysis. TRI existed not just to achieve legal goals but also to preserve and spread the Christian gospel. Whitehead might have noted that believers cannot continue to preach their Christian message if religion's sphere of activity remained restricted. To maintain its integrity and influence, faith must be protected; indeed, if it has a fair chance in the marketplace of ideas, one could be confident that faith would not only be protected, it would thrive. From this perspective, there was no shame in preserving Christian liberty through pragmatic means if heaven became more crowded as a result.

However plausible and reasonable such imagined rejoinders might seem, other larger, potentially more significant compromises came with adopting the religion-as-speech strategy.[47] First, that tactic may have very real practical limitations. One scholar has contended that "the free speech clause can never be an effective long-term ally of the New Christian Right": some cases ill fit this hermeneutical template, and the key victories already won by virtue of this argument pertained almost exclusively to educational settings.[48] Certainly The Rutherford Institute always highlighted the critical, worldview-forming role of public schools, but this was not an exclusive interest. If the religion-as-speech strategy worked infrequently in other cases, then comprehensive, long-term success might depend upon developing other persuasive tactics.

Second, arguing that religion should be treated equally because it is merely another form of protected speech may actually provide justification for many decisions that would cancel out any free-exercise victories. If religion truly does not differ from any other form of expression, little reason remains for the government to treat religious institutions as somehow special. If the religion-as-speech argument is pursued to its logical end, Derek Davis argues, then "no valid reason remains for exempting churches and religious organizations from tax requirements or government regulations." Nor would there any longer be justification for allowing churches to discriminate in hiring practices or for religious schools to teach an unregulated curriculum. "Equal treatment," Davis has concluded, "could become the Pandora's box that drives government regulation and government interference every bit as much in the sanctuary as it does in other places in soci-

47. It should be noted that these possible critiques did not noticeably affect The Rutherford Institute. Whitehead's own writings and TRI's materials did not indicate that anyone ever raised theological objections to the religion-as-speech tactic, much less that TRI agreed with any of these imagined responses.

48. Brown, *Trumping Religion,* 142.

ety."[49] Treating religion "equally" in this way may indeed create more room for religious expression in public, but it also risks making majoritarian standards override particular religious ones.

This religion-as-speech strategy also formed part of a wider secularization of the Christian conservative movement in the late twentieth century. Having viewed the success of African Americans, women, and homosexuals in raising issues of fairness and discrimination both in society and in the courts, conservative Christians adopted a similar tactic to justify their political activism. Some evangelicals and fundamentalists claimed that they, too, constituted a persecuted minority, one unfairly denied the right to participate fully in politics.

As with the parallel religion-as-speech argument, this political strategy met with some success. But, similarly, conservative Christians made their case in rhetorically secular terms, engendering similar and presumably negative consequences. Analyzing the New Christian Right, Steve Bruce has argued that "adopting some of the rhetoric of the modern pluralistic liberal society is self-defeating because it is asking to be judged by the rules of a game in which religious orthodoxy is an irrelevance."[50] In macrocosm, then, conservative Christians committed the same tactical error in politics that The Rutherford Institute and others committed in the legal realm. Adopting antidiscrimination language, conservative Christian legal advocates may, in the short term, have succeeded in hoisting liberal proponents of equality on their own petards. However, in the long run Christians may not have been reframing a secularist discourse; the discourse may have been reframing them.

2. The Rutherford Institute in Context

This analysis of The Rutherford Institute's legal arguments raises questions about its ability to achieve long-term success. Despite noteworthy support for reversing incorporation, Whitehead and his fellow advocates chose not to press the courts to do so. In adopting its most immediately successful legal tactic — treating religion as a form of constitutionally pro-

---

49. Davis, "Equal Treatment," 156.

50. Steve Bruce, *The Rise and Fall of the New Christian Right: Conservative Protestant Politics in America, 1978-1988* (New York: Oxford University Press, 1988), 125.

tected speech — TRI forsook the hermeneutical originalism that seemed to propel much of its advocacy. All the while pushing to get the "octogovernment" out of people's lives, TRI extended antidiscrimination language many times to argue that the government's enormous size demanded that religion be granted more cultural room to breathe in order to remain faithful to the founders' intentions. But in doing so, TRI may have unwittingly undermined its mission by reinforcing rather than razing the state's secularist superstructure.

However, there are other ways to measure TRI's success. Having made some legal compromises with little detectable anguish, Whitehead nevertheless seemed wary of other dangers that could threaten his organization's mission and method. One such peril, in Whitehead's estimation, was the potential loss of TRI's independence. When Whitehead created TRI in 1982, he and his organization had much of the terrain to themselves. But in the early 1990s other conservative Christians sought to perform similar legal advocacy work, inevitably raising questions about the utility of combining efforts. Despite the fact that some of TRI's supporters urged consolidation, Whitehead resisted any alliances with apparent theological and legal soul mates.[51] Staunchly maintaining TRI's autonomy, Whitehead signaled clearly that any compromises he might make in court would not be matched by organizational compromises that might restrict his own freedom. TRI's success could certainly be measured in legal terms, but for Whitehead success also meant maintaining TRI's organizational and financial independence in an increasingly crowded, competitive legal marketplace.

At times Whitehead went to great lengths to preserve his organization's sovereignty. In the 1990s two governmental directives gained support from a wide range of religious advocacy groups — but not from The Rutherford Institute. The Religious Freedom Restoration Act (RFRA), passed by Congress in 1993, had been endorsed by perhaps the broadest coalition of religious groups — liberal and conservative — in American history. However, in an article in the *Washburn Law Journal*, Whitehead explained that he had "important reservations . . . about resorting to majoritarian remedies such as RFRA, at either the state or federal level, to protect or create religious rights."[52] The second, President Clinton's directive on religion in the public schools, had been issued by the Department of

51. See chapter 3.
52. John W. Whitehead, "Religious Freedom in the Nineties: Betwixt and between *Flores* and *Smith*," *Washburn Law Journal* 37 (1997): 112.

Education in 1995 with a similarly broad base of support. But TRI again held its applause. One observer noted that "Not only did the Institute not join this laudable effort, they attacked it."[53] Opposing these broadly popular measures hardly endeared TRI to religious conservatives; indeed, such singular public stances led one observer to conclude that TRI "has long been viewed as the black sheep of the New Christian Right legal family."[54]

This deliberate organizational standoffishness occasionally came with a significant price. When Ronald Rosenberger needed help suing the University of Virginia, he first contacted TRI, who declined to represent him. He then turned to lawyers connected with the recently created Alliance Defense Fund (ADF), which supported him in what became one of the most significant church-state cases of the 1990s. The ADF consequently featured Rosenberger's victory — presumably to good effect — in its fund-raising materials.[55] TRI, meanwhile, had refused even to file an amicus brief in the case. Whitehead's organization willingly paid whatever price this deliberate lone-wolf behavior required, it claimed, so that it might remain free to pursue cases of its own choosing in whatever fashion it deemed appropriate. Independence trumped most other concerns; as Whitehead himself admitted, "We don't like holding hands. It gets all sweaty."[56]

It was not just Whitehead's maverick streak that kept TRI from joining forces with other Christian legal organizations. By the 1990s TRI's ideology and practice had shifted just enough to make religious conservatives uncomfortable with the prospect of aligning themselves with Whitehead's operation. Although strongly influenced early in his career by Christian Reconstructionism, Whitehead publicly distanced himself in the 1990s from the more exclusivist elements of this theological worldview.[57] For example, in 1994 Whitehead voluntarily contrasted TRI's more ecumenical nature with the narrower mind-set of his competitors: of Pat Robertson, the ACLJ's founder, he asserted that "his goal is to Christianize America." In contrast, "We don't have any of that. We provide free legal aid for real peo-

53. Robert Boston, *Close Encounters with the Religious Right: Journeys into the Twilight Zone of Religion and Politics* (Amherst, N.Y.: Prometheus Books, 2000), 149.

54. Brown, *Trumping Religion*, 35.

55. Brown, *Trumping Religion*, 51, notes this missed opportunity.

56. Moore, "The Lord's Litigators."

57. He directly addressed and dismissed Reconstructionism in John W. Whitehead, *Religious Apartheid: The Separation of Religion from American Public Life* (Chicago: Moody Press, 1994); see above, chapter 3.

ple who need help."[58] A further sign that Whitehead wanted to soften his image: TRI stopped selling the quite strident book and movie *Religious Apartheid* in 1997. An interviewer the next year found him "clearly uncomfortable with the video."[59]

Over the course of its first two decades, The Rutherford Institute had incrementally widened its legal purview, morphing from a virtually exclusivist Christian organization driven by a crypto-Reconstructionist into an institution with a much broader agenda. By 2003 TRI's motto did not even mention religion, much less Christianity: instead, visitors to its Web site encountered an organization "Dedicated to the defense of civil liberties and human rights."[60] Areas of institutional concern included not just "Religious Freedom," "Church Rights," and "Sanctity of Life" — all readily identifiable as religious concerns — but also more secular topics such as "Free Speech," "Parents Rights," "Zero Tolerance," "Search & Seizure," "Sexual Harassment," "Death Penalty," and "International." Although religious motivation lay beneath the surface of these more generic concerns, a casual encounter with TRI provided no immediate indication that Christian faith remained the wellspring of its efforts.

This partial de-religiocification matched a wider trend among some conservative activists in the late twentieth century. After gaining political traction in the late 1970s and early 1980s, some Christian conservative leaders began to drop religious references from their organizational titles and promotional literature in order to smooth the way for broader political alliances.[61] They also attempted to shake loose the particularism of some rhetoric, as when, for example, "creationism" gave way to "creation science."[62] Among Christian legal organizations, TRI made the most intentional effort to broaden its legal and cultural boundaries. The Christian magazine *World* observed in 1998 a "kinder, gentler Whitehead"; since the 1980s Whitehead "has muted his positions . . . and has begun to 'grow' po-

---

58. Quoted in Moore, "The Lord's Litigators."

59. Boston, *Close Encounters*, 153. The content of *Religious Apartheid* is discussed in chapter 3.

60. In early 2003, The Rutherford Institute's Web site could be found at http://rutherford.org.

61. See especially Matthew C. Moen, *The Transformation of the Christian Right* (Tuscaloosa: University of Alabama Press, 1992). An obvious and important exception to this was the Christian Coalition, founded in 1989 by Pat Robertson.

62. Bruce, *Rise and Fall*, 97. Bruce also points to the Creation Research Society's requirement that all members hold a degree in science.

litically." As evidence, *World* noted that only TRI among conservative legal organizations had defended gay men from sexual harassment in the workplace or resisted discrimination against an HIV-positive teenager.[63] Groups such as the ACLJ and the Liberty Counsel broadened their agendas slightly as they pressed religion-as-speech arguments, but only TRI included such matters as sexual harassment, random drug testing, zero-tolerance policies in public schools, and police search-and-seizure powers under its legal aegis.[64] Both in scope and in flexibility, The Rutherford Institute continued to be an institutional breed apart.

Critics still found reason to question the authenticity of the "new, improved" Whitehead. TRI's expanded interests may have signaled a more "mature" understanding of individual liberties and their interconnections; viewed from a different angle, this purported ideological evolution could instead be seen as the surreptitious strategy of an organization increasingly outflanked by competitors and thirsty for new funds. Whitehead's adoption of Paula Jones's cause in 1997 reeked of desperation and publicity mongering. Notwithstanding the publication of Whitehead's *Women's Rights and the Law* the year before, sexual harassment still remained far, far afield from TRI's core concerns. Whitehead could point to a long record of helping individuals resist the government's oppressive power, but it was still a stretch to pour the very personal drama of *Jones v. Clinton* into that mold.

Ironically it was this grand leap outside The Rutherford Institute's customary purview that most cemented public perceptions of Whitehead as the leader of a far-right Christian organization. For many observers, Whitehead's appearance at Jones's side confirmed his status as a leading player in the "vast right-wing conspiracy" Hillary Rodham Clinton had claimed was out to get her husband.[65] Whitehead later insisted, "There ain't no vast right-wing conspiracy. That's a joke. First, I'm not right-wing."[66] But a quick scan of his publications provided ample proof that TRI's founder had more than a few antidemocratic, antigovernment ten-

---

63. Chris Stamper, "A Surreal Legal Thriller: Jones Case Hero Whitehead Has Eclectic Tastes," *World,* 28 Nov. 1998.

64. This began to change slightly after the terrorist attacks of 11 Sept. 2001. As Attorney General John Ashcroft — former senator and Pentecostal, customarily an ally of conservative Christians — sought more governmental power to track American citizens, other Christian legal organizations joined TRI in protesting this development.

65. Hillary Rodham Clinton made her infamous statement on NBC's *Today Show,* 27 Jan. 1998, in an interview with Matt Lauer.

66. Quoted in Stamper, "A Surreal Legal Thriller."

dencies. And when his autobiography, *Slaying Dragons*, appeared in 1999, Whitehead linked the Jones case directly with the cause of Christ. Critics could marshal ample evidence to argue that Whitehead and TRI wanted much more than simple justice for a wronged woman.

While impossible for The Rutherford Institute to shake its conservative Christian connections — something it never explicitly sought to do — this stark portrait painted by Whitehead's enemies should have been more complex. In addition to his self-imposed distance from other Christian legal organizations, Whitehead also claimed that Clinton had been a friend for religious freedom, that the death penalty was wrong, and that Jesus Christ would not have shunned homosexuals — all heterodox positions for most Christian-right leaders involved in legal advocacy. In surveying conservative Christian organizations, most public commentators agreed with a lawyer for the Council on Religious Freedom, a separationist group, who a few years earlier claimed of all such organizations, "When you scratch the surface, what they really believe is that this is a Christian nation."[67] But lumping Whitehead and TRI in with others obscured important strategic, ideological, and teleological gradations. To those who bothered to look carefully, a more complicated picture existed, one that intimated a repudiation of Christian exclusivism.[68] In 2000 a longtime staffer at TRI's most vigilant and vehement opponent, Americans United for the Separation of Church and State, confessed: "If I had to be trapped in an elevator for three hours with the Religious Right figure of my choosing, I'd pick Whitehead. He is at least interesting to talk to and speaks with passion."[69] Regrettably, few in the media noticed, much less highlighted, these complexities.[70]

Indeed, as Whitehead and TRI became more difficult to categorize, fellow conservative Christians did not always approve. In a profile of Whitehead, one conservative Christian weekly described "a bohemian side you don't see in the courtroom."[71] Institute publications began to reflect some concern among its supporters at the blurring of once-clear political

67. Lee Boothby, quoted in Moore, "The Lord's Litigators."

68. Whitehead's early publications demonstrated clearly the strong influence of Christian Reconstructionism; see chapter 2.

69. Boston, *Close Encounters*, 163.

70. See Nat Hentoff, "A Conspirator for the Constitution," *Washington Post*, 5 June 1999, A21, for one of the few balanced media considerations of Whitehead and TRI. Ian Brodie, "Jones Case Catapults Christian Lawyers into the Big Time," *The Times*, 27 Jan. 1998, also provided a more nuanced, if briefer, assessment.

71. Stamper, "A Surreal Legal Thriller."

boundaries: many subscribers to *Rutherford* protested Whitehead's inter-
views with gay activists and disdained his rhetorical riffs on 1960s protest
music. (As a result, TRI eventually created an institutional firewall separating cultural interests from legal endeavors.)[72] Whitehead certainly remained aware, even proud, of his pariah status, telling a reporter in the late
1990s that "I'm getting as many attacks from the Right now as I ever got on
the left."[73] He and his organization pointed to this as proof of TRI's organizational independence and of its carefully cultivated distinction between it
and other conservative Christian advocates. Whitehead was "especially
blunt about those that would use the law to 'Christianize' America," according to one observer. With groups like the ACLJ undoubtedly in mind,
Whitehead averred: "If you don't want others ramming their views down
your throat, you can't ram your views down theirs. . . . Our agenda is not to
have a Christian nation, but to enable religious people to survive."[74]

If success in a complicated, competitive landscape meant persever-
ance while preserving institutional independence, TRI certainly succeeded.
More than others, Whitehead may have recognized and therefore refused
the compromises that inevitably come with joining even the most like-
minded of coalitions. Analyses of the New Christian Right have suggested
that as the movement sought more political success, it inevitably was
forced to play down the distinctive ideological elements that defined its activism in the first place. Steve Bruce concluded in 1988 that "the conditions
for expanding the movement are also conditions which weaken its core." In
the late twentieth century, making alliances inevitably required the
compartmentalization of distinctiveness — a signal feature of modernity,
according to Bruce. But as conservative Christians muted their most divi-

72. TRI's publications took on many different forms over time; see chapter 3,
n. 87. Earlier publications combined legal news and information with pop-culture fea-
tures, but in the late 1990s TRI completely separated the cultural (the bimonthly *Gadfly*)
from the specifically legal (the *Religious Liberty Bulletin*).

73. Quoted in Boston, *Close Encounters,* 156.

74. Brown, *Trumping Religion,* 35. This statement directly echoed Ed Dobson's defense of the Moral Majority's intentions: "The Moral Majority was founded as a reaction
against a secular society that was increasingly hostile to conservative Christians. Christians believed that they were an oppressed minority and that if they did not stand up,
they would be buried by the secularists and the humanists. The Moral Majority . . . was a
fortress to protect, not a battleship to attack. We were not interested in taking over
America. We were only interested in making sure we did not get overtaken"; Cal Thomas
and Ed Dobson, *Blinded by Might: Can the Religious Right Save America?* (Grand Rapids:
Zondervan, 1999), 36.

sive characteristics in order to make common cause with others, they risked losing much of their core identity in the process. Bruce concluded that "the very limited successes enjoyed by the movement have been won at the cost of submitting to modernity and abandoning the ethos of orthodox separatism which has been characteristic of fundamentalism."[75]

In the 1990s, conservative Christian leaders publicly reassessed the wisdom of political activism, a heated debate sparked in part because of the inevitable concessions politics seemed to require. In the legal genus of this larger conservative Christian species, Whitehead and TRI had to wrestle with similar concerns about compromising their integrity of vision. Avoiding cooperation, however, meant that TRI had no personal stake in this wider debate — its independence immunized it against this kind of corruption. Like Roger Williams, the self-proclaimed "Seeker" who eventually concluded that theological purity demanded his individual spiritual independence from all denominations, Whitehead remained zealously separatist, hermetically sealed off from infection by even the most like-minded of others. Although critics at both ideological poles often viewed this as mere stubbornness, TRI's institutional misanthropy prevented the compartmentalization to which the wider conservative Christian movement fell victim. Viewed in this light, Whitehead — forever unwilling to compromise The Rutherford Institute's theological or strategic independence — may have demonstrated, via his recalcitrance, some valuable prescience.

In pointing to the power of the federal courts in shaping American culture, Whitehead also demonstrated notable foresight. Although many had rued specific Supreme Court decisions such as *Engel v. Vitale* (1962) and *Roe v. Wade* (1973), few conservatives — religious or not — had marshaled a comprehensive critique of the role judges had played in creating late twentieth-century social conditions. Much less did others provide a strategy for solving the problem. By the mid-1980s Whitehead had over a half-dozen books, an article in a law journal, and a nonprofit organization to his credit, all devoted to educating the public and confronting the crisis directly. Soon copied and in many ways superseded, Whitehead and TRI could still fairly claim pioneer status.

One noteworthy example highlighted the "early" nature of White-

75. Bruce, *Rise and Fall,* 127, 92-93. Reflecting in 1999, former Moral Majority director of communications Cal Thomas complained about just this facet of modernity reproducing itself at the individual level: "Too often believers treat their faith as just one of the many things competing for their attention. They take it seriously, but it is compartmentalized"; Thomas and Dobson, *Blinded by Might,* 144.

head's arrival. In November 1996 the conservative monthly *First Things* suggested that America had experienced "the end of democracy" because of the "judicial usurpation of politics." According to the editors, "What is happening now is the displacement of a constitutional order by a regime that does not have, will not obtain, and cannot command the consent of the people." Indeed, they stated that the situation had become so dire that it was appropriate to ask "whether we have reached or are reaching the point where conscientious citizens can no longer give moral assent to the existing regime."[76] One appropriate response — if current trends continued — might even be "morally justified revolution."[77] The symposium and the ensuing controversy gained widespread public attention . . . *fourteen years* after Whitehead had accused Supreme Court justices of attempting to steal America (*The Stealing of America,* 1983). Part of the *First Things* controversy stemmed from comparing the moral illegitimacy of the current American state to that of Nazi Germany . . . a full *twenty years* after Whitehead had made the same inflammatory comparison. This is not to say that Whitehead was first in line for complaining about the judicial hijacking of American culture.[78] But Whitehead had joined the game near the beginning and, especially for his grassroots Christian supporters, was likely the first to frame these important issues.

*   *   *

Before the 1980s, legal advocacy groups did not reflect the worldview or interests of religious conservatives. Hence, in entering the courts The Rutherford Institute filled a vacuum, creating a counterbalance to already active liberal organizations that could contend for alternative legal and cultural outcomes. The threat to individual religious liberty, so amplified in

76. Richard John Neuhaus, ed., *The End of Democracy? The Judicial Usurpation of Politics; The Celebrated* First Things *Debate with Arguments Pro and Con* (Dallas: Spence Publishing, 1997), 3.

77. Neuhaus, *The End of Democracy?* 3, 8. The entire symposium, along with published responses and articles in other periodicals, was collected in this volume.

78. Raoul Berger, *Government by Judiciary: The Transformation of the Fourteenth Amendment,* 2nd ed. (Indianapolis: Liberty Fund, 1997), first published in 1977, laid out this argument in much more lucid, exhaustive detail. And in response to the 1996 symposium, *Commentary* editor Norman Podhoretz noted that "Far from having discovered this threat, *First Things* has merely joined in a clamor over the imperial judiciary that some of us have been raising for over twenty-five years"; Neuhaus, *The End of Democracy?* 101.

both Whitehead's own writings and TRI's materials, was not necessarily invented or even exaggerated. For instance, of seventeen free exercise claims before the Supreme Court between 1963 and 1990, only four succeeded. In the 1980s, appeals courts granted only twelve of ninety-seven free exercise claims. And a similarly small percentage of free exercise claims prevailed in a study of around one hundred cases before federal courts of appeal and state supreme courts.[79] Without TRI and other similar organizations — both conservative and liberal — the situation for religious liberty might have been even worse. Whitehead himself believed as much, suggesting in 2000 that although there was plenty more work to be done, "partly through our efforts, things have gotten better out there."[80]

However, there was a significant, little-acknowledged downside to filling this vacuum: in taking up once-empty space, The Rutherford Institute and its cohorts made it more difficult for everyone to move around. In an analysis of parachurch groups in 1981 — the year before Whitehead founded TRI — J. Alan Youngren complained of their "unchecked" and "extravagant proliferation." So many now existed, Youngren wrote, that "their effect is like that of the algae in the fish pond: when they have multiplied enough, everything around them will be killed off."[81] If this was true of parachurch groups in general, by century's end it was equally true of conservative Christian legal groups in particular. Beginning in 1982, The Rutherford Institute stood as a ready ally for religious citizens who found their liberties threatened, and it helped to ensure that a conservative Christian voice would be heard in the nation's highest courts. But having spawned both imitators and enemies, TRI soon came to be only one voice among a multitude of advocates in an increasingly clogged and competitive arena. By century's end the marketplace of ideas was a noisy and crowded place indeed. Through legal activism, John Whitehead and The Rutherford Institute simultaneously helped and hindered the ability of conservative Christian voices to be heard above the din.

79. Mark Tushnet, "The Rhetoric of Free Exercise Discourse," *Brigham Young University Law Review*, 1993, 121-22. Tushnet's data came from James E. Ryan, "*Smith* and the Religious Freedom Restoration Act: An Iconoclastic Assessment," *Virginia Law Review* 78 (1992): 1458-62, and Anthony A. Cavallo, "The Free Exercise of Religion: Is It Truly Free or Merely Convenient to the States?" (unpublished manuscript, Spring 1990, on file with the author).

80. Quoted in Boston, *Close Encounters*, 159.

81. J. Alan Youngren, "Parachurch Proliferation: Caught in Traffic," *Christianity Today*, 6 Nov. 1981.

Bibliography

Published Works

Ahlstrom, Sydney E. *A Religious History of the American People*. New Haven: Yale University Press, 1972.

Armey, Richard K. *The Freedom Revolution: The Republican House Majority Leader Tells Why Big Government Failed, Why Freedom Works, and How We Will Rebuild America*. Washington, D.C.: Regnery, 1995.

Augustine, Karen. "Interview." *Rutherford* 3, no. 1 (Jan. 1994): 12-13.

Baker, Peter. "Paula Jones Lawyers Ask to Quit Case: 'Fundamental Differences' Cited after Apparent Collapse of Settlement." *Washington Post*, 9 Sept. 1997, A1.

Banner, Lois W. "Religious Benevolence as Social Control: A Critique of an Interpretation." *Journal of American History* 50 (1973): 23-41.

Becker, Susan J. "Amicus Filings on the Rise." *Litigation News* 23, no. 1 (1998).

Bennett, Linda L. M. *Living with Leviathan: Americans Coming to Terms with Big Government*. Lawrence: University Press of Kansas, 1990.

Berger, Raoul. *Government by Judiciary: The Transformation of the Fourteenth Amendment*. 2nd ed. Indianapolis: Liberty Fund, 1997.

Boston, Robert. *Close Encounters with the Religious Right: Journeys into the Twilight Zone of Religion and Politics*. Amherst, N.Y.: Prometheus Books, 2000.

Branegan, Jay. "In Paula We Trust: With *Jones v. Clinton*, a Christian-Right Legal Group Makes Its Case." *Time*, 24 Nov. 1997, 54.

Brodie, Ian. "Jones Case Catapults Christian Lawyers into the Big Time." *The Times*, 27 Jan. 1998.

Brown, Steven P. *Trumping Religion: The New Christian Right, the Free Speech Clause, and the Courts.* Tuscaloosa: University of Alabama Press, 2002.

Bruce, Steve. *The Rise and Fall of the New Christian Right: Conservative Protestant Politics in America, 1978-1988.* New York: Oxford University Press, 1988.

Burlein, Ann. *Lift High the Cross: Where White Supremacy and the Christian Right Converge.* Durham, N.C.: Duke University Press, 2001.

Butler, Jon. *Awash in a Sea of Faith: Christianizing the American People.* Cambridge: Harvard University Press, 1990.

———. "Why Revolutionary America Wasn't a 'Christian Nation.'" In *Religion and the New Republic: Faith in the Founding of America,* edited by James H. Hutson, 187-202. Lanham, Md.: Rowman and Littlefield, 2000.

Carpenter, Joel A. *Revive Us Again: The Reawakening of American Fundamentalism.* New York: Oxford University Press, 1997.

Carwardine, Richard. *Evangelicals and Politics in Antebellum America.* Knoxville: University of Tennessee Press, 1997.

Clarkson, Frederick. "Radical Reconstruction." *In These Times* 22, no. 7 (1998): 16.

Colson, Charles. "What's Right about the Religious Right." *Christianity Today,* 6 Sept. 1999, 58.

Cord, Robert L. *The Separation of Church and State: Historical Fact and Current Fiction.* New York: Lambeth Press, 1982.

Covey, Frank M., Jr. "Amicus Curiae: Friend of the Court." *DePaul Law Review* 9 (1959-60).

Crapanzo, Vincent. *Serving the Word: Literalism in America from the Pulpit to the Bench.* New York: New Press, 2000.

Curry, Thomas J. *Farewell to Christendom: The Future of Church and State in America.* New York: Oxford University Press, 2001.

———. *The First Freedoms: Church and State in America to the Passage of the First Amendment.* New York: Oxford University Press, 1986.

Davis, Derek H. "Equal Treatment: A Christian Separationist Perspective." In *Equal Treatment of Religion in a Pluralistic Society,* edited by Stephen V. Monsma and J. Christopher Soper, 136-57. Grand Rapids: Eerdmans, 1998.

Diamond, Sara. *Not by Politics Alone: The Enduring Influence of the Christian Right.* New York: Guilford Press, 1998.

————. *Spiritual Warfare: The Politics of the Christian Right.* Boston: South End Press, 1989.

Dobson, James. "The New Cost of Discipleship." *Christianity Today,* 6 Sept. 1999, 56.

Dolan, Jay P. *The American Catholic Experience: A History from Colonial Times to the Present.* Notre Dame, Ind.: University of Notre Dame Press, 1985.

Dreisbach, Daniel L. *Real Threat and Mere Shadow: Religious Liberty and the First Amendment.* TRI Report 5. Westchester, Ill.: Crossway, 1987.

Ennis, Bruce J. "Symposium on Supreme Court Advocacy: Effective Amicus Briefs." *Catholic University Law Review* 33 (1984): 603-9.

Falwell, Jerry. "I'd Do It All Again." *Christianity Today,* 6 Sept. 1999, 50.

Findlay, James F., Jr. *Dwight L. Moody: American Evangelist, 1837-1899.* Chicago: University of Chicago Press, 1969.

Fowler, Robert Booth, and Allen D. Hertzke. *Religion and Politics in America: Faith, Culture, and Strategic Choices.* Boulder, Colo.: Westview, 1995.

Frady, Marshall. *Billy Graham: A Parable of American Righteousness.* Boston: Little, Brown, 1979.

Fraser, James W. *Between Church and State: Religion and Public Education in a Multicultural America.* New York: St. Martin's Press, 1999.

Gaustad, Edwin S., ed. *A Documentary History of Religion in America.* 2nd ed. Vol. 2. Grand Rapids: Eerdmans, 1993.

Gerlin, Andrea. "With Free Help, the Religious Turn Litigious." *Wall Street Journal,* 17 Feb. 1994, B1.

Gleick, Elizabeth. "Onward Christian Lawyers." *Time,* 13 Mar. 1995.

Grace, J. Peter. *The Problem of Big Government.* Bellevue, Wash.: Washington Institute for Policy Studies, 1998.

Graham, Billy. *Just as I Am: The Autobiography of Billy Graham.* San Francisco: HarperSanFrancisco, 1997.

Green, Steven K. "Of (Un)Equal Jurisprudential Pedigree: Rectifying the Imbalance between Neutrality and Separationism." *Boston College Law Review* 43 (Sept. 2002): 1111-37.

Handy, Robert T. *A Christian America: Protestant Hopes and Historical Realities.* New York: Oxford University Press, 1971.

————. *Undermined Establishment: Church-State Relations in America, 1880-1920.* Princeton: Princeton University Press, 1991.

Hartog, Hendrik. "The Constitution of Aspiration and 'the Rights That Belong to Us All.'" *Journal of American History* 74 (1987): 1013-74.

Harvey, Elizabeth A. "Casenote: *Freiler v. Tangipahoa Board of Education;* Squeeze the *Lemon* Test out of Establishment Clause Jurisprudence." *George Mason Law Review* 10 (2001): 299-320.

"Haunted by Scots Preacher." *Scotland on Sunday,* 25 Jan. 1998, 11.

Hedge, Scott A., ed. *Balancing America's Budget: Ending the Era of Big Government.* Washington, D.C.: Heritage Foundation, 1997.

Hentoff, Nat. "A Conspirator for the Constitution." *Washington Post,* 5 June 1999, A21.

Howe, Mark DeWolfe. *The Garden and the Wilderness: Religion and Government in American Constitutional History.* Chicago: University of Chicago Press, 1965.

Hutchison, William R. *The Modernist Impulse in American Protestantism.* Durham, N.C.: Duke University Press, 1992.

Hutson, James H., ed. *Religion and the New Republic: Faith in the Founding of America.* Lanham, Md.: Rowman and Littlefield, 2000.

Justice for All: The Rutherford Institute Story. Pamphlet. Charlottesville, Va.: The Rutherford Institute, 1994.

Kearney, Joseph D., and Thomas W. Merrill. "The Influence of Amicus Curiae Briefs on the Supreme Court." *University of Pennsylvania Law Review* 148 (2000): 743-829.

Kennedy, James R., and Walter D. Kennedy. *Why Not Freedom! America's Revolt against Big Government.* Gretna, La.: Pelican Publishing, 1995.

Kennedy, John. "Do We Really Need Prayer in Public School?" *Rutherford* 4, no. 9 (Sept. 1995): 7-11.

Krislov, Samuel. "The Amicus Curiae Brief: From Friendship to Advocacy." *Yale Law Journal* 72 (1963): 694-704.

Larson, Edward J. *Summer of the Gods: The Scopes Trial and America's Continuing Debate over Science and Religion.* New York: Basic Books, 1997.

Lash, Kurt T. "The Second Adoption of the Establishment Clause: The Rise of the Nonestablishment Principle." *Arizona State Law Journal* 27 (1995): 1085-1154.

Laycock, Douglas. "Formal, Substantive, and Disaggregated Neutrality toward Religion." *DePaul Law Review* 39 (1990).

Levy, Leonard W. *The Establishment Clause: Religion and the First Amendment.* 2nd rev. ed. Chapel Hill: University of North Carolina Press, 1994.

Lienesch, Michael. *Redeeming America: Piety and Politics in the New Christian Right.* Chapel Hill: University of North Carolina Press, 1993.

Longfield, Bradley J. *The Presbyterian Controversy: Fundamentalists, Modernists, and Moderates*. Oxford: Oxford University Press, 1991.

Lowman, Michael K. "Comment: The Litigating Amicus Curiae; When Does the Party Begin after the Friends Leave?" *American University Law Review* 41 (1992): 1243-99.

Machen, J. Gresham. *Christianity and Liberalism*. New York: Macmillan, 1923.

Marsden, George M. *Fundamentalism and American Culture: The Shaping of Twentieth-Century Evangelicalism, 1870-1925*. Oxford: Oxford University Press, 1980.

———. *The Outrageous Idea of Christian Scholarship*. New York: Oxford University Press, 1997.

———. *Reforming Fundamentalism: Fuller Seminary and the New Evangelicalism*. Grand Rapids: Eerdmans, 1987.

———, ed. *The Fundamentals: A Testimony to the Truth*. Edited by Joel A. Carpenter. 4 vols. Fundamentalism in American Religion, 1880-1950. New York: Garland, 1988.

Martin, William. *A Prophet with Honor: The Billy Graham Story*. New York: Morrow, 1991.

———. *With God on Our Side: The Rise of the Religious Right in America*. New York: Broadway Books, 1996.

Marty, Martin E. *Modern American Religion*. Vol. 1, *The Irony of It All, 1893-1919*. Chicago: University of Chicago Press, 1986.

———. *Modern American Religion*. Vol. 2, *The Noise of Conflict, 1919-1941*. Chicago: University of Chicago Press, 1991.

———. *Modern American Religion*. Vol. 3, *Under God, Indivisible, 1941-1960*. Chicago: University of Chicago Press, 1996.

———. *Righteous Empire: The Protestant Experience in America*. 1st ed. New York: Dial Press, 1970.

McConnell, Michael W. "Freedom from Persecution or Protection of the Rights of Conscience? A Critique of Justice Scalia's Historical Arguments in *City of Boerne v. Flores*." *William and Mary Law Review* 39 (1998): 819-47.

———. "The Origins and Historical Understanding of the Free Exercise of Religion." *Harvard Law Review* 103 (May 1990): 1409-1517.

———. "The Problem of Singling Out Religion." *DePaul Law Review* 50, no. 1 (2000): 1-47.

McDonald, Forrest. *Novus Ordo Seclorum: The Intellectual Origins of the Constitution*. Lawrence: University Press of Kansas, 1985.

McGirr, Lisa. *Suburban Warriors: The Origins of the New American Right.* Princeton: Princeton University Press, 2001.

McLoughlin, William G. Introduction to *The American Evangelicals, 1800-1900: An Anthology,* edited by William G. McLoughlin. New York: Harper and Row, 1968.

McThenia, Sheila. "Religious Apartheid." *Rutherford* 3, no. 6 (June 1994): 5.

Mead, Sidney E. *The Lively Experiment: The Shaping of Christianity in America.* New York: Harper and Row, 1963.

Miller, Robert T., and Ronald B. Flowers. *Toward Benevolent Neutrality: Church, State, and the Supreme Court.* 3rd ed. Waco, Tex.: Markham Press Fund, 1987.

Moen, Matthew C. *The Transformation of the Christian Right.* Tuscaloosa: University of Alabama Press, 1992.

Monsma, Stephen V. *When Sacred and Secular Mix: Religious Nonprofit Organizations and Public Money.* Lanham, Md.: Rowman and Littlefield, 1996.

Moore, R. Laurence. *Religious Outsiders and the Making of Americans.* New York: Oxford University Press, 1986.

Moore, R. Laurence, and Isaac Kramnick. *The Godless Constitution: The Case against Religious Correctness.* New York: Norton, 1996.

Moore, W. John. "The Lord's Litigators." *National Journal,* 2 July 1994.

Moriss, Andrew P. "Symposium: Private Amici Curiae and the Supreme Court's 1997-1998 Term; Employment Law Jurisprudence." *William and Mary Bill of Rights Journal* 7 (1999): 823-911.

Nelson, William E. *The Fourteenth Amendment: From Political Principle to Judicial Doctrine.* Cambridge: Harvard University Press, 1988.

Neuhaus, Richard John, ed. *The End of Democracy? The Judicial Usurpation of Politics; The Celebrated* First Things *Debate with Arguments Pro and Con.* Dallas: Spence Publishing, 1997.

Noll, Mark A. "Evangelicals in the American Founding and Evangelical Political Mobilization Today." In *Religion and the New Republic,* edited by James H. Hutson, 137-58. Lanham, Md.: Rowman and Littlefield, 2000.

————. *A History of Christianity in the United States and Canada.* Grand Rapids: Eerdmans, 1992.

Noonan, John T., Jr. *The Believer and the Powers That Are: Cases, History, and Other Data Bearing on the Relation of Religion and Government.* New York: Macmillan, 1987.

————. *The Lustre of Our Country: The American Experience of Religious Freedom.* Berkeley: University of California Press, 1998.

Nord, Warren A. *Religion and American Education: Rethinking a National Dilemma.* Chapel Hill: University of North Carolina Press, 1995.

Numbers, Ronald L. *The Creationists: The Evolution of Scientific Creationism.* Berkeley: University of California Press, 1992.

Olsen, Ted. "The Dragon Slayer." *Christianity Today,* 7 Dec. 1998, 36.

Ostling, Richard N., and Joan K. Ostling. *Mormon America: The Power and the Promise.* New York: HarperCollins, 1999.

Patrick, John J., and Gerald P. Long, eds. *Constitutional Debates on Freedom of Religion: A Documentary History.* Westport, Conn.: Greenwood Press, 1999.

Perry, Michael J. *We the People: The Fourteenth Amendment and the Supreme Court.* New York: Oxford University Press, 1999.

Peters, Charles, and Michael Nelson, eds. *The Culture of Bureaucracy.* New York: Holt, Rinehart and Winston, 1979.

Reed, Ralph. "We Can't Stop Now." *Christianity Today,* 6 Sept. 1999, 46.

"Religious Apartheid on Tour." *Rutherford* 4, no. 2 (Feb. 1995): 5.

Rosenfeld, Megan. "On the Case for Paula Jones." *Washington Post,* 17 Jan. 1998, 1.

Rushdoony, Rousas John. *The Institutes of Biblical Law.* 3 vols. Vol. 1. Nutley, N.J.: Craig Press, 1973.

————. *The Nature of the American System.* Nutley, N.J.: Craig Press, 1965.

Ryan, James E. "*Smith* and the Religious Freedom Restoration Act: An Iconoclastic Assessment." *Virginia Law Review* 78 (1992): 1407-62.

Schaeffer, Francis A. *How Should We Then Live? The Rise and Decline of Western Thought and Culture.* Old Tappan, N.J.: Revell, 1976.

Sekulow, Jay. *From Intimidation to Victory: Regaining the Christian Right to Speak.* Lake Mary, Fla.: Creation House, 1990.

Sekulow, Jay, and Keith Fournier. *And Nothing but the Truth: Real-Life Stories of Americans Defending Their Faith and Protecting Their Families.* Nashville: Nelson, 1996.

Shelley, Bruce L. "Evangelicalism." In *The Dictionary of Christianity in America,* edited by Daniel G. Reid et al., 413-16. Downers Grove, Ill.: InterVarsity, 1990.

————. "Parachurch Groups (Voluntary Societies)." In *The Dictionary of Christianity in America,* edited by Daniel G. Reid et al., 863-65. Downers Grove, Ill.: InterVarsity, 1990.

Shipps, Jan. *Mormonism: The Story of a New Religious Tradition.* Urbana: University of Illinois Press, 1985.

Smith, Nathaniel. "Religious Liberty Wars: The Rutherford Institute Leading the Way." *Rutherford,* Feb. 1995, 6-9, 18-19.

Smith, Steven D. *Foreordained Failure: The Quest for a Constitutional Principle of Religious Freedom.* New York: Oxford University Press, 1995.

———. *Getting over Equality: A Critical Diagnosis of Religious Freedom in America.* New York: New York University Press, 2001.

Stafford, Tim. "Move Over, ACLU: A Host of New Public-Interest Law Firms Are Helping American Christians Fight for Their Religious Liberties." *Christianity Today,* 25 Oct. 1993, 20-24.

Stamper, Chris. "A Surreal Legal Thriller: Jones Case Hero Whitehead Has Eclectic Tastes." *World,* 28 Nov. 1998, 22.

Stanciu, T., and Nisha N. Mohammed. "Committed to the 'Little Guy' (Interview with Alexis Crowe)." *Rutherford* 4, no. 2 (Feb. 1995): 13-15.

———. "Letter from the Editors." *Rutherford* 4, no. 2 (Feb. 1995): 2.

Sullivan, Winnifred Fallers. "The Difference Religion Makes: Reflections on *Rosenberger.*" *Christian Century,* 13 Mar. 1996, 292-95.

———. *Paying the Words Extra: Religious Discourse in the Supreme Court of the United States.* Cambridge: Harvard University Press, 1994.

Thomas, Cal, and Ed Dobson. *Blinded by Might: Can the Religious Right Save America?* Grand Rapids: Zondervan, 1999.

Travisano, Jim. "Fighting for Religious Freedom." *Rutherford* 3, no. 1 (Jan. 1994): 3-11.

Trollinger, William Vance, Jr. *God's Empire: William Bell Riley and Midwestern Fundamentalism.* Madison: University of Wisconsin Press, 1990.

Trotter, Andrew. "Religious Apartheid: The Film." *Rutherford,* June 1994, 18-19.

Tushnet, Mark. "Religion and Theories of Constitutional Interpretation." *Loyola Law Review* 33 (1987): 221-40.

———. "The Rhetoric of Free Exercise Discourse." *Brigham Young University Law Review,* 1993, 117-40.

Vanourek, Gregg, Scott W. Hamilton, and Chester E. Finn, Jr. *Is There Life after Big Government? The Potential of Civil Society.* Indianapolis: Hudson Institute, 1996.

Vatter, Harold G., and John F. Walker. *The Inevitability of Government Growth.* New York: Columbia University Press, 1990.

Walker, John F., and Harold G. Vatter, eds. *The Rise of Big Government in the United States.* Armonk, N.Y.: M. E. Sharpe, 1997.

Weber, Paul J., and W. Landis Jones. *U.S. Religious Interest Groups: Institutional Profiles.* Westport, Conn.: Greenwood Press, 1994.

Weber, Timothy P. *Living in the Shadow of the Second Coming: American Premillennialism, 1875-1925.* New York: Oxford University Press, 1979.

White, Jerry. *The Church and the Parachurch: An Uneasy Marriage.* Portland, Ore.: Multnomah, 1983.

Whitehead, Carol. "Looking Back at the Early Days." *Rutherford* 3, no. 1 (Jan. 1994): 14.

Whitehead, John W. *An American Dream.* Westchester, Ill.: Crossway, 1987.

————. *Censored on the Job: Your Religious Rights.* Faith and Freedom series. Chicago: Moody Press, 1994.

————. *The Christian and Political Involvement: Responsibility and Stewardship.* Pamphlet. Charlottesville, Va.: TRI, 1992.

————. *Christians Involved in the Political Process.* Faith and Freedom series. Chicago: Moody Press, 1994.

————. "Christ Was Controversial and Dogmatic." *Rutherford* 3, no. 3 (Mar. 1994): 6-7.

————. *Church vs. State.* Faith and Freedom series. Chicago: Moody Press, 1996.

————. "The Conservative Supreme Court and the Demise of the Free Exercise of Religion." *Temple Political and Civil Rights Law Review* 7 (1997): 1-71.

————. *The End of Man.* Westchester, Ill.: Crossway, 1986.

————. *Engaging the Culture.* Charlottesville, Va.: The Rutherford Institute, 1993.

————. *The Freedom of Religious Expression in Public High Schools.* 1st ed. TRI Report 1. Westchester, Ill.: Crossway, 1983.

————. *The Freedom of Religious Expression in Public Universities and High Schools.* 2nd ed. TRI Report 1. Westchester, Ill.: Crossway, 1986.

————. *Grasping for the Wind: Humanity's Search for Meaning.* Directed by Franky Schaeffer. 7 episodes. MPI Home Video, 1998. Videocassette.

————. *The New Tyranny: The Ominous Threat of State Authority over the Church.* Ft. Lauderdale, Fla.: Coral Ridge Ministries, 1982.

————. "No Political Agenda." *Washington Post,* 15 Nov. 1997, 23.

————. *Politically Correct: Censorship in American Culture.* Faith and Freedom series. Chicago: Moody Press, 1995.

————. "Political Stones or Spiritual Bread?" *Rutherford* 4, no. 4 (Apr. 1995): 11.

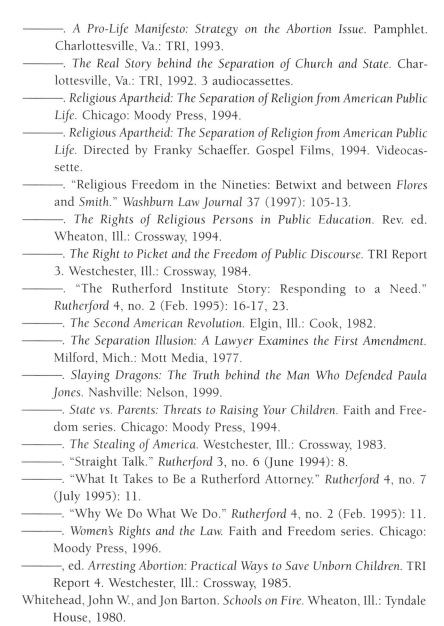

————. *A Pro-Life Manifesto: Strategy on the Abortion Issue*. Pamphlet. Charlottesville, Va.: TRI, 1993.

————. *The Real Story behind the Separation of Church and State*. Charlottesville, Va.: TRI, 1992. 3 audiocassettes.

————. *Religious Apartheid: The Separation of Religion from American Public Life*. Chicago: Moody Press, 1994.

————. *Religious Apartheid: The Separation of Religion from American Public Life*. Directed by Franky Schaeffer. Gospel Films, 1994. Videocassette.

————. "Religious Freedom in the Nineties: Betwixt and between *Flores* and *Smith*." *Washburn Law Journal* 37 (1997): 105-13.

————. *The Rights of Religious Persons in Public Education*. Rev. ed. Wheaton, Ill.: Crossway, 1994.

————. *The Right to Picket and the Freedom of Public Discourse*. TRI Report 3. Westchester, Ill.: Crossway, 1984.

————. "The Rutherford Institute Story: Responding to a Need." *Rutherford* 4, no. 2 (Feb. 1995): 16-17, 23.

————. *The Second American Revolution*. Elgin, Ill.: Cook, 1982.

————. *The Separation Illusion: A Lawyer Examines the First Amendment*. Milford, Mich.: Mott Media, 1977.

————. *Slaying Dragons: The Truth behind the Man Who Defended Paula Jones*. Nashville: Nelson, 1999.

————. *State vs. Parents: Threats to Raising Your Children*. Faith and Freedom series. Chicago: Moody Press, 1994.

————. *The Stealing of America*. Westchester, Ill.: Crossway, 1983.

————. "Straight Talk." *Rutherford* 3, no. 6 (June 1994): 8.

————. "What It Takes to Be a Rutherford Attorney." *Rutherford* 4, no. 7 (July 1995): 11.

————. "Why We Do What We Do." *Rutherford* 4, no. 2 (Feb. 1995): 11.

————. *Women's Rights and the Law*. Faith and Freedom series. Chicago: Moody Press, 1996.

————, ed. *Arresting Abortion: Practical Ways to Save Unborn Children*. TRI Report 4. Westchester, Ill.: Crossway, 1985.

Whitehead, John W., and Jon Barton. *Schools on Fire*. Wheaton, Ill.: Tyndale House, 1980.

Whitehead, John W., and Wendell R. Bird. *Home Education and Constitutional Liberties: The Historical and Constitutional Arguments in Support of Home Instruction*. TRI Report 2. Westchester, Ill.: Crossway, 1984.

Whitehead, John W., and John Conlan. "The Establishment of the Religion of Secular Humanism and Its First Amendment Implications." *Texas Tech Law Review* 10, no. 1 (1978): 1-66.

Whitehead, John W., and Alexis Irene Crowe. *Home Education: Rights and Reasons.* Wheaton, Ill.: Crossway, 1993.

Williams, Peter W. *America's Religions: Cultures and Traditions.* Urbana: University of Illinois Press, 1998. Reprint, Illini Books.

Willmer, Wesley K., and J. David Schmidt. *The Prospering Parachurch: Enlarging the Boundaries of God's Kingdom.* San Francisco: Jossey-Bass, 1998.

Wuthnow, Robert. *The Restructuring of American Religion: Society and Faith Since World War II.* Princeton: Princeton University Press, 1988.

Youngren, J. Alan. "Parachurch Proliferation: Caught in Traffic." *Christianity Today*, 6 Nov. 1981, 38-41.

Court Cases

Agostini v. Felton, 000 U.S. 96-552 (1997)

Aguilar v. Felton, 473 U.S. 402 (1985)

Allegheny County v. Greater Pittsburgh ACLU, 492 U.S. 573 (1989)

Bender et al. v. Williamsport Area School District et al., 475 U.S. 534 (1986)

Board of Education of the Westside Community Schools v. Mergens, 496 U.S. 226 (1990)

Board of Regents v. Southworth, 529 U.S. 217 (2000)

Bob Jones University v. United States, 461 U.S. 574 (1983)

Cantwell v. Connecticut, 310 U.S. 296 (1940)

Davis v. Beason, 133 U.S. 333 (1890)

District of Abington Township v. Schempp, 374 U.S. 203 (1963)

Edwards v. Aguillard, 482 U.S. 578 (1987)

Engel v. Vitale, 370 U.S. 421 (1962)

Epperson v. Arkansas, 399 U.S. 97 (1968)

Everson v. Board of Education, 330 U.S. 1 (1947)

Frazee v. Illinois Department of Employment Security, 489 U.S. 829 (1989)

Lamb's Chapel v. Center Moriches School District, 508 U.S. 384 (1993)

Lee v. Weisman, 505 U.S. 577 (1992)

Lemon v. Kurtzman, 403 U.S. 602 (1971)

Lynch v. Donnelly, 465 U.S. 668 (1984)

Marsh v. Chambers, 463 U.S. 783 (1983)

McCollum v. Board of Education, 333 U.S. 203 (1948)

Murdock v. Pennsylvania, 319 U.S. 105 (1943)

Reynolds v. United States, 98 U.S. 145 (1878)

Roe v. Wade, 410 U.S. 113 (1973)

Rosenberger, et al., Petitioners v. University of Virginia et al., 515 U.S. 819 (1995)

Santa Fe Independent School District v. Doe, 539 U.S. 290 (2000)

Stone v. Graham, 449 U.S. 39 (1980)

Torcaso v. Watkins, 367 U.S. 488 (1961)

Wallace v. Jaffree, 472 U.S. 38 (1985)

Walz v. Tax Commission, 397 U.S. 664 (1970)

Widmar v. Vincent, 454 U.S. 263 (1981)

Witters v. Washington Department of Services for the Blind, 474 U.S. 481 (1986)

Zelman v. Simmons-Harris, 000 U.S. 00-1751 (2002)

Zorach v. Clauson, 343 U.S. 306 (1952)

Amicus Curiae Briefs

1982 Brief Amici Curiae of the Coalition for Religious Liberty and the Freedom Council on Writ of Certiorari to the U.S. Court of Appeals for the First Circuit in Support of Petitioners, Lynch, et al., No. 82-1256.

1983 Brief Amicus Curiae of the Freedom Council on Appeal from the U.S. Court of Appeals for the Eleventh Circuit in Support of the Appellants, Wallace et al., No. 83-812, No. 83-929.

1984 Brief Amicus Curiae of The Rutherford Institute on Writ of Certiorari to the U.S. Court of Appeals for the Third Circuit in Support of the Petitioners, Bender et al., No. 84-773.

Brief Amicus Curiae of The Rutherford Institute on Writ of Certiorari to the Supreme Court of Washington in Support of the Petitioner, Witters, No. 84-1070.

Brief Amicus Curiae of The Rutherford Institute on Writ of Certiorari to the U.S. Court of Appeals for the District of Columbia in Support of the Petitioner, Goldman, No. 84-1097.

Brief Amicus Curiae of The Rutherford Institute on Appeal from U.S. District Court for the Middle District of Pennsylvania in Support of Appellees, Roy et al., No. 84-780.

1985   Brief Amici Curiae of the Rabbinical Alliance of America, et al., in Support of the Appellants, Aguillard, et al., No. 85-1513.

Brief Amicus Curiae of The Rutherford Institute on Appeal from the District Court of Appeal of the State of Florida, Fifth District, in Support of Appellant, Hobbie, No. 85-993.

Brief Amicus Curiae of The Rutherford Institute on Writ of Certiorari to the Eleventh Circuit Court of Appeals in Support of Petitioner, Bowers, No. 85-140.

Brief Amicus Curiae of The Rutherford Institute on Appeal from the Sixth Circuit Court of Appeals in Support of the Appellees, Dayton Christian Schools, No. 85-488.

Brief Amicus Curiae of The Rutherford Institute on Writ of Certiorari to the U.S. Court of Appeals for the Third Circuit in Support of Appellants, Karcher et al., No. 85-1551.

1986   Brief Amicus Curiae of The Rutherford Institute on Writ of Certiorari to the U.S. Court of Appeals for the Ninth Circuit in Support of Respondents, Jews for Jesus, Inc., No. 86-104.

1987   Brief Amicus Curiae of The Rutherford Institute on Writ of Certiorari to the U.S. Court of Appeals for the Third Circuit in Support of Appellant, Bowen, No. 87-253.

1988   Brief Amicus Curiae of The Rutherford Institute on Appeal from the U.S. Court of Appeals for the Eighth Circuit in Support of Appellants, Webster et al., 1988 U.S. Briefs 605.

Brief Amicus Curiae of The Rutherford Institute on Writ of Certiorari to the Missouri Supreme Court in Support of Respondents, Harmon et al., 1988 U.S. Briefs (1503).

Brief Amicus Curiae of The Rutherford Institute on Appeal from the U.S. Court of Appeals for the Seventh Circuit in Support of Appellants, Turnock et al., No. 88-790.

Brief Amicus Curiae of The Rutherford Institute on Writ of Certiorari to the U.S. Court of Appeals for the Eighth Circuit in Support of Respondents, Mergens et al., 1988 U.S. Briefs 1597.

Brief Amicus Curiae of The Rutherford Institute on Writ of Certiorari to the U.S. Court of Appeals for the First Circuit in Support of Petitioners, Lee et al., 1990 U.S. Briefs 1014.

1991   Brief Amicus Curiae of The Rutherford Institute on Writ of Certiorari on Appeal from the U.S. Court of Appeals for the Second Circuit in Support of Appellants, Lamb's Chapel et al., 1991 U.S. Briefs 2024.

Brief Amicus Curiae of The Rutherford Institute on Writ of Certiorari to the U.S. Court of Appeals for the Eleventh Circuit in Support of Petitioners, Church of the Lukumi Babalu Aye, Inc., and Ernest Picardo, 1991 U.S. Briefs 948.

1993   Brief Amicus Curiae of The Rutherford Institute on Writ of Certiorari to the New York Court of Appeals in Support of Petitioners, Board of Education of the Kiryas Joel Village School District et al., 1993 U.S. Briefs 517.

1995   Brief Amicus Curiae of The Rutherford Institute on Writ of Certiorari to the U.S. Court of Appeals for the Fifth Circuit in Support of Respondents, Flores and U.S.A., 1995 U.S. Briefs 2074.

Brief Amicus Curiae of The Rutherford Institute on Writ of Certiorari to the U.S. Court of Appeals for the Second Circuit in Support of Petitioners, Schenck and Saunders, 1995 U.S. Briefs 1065.

1998   Brief Amicus Curiae of The Rutherford Institute on Writ of Certiorari to the U.S. Court of Appeals for the Seventh Circuit in Support of Respondents, Southworth et al., 1998 U.S. Briefs 1189.

1999   Brief Amicus Curiae of The Rutherford Institute on Writ of Certiorari to the U.S. Court of Appeals for the Fifth Circuit in Support of Respondents, Doe and Doe, 1999 U.S. Briefs 62.

Acknowledgments

In the course of this project, I have accrued many debts that cannot be repaid but deserve to be acknowledged. I am deeply grateful to Martin Marty, who as teacher, adviser, mentor, and collaborator, has immeasurably influenced my own work. Chris Gamwell of the University of Chicago Divinity School and Craig Mousin of the DePaul University School of Law each read the entire manuscript and offered helpful comments, as did an anonymous reviewer for Eerdmans. John Witte of the Emory University School of Law provided unflagging encouragement as this project came to fruition.

On a more personal level, I am grateful for Audrey and Robert Moore, parents and educators who first taught me how to learn and how to question. And, finally, thanks to my wife, Marita, without whose love and patience (and income!) this book would never have been finished.

Index